THE TWENTIETH CENTURY IN POETRY

How has the twentieth century been represented in poetry?

The Twentieth Century in Poetry examines both 'English' poetry through the events of the twentieth century, and British history through its representations in recent poetry. It builds a narrative not of poetry in the twentieth century but of the twentieth century in poetry.

A high proportion of literature courses include an exploration of questions of gender, ethnicity, theory, nationality, politics, and social class. But until now most teaching has focused on the novel as the most useful way of raising these issues. In *The Twentieth Century in Poetry* Peter Childs demonstrates that all poetry is historically produced and consumed, and is part of our understanding of society and identity. This student-friendly critical survey includes chapters on:

* the Georgians
* poetry of World War I
* Eliot
* Yeats
* the 1930s
* postwar poetry
* contemporary anthologies
* women's poetry
* Northern Irish and black British poets

Placing literature in a wider social context, this book is a fascinating examination of the way in which recent theory has questioned divisions between 'history' and literature, between 'text' and 'event', between society and the individual.

Peter Childs is Senior Lecturer in Literary Studies at John Moores University, Liverpool.

THE TWENTIETH CENTURY IN POETRY

A critical survey

Peter Childs

London and New York

First published 1999
by Routledge
11 New Fetter Lane, London EC4P 4EE

Simultaneously published in the USA and Canada
by Routledge
29 West 35th Street, New York, NY 10001

© 1999 Peter Childs

The right of Peter Childs to be identified as the Author of this Work
has been asserted by him in accordance with the Copyright, Designs
and Patents Act 1988

Typeset in Goudy by Routledge
Printed and bound in Great Britain by
Creative Print and Design (Wales), Ebbw Vale

British Library Cataloguing in Publication Data
A catalogue record for this book is available from the British Library

Library of Congress Cataloguing in Publication Data
Childs, Peter, 1962–
The twentieth century in poetry / Peter Childs.
p. cm.
Includes bibliographic references and index.
1. English poetry–20th century–History and criticism.
2. Literature and history–Great Britain–History–20th century.
3. Literature and society–Great Britain–History–20th century.
I. Title.
PR605.H5C48 1999
821'.9109–dc21   98–7836

ISBN 0–415–17101–6 (pbk)
ISBN 0–415–17100–8 (hbk)

TO MY PARENTS, JOHN AND
PATRICIA CHILDS

CONTENTS

PREFACE AND
ACKNOWLEDGEMENTS

In the *Times Higher Educational Supplement* on 29 August 1997, Peter Barry, Secretary of the English Association, was quoted as saying that the teaching of poetry had come increasingly 'under threat' in literature departments. He put this trend down to modularisation and the rise of student choice. The message would appear to be that nowadays students who are not forced to will seldom elect to study poetry. This phenomenon has perhaps two chief causes: students associate poetry with difficulty, in terms of form and sense, and they dissociate it from society, which seems to them more adequately treated in the longer, polyphonic narratives of fiction.

The Twentieth Century in Poetry is in part an attempt to resist this trend by plotting connections between society, history, narrative and poetry. The book's premise is that poetry can be effectively used to explore questions of gender, ethnicity, national identity, politics, and class that are now the core issues of a high proportion of literature courses but which are most frequently raised in connection with the novel. The reverse is also true and these same issues should be employed to analyse poetry in terms of social history.

Consequently, my chief aim is to reassert that all poetry is historically produced and consumed, and is part of the intertextual weave of discourses that structure our understanding of society and identity. To suggest the variety of levels at which poetry can be approached in terms of history, different chapters in the first half of the book respectively cover one poem (*The Waste Land*), one poet (Yeats), one decade (the 1930s), one event (World War I), and one 'style' (Georgian poetry). To a degree, the chapters' complexity reflects that of the poetry, and the more in-depth discussions of the modernists, Eliot and Yeats, are less straightforward and more theoretical than the others. Chapters in the second half aim to delineate in poetry the social fracturing and restructuring of postwar British society – two chapters offer period-based reviews of the poetic 'mainstream' and two chapters concentrate on the 'alternative currents' of women's and 'post-colonial' poetry which are increasingly producing the most innovative, socially relevant poetry.

It is impossible in a short overview such as this to give adequate coverage to even the best-known twentieth-century British poets (e.g. Ted Hughes and Dylan Thomas are mentioned only briefly). However, a large number of the most commonly taught poems, poets, and collections have been chosen for consideration and they are augmented by texts which seem to require more attention given the book's general approach. For purposes of accessibility, examples have been drawn from widely available anthologies wherever possible – in most instances, the poets' more well-known works are the ones discussed and cited. The detail of the analyses varies greatly and very few poems are interpreted closely or quoted at length, in keeping with the book's aim to situate the texts less as significant personal utterances than as literary interventions in social discourses.

I would like to thank Michael Storry and Edmund Cusick for reading portions of the manuscript. For copyright permission I am grateful to: A.P. Watt on behalf of The National Trust for Rudyard Kipling's 'The Storm Cone' and 'The Female of the Species'; Bloodaxe Books for poems from Fred D'Aguiar's *British Subjects*, Selima Hill's *Trembling Hearts in the Bodies of Dogs: New and Selected Poems*, Peter Reading's *Collected Poems 2: Poems 1985–1996*, Tony Harrison's *V*, Simon Armitage's *Zoom!*, Peter Didsbury's *The Butchers of Hull*, Linton Kwesi Johnson's *Tings an Times: Selected Poems*, Anne Rouse's *Sunset Grill*, Jo Shapcott's *Electroplating the Baby*, and Benjamin Zephaniah's *City Pslams*; Carcanet Press for Hugh MacDiarmid's 'In the Slums of Glasgow' and Elizabeth Daryush's *Selected Poems*; Chatto & Windus, for Fred D'Aguiar's 'Angry Mama Dot' and 'Letter from Mama Dot'; David Higham for lines from Louis MacNeice's 'Bagpipe Music' and Elizabeth Jenning's 'Answers'; Faber and Faber for lines from Louis MacNeice's *Collected Poems* and Sassoon's 'Counter-Attack', © Siegfried Sassoon by permission of George Sassoon; John Murray for John Betjeman's 'In Westminster Abbey'; Jonathan Cape for W.H. Davies's 'Heaven' from *Collected Poems*; John Lehmann for 'This Excellent Machine'; Oxford University Press for selections from Peter Porter's *Collected Poems*, for Ann Stevenson's 'A Love Letter', and for Ivor Gurney's 'To the Prussians of England', © Robin Haines, Sole Trustee of the Gurney Estate 1982 (reprinted from *Collected Poems of Ivor Gurney* edited by P.J. Kavanagh (1982)); and Papermac for Thomas Hardy's 'The Convergence of the Twain' and 'Christmas 1924'. Lines from Medbh McGuckian's *The Flower Master and Other*

Poems (1993) are reprinted by kind permission of the author and The Gallery Press. Lines from *The Complete Poem*, by C. Day Lewis, published by Sinclair-Stevenson (1992), © 1992 in this edition The Estate of C. Day Lewis.

Every effort has been made to obtain permission to reproduce copyright material. If any proper acknowledgement has not been made, we would invite copyright holders to inform us of the oversight.

INTRODUCTION

Can anyone but a philistine, you will ask, talk about lyric
poetry and society?

                                                      (Adorno 1989)

As its title indicates, this book tries to do two things: to sketch the
ways in which poetry since 1900 has engaged with historical events
and to construct a narrative of the century through the poetry it has
produced. Yet, to regard poetry as distinct from history has to an extent
become an inevitable 'habit of reading' in critical practice. Terry
Eagleton observes that 'poetry is of all literary genres the one most
apparently sealed from history, the one where "sensibility" may play in
its purest, least socially tainted form' (Eagleton 1983: 51). Among the
literary genres, poetry is seen as the most personal, the most emotional
and introspective, the least social or political. If the novel orchestrates
a number of characters, and drama functions through dialogue, then
poetry appears to be sealed, sometimes almost hermetically, from the
outside world, as the isolated writer communicates a personal message
to the solitary reader. However, to take just the Romantics, this ahistorical view would obviously be frustrated by any analysis of Shelley's
'The Mask of Anarchy' or Byron's 'The Vision of Judgement'. These
are poems whose content engages explicitly, though imaginatively,
with contemporary politics – poems of the variety found in Kenneth
Baker's anthology, *The Faber Book of English History in Verse*, which
represents one attempt to place poems in terms of their reaction to
social events and to construct a historical narrative, however scanty,
through poetry. From another perspective, we need also to remember
that it is only since the invention of the printing press that reading
poetry has gradually come to replace the more traditional activity of
the poetry reading (revived since the 1960s by an increased interest in
performance poetry).

However, these are elementary connections between poetry and society, and there are other ways of linking the two than through an attention to a poem's overt message or its social performance. On the one hand, poetry may not frequently comment on the historical situation in which it was written but its subject matter will nevertheless be a product of that moment, of the ideologies, beliefs, convictions, and attitudes of its time. On the other hand, what we call the 'form' of a poem is also fashioned by contemporary preferences and orthodoxies: the sonnet *appears* ideal for love poetry, the iambic pentameter *seems* to give the best rhythm to the English language. Form is in fact neither autonomous nor separable from content, because it is shaped by literary history, by dominant ideological structures, and by the relationship between writer and reader (Eagleton 1976b: 26).

The prevailing view of the twentieth century, since the interventions in the 1920s of critics such as T.S. Eliot and I.A. Richards, is that a poem's meaning exists in the words on the page. Which means that no outside or extraneous knowledge, such as the author's biography, is needed to uncover a poem's significance or quality; as a distinct artefact the self-sufficient poem stands aside from author, reader, and history. The belief underlying this view is that a well-made poem, like a good detective novel, contains in itself all the clues necessary for the reader's understanding – a theory which actually, though denying it, locates the 'truth' in the author once again: in the author's success in embodying his or her intended meaning in the poem's language and form. It is assumed that the poem has a common subject and the author's task is to achieve a complex unity of all the poem's aspects in expressing that universal theme (mortality, unrequited love, the glory/horror of war), while the reader's task is to assess the poem's – which is in fact to say the author's – methodology and success. New Criticism, to give this approach a name, despite its valorisation of irony and paradox, seems both to fix the poem's meaning too rigidly and to ignore the conditions of its material production and consumption.[1] Other theories, which locate meaning in the reader's encounter, in a specific cultural situation, with the particular poem, produced at a certain time and place, free meaning from the 'words on the page' and locate it instead in the processes of social language and the discourses of history.[2] In other words, a reader in 1850 will ascribe a different meaning to *Hamlet* from a reader in 1990, and a reader in Delhi is likely to react differently to Kipling's poetry from a reader in Oslo. It is also a point made in a short story by Jorge Luis Borges that, in his example, *Don Quixote* would 'mean' something very different had it been authored by a twentieth-century Frenchman and not a seventeenth-century Spaniard.[3] To stress the importance of literature's time of production, critics often also make distinctions between texts written about their own time and 'historical writing'.

When considering the relation between literature and history, we should additionally register the fact that many recent theorists, from the institutional disciplines of history and English, have questioned the traditional boundary between the two. While literary critics have increasingly incorporated historical perspectives into their analyses, historians such as Hayden White have insisted on the constructed nature of all historiography, which is to say its use of narrative, conjecture, metaphor, perspective, and imagery.[4] All writing, whether it be historical or poetical, is published from one location at one point in time, and is addressed to a particular and almost invariably contemporary audience; which is not to say that we cannot make distinctions between poetry and history, but that we must remember that both are constructed in language and in social situations. A similar interrogation of the difference between text and event has taken place. If an event, such as the Battle of the Somme or the 1968 Olympics, is only available to us as a series of accounts in books and films then its difference from any other text is only marked by our acceptance of its roots in a particular occurrence in the real world: we only have access to the event through written or recorded accounts, through texts.

It is partly the 'form' in which history is written that leads us to accept it as more objective than subjective. In relation to this, Catherine Belsey explains a distinction made by the critic Emile Benveniste between discourse, which we associate with literature, and history:

> History narrates events apparently without the intervention of a speaker. In history there is no mention of 'you' and 'I'; 'the events seem to narrate themselves.' Discourse on the other hand, assumes a speaker and a hearer, the 'you' and 'I' of dialogue.
>
> (Belsey 1980: 71)

In this respect, biography sits alongside history, which is partly why a writer such as Peter Ackroyd has tried to experiment with the genre's form in his 'life narratives' of writers such as Dickens: by introducing imaginary dialogues, conjectured situations, and first-person interventions into his own third-person account.

In general, the presence of a third-person omniscient narrator will nearly always privilege 'history' as authoritative; despite the fact that there are likely to be several competing accounts of a period or subject. Similarly, first-person writing, as poetry often is, more often meets with an emotional response because the reader identifies with the position of the speaker. A related point to make but not labour is that just as history can become the subject of poetry, poetry is a part of history, produced within it and adding to it (e.g. Shakespeare probably provides the most familiar images of Richard III). Consequently, this book considers history alongside poetical texts. However, as I've already argued, history is also textual and, while I'll be talking about contexts, the distinction between texts and contexts is really that between one set of texts and another set – between texts and inter-texts.[5] Which is to say that everything is textual, and therefore we cannot invoke 'history' in any absolute sense because

> all we can hope to recover of the past is other representations of it.... But if we can compare a poem, as a discursive account of reality, with other contemporary accounts, we can begin to understand it...as the embodiment of a partial view of the world in competition with other partial views; as political, and not as universal.
>
> (Barrell 1988: 12)

Another traditional division we need to consider briefly in this introduction is that between society and the individual, a separation often associated with the difference between history, a collective experience, and poetry, a personal expression. (A similarly aligned opposition between 'fact' and 'feeling' might also be challenged.) This should be considered in several ways. Since the Romantics, 'the individual' has become an especially privileged category, and particularly in poetry, as the writer has come to be seen not as 'holding a mirror up to reality' but as generating light from an internal lamp – the individual as not reflection but fount(ain). Inspiration, feeling, and individual genius come to be treated as more important than social codes and values. Matthew Arnold's lost spirit on 'Dover Beach' expresses this isolation, as does D.H. Lawrence's assertion that the only clue to the universe is the individual soul within the individual being (Lawrence 1971: 150). This championing of the self can be read in terms of other ideologies, such as the principles of capitalist society – in distinction from the collectivism of socialism – which rely on competition and the entrepreneur. Again, as Toril Moi writes in her attack on 'traditional bourgeois humanism of a liberal-individualist kind', modern Western society has modelled its idea of the author in terms akin to divinity: 'In this humanist ideology the self is the sole author of history and of the literary text: the humanist creator is potent, phallic and male – God in relation to his world, the author in relation to his text' (Moi 1985: 6–8). In contrast to this, recent critical and cultural theory emphasises that the individual cannot be separated off from society, that people's views are not the product of their own autonomous deliberations but of discourses that vie for their identification (their self-recognition or agreement) from the moment they are born. Also, we should remember that the period examined in this book is that of mass state expansion, of new global technologies, and of multinational corporations, all of which dispense with the category of the individual in favour of the citizen, the viewer, the customer or the consumer.

One way of starting to look at twentieth-century poetry is through the anthologies that have outlined and influenced opinion at particular moments. That is to say, the century can be divided into 'key' though contentious anthologies which have sought to rank the poets and the poetry of their generation. The vogue for anthologies was set by the archetypal collection of the later nineteenth century, F.T. Palgrave's *The Golden Treasury of the Best Songs and Lyrical Poems in the English Language* (1861), which attempted to restrict the canon to lyric poetry. The authoritative status of *The Golden Treasury* itself is illustrated by the fact that it is still in print today, updated to include recent writers such as Fleur Adcock and Tony Harrison. However, Palgrave's was displaced as *the* definitive collection after 1900 by the original *Oxford Book of English Verse*, edited by Sir Arthur Quiller-Couch (while Palgrave had become Oxford Professor of Poetry, Quiller-Couch was appointed in 1912 the first King Edward VII Professor of *English Literature* at Cambridge). The first significant collection of twentieth-century poets was Edward Marsh's ultraEnglish *Georgian Poetry 1911–1912*, soon followed by Ezra Pound's unEnglish *Des Imagistes* in 1914. These two volumes defined the poles of poetry for the next fifteen years, ranging from the innovative but never widely popular work of the modernists to the largely unexceptionable but also unexceptional verse of the Georgians, whose continuing appeal can be gauged by the fact that Sir Algernon Methuen's predominantly Georgian *Anthology of Modern Verse* was reprinted nearly eighty times between 1921 and the end of World War II.

The 1930s was chiefly notable for three highly praised left-wing collections edited by Michael Roberts. Together, these publications helped to make W.H. Auden the undoubted pre-eminent poet of the time: *New Signatures* (1932), *New Country* (1933), and the long-lasting *Faber Book of Modern Verse* (1936). Consequently, Auden, Louis

MacNeice, Stephen Spender and Cecil Day Lewis, disparagingly lumped together by some as 'MacSpaunday', were also known at the time as not the 'Thirties poets' but the 'New Country' poets. Their admiration for Eliot, the war poets, Yeats, and some aspects of prewar verse suggested a *new* poetry that might form a bridge between the conservative Georgian and radical modernist styles that were splitting 'English poetry' apart. *New Signatures* effectively signalled a fresh literary direction which almost immediately made redundant Harold Monro's somewhat premature and perhaps ill-timed *Twentieth-Century Poetry* (1929).

Since World War II, a good number of influential anthologies have been published, beginning in 1950 with Hermann Peschmann's retro-spective *The Voice of Poetry 1930–1950*. However, the first of great importance was Robert Conquest's 1956 *New Lines* which heralded the emergence of 'The Movement' poets and Philip Larkin in particular (Conquest's introduction is seen as a kind of manifesto, one which defends the conversational style and formal conservatism of his chosen poets and attacks in particular the 'Apocalyptic' poets of the 1940s, such as J.F. Hendry, Vernon Watkins, Norman MacCaig, and Nicholas Moore).[6] As a response to Conquest's book, A. Alvarez published *The New Poetry* in 1962 (and re-published it in 1966, foregrounding writers including Sylvia Plath). Partly because of its polemical prefatory remarks, *The New Poetry* soon became established as *the* significant postwar anthology, with Alvarez replying to *New Lines* by insisting that modern poetry must engage with contemporary society. Although in 1962 Penguin relaunched Kenneth Allot's 1950s collection of the *Penguin Book of Contemporary Verse*, now covering 1918–60, and in 1965 issued David Wright's *The Mid-Century: English Poetry 1940–1960*, Alvarez's book, with its argumentative and agenda-setting preface, remained the important collection.[7] In 1970 Penguin published Edward Lucie-Smith's capacious *British Poetry Since 1945*, which has been repeatedly revised but has always seemed too disparate, as has D.J. Enright's *Oxford Book of Contemporary Verse 1945–1980*. The most influential collections have remained those that are closely focused and seem to be 'of the moment'. In 1982 Blake Morrison and Andrew Motion published the next anthology to gain wide accep-tance, *The Penguin Book of Contemporary British Poetry* – a very judgemental selection, rather than collection, of twenty poets. Its stated aim was to mark the eclipse of Alvarez's anthology and to delin-eate another new poetry characterised by narrative, extreme metaphor, observation, and postmodernism. Since then poetry publication has undergone a number of changes, most notable of which is perhaps the continued emergence of influential presses away from the English south-east, particularly Bloodaxe books in Newcastle. In 1993, to echo Alvarez's book and to attempt an overthrow of the 1982 Penguin anthology, Michael Hulse, David Kennedy, and David Morley published their Bloodaxe collection, *The New Poetry*, which 'represents what we believe to be the best poetry published in the British Isles in the 1980s and early 1990s'. It features none of the score of poets elevated by the Morrison and Motion book, and is curiously homogenising in its introductory remarks, claiming a new cohesiveness and the end of 'British poetry's tribal divisions'.

Against such gestures towards commonality, since the mid-1980s the politics of anthologies has been trenchantly debated, and many more alternative, regional, or specialised anthologies have also been published. Even those with an overarching aim, such as Paladin's *The New British Poetry* (1988), stress gender and ethnicity in their selections. Volumes of English language poetry from India or Africa had been available long before this, but there has been a recent growth in surveys such as anthologies of Caribbean poetry (*Hinterland*, 1989, and *The Penguin Book of Caribbean Verse in English*, 1986). Since the 1980s there has also been a proliferation of women-only collections (for example, *The Faber Book of Twentieth-Century Women's Poetry*, 1987, and *The Bloodaxe Book of Contemporary Women Poets*, 1985). These are catering for different markets but also challenging the hegemony of the tradition of white, male-dominated anthologies like *The Penguin Book of Contemporary British Poetry* (which has no black and only five women poets, none with more than seven poems, as opposed to Heaney's twenty and Christopher Reid's or Tom Paulin's eleven). Such specificity is a refusal of universalism in favour of collections which acknowledge the politics of gender, nation, sexuality, region, or genre. The liking for definitive epoch-making anthologies survives, as with Bloodaxe's *The New Poetry*, but many editors eschew introducing an hierarchical order of merit. Carol Rumens has suggested that perhaps 'the desire to elect leaders and order everyone else to fall into step behind is a quirk peculiar to English male anthologists' (Longley 1996: 9).

The clearest message from this very brief summary should be that anthologists have reacted against each other – that each widely accepted and adopted collection (as well as many neglected ones) has sought to challenge the view of poetry advocated by a previous editor.[8] 'New' remains the most common adjective in poetry anthologies. It is also worth noting that the foremost poets of their generation have often been asked to compile modern anthologies although these have rarely become the standard textbooks of their time: from Yeats's *Oxford*

Book of Modern Verse 1892–1935 (1936), Auden's *Oxford Book of Light Verse* (1939), Larkin's *Oxford Book of Twentieth-Century English Verse* (1973), and Heaney and Hughes's *The Rattle Bag* (1985) through to Fleur Adcock's *Faber Book of Twentieth Century Women's Poetry* (1987). Unlike Palgrave's *Golden Treasury*, influential twentieth-century anthologies have generally been those that choose a small selection of emergent poets and argue that they constitute a new generation or a shift in poetic sensibility.

A second way of beginning to introduce poetry since 1900 is to consider the two influential poets, both equally well known for their fiction, who stand at the gate of the twentieth century: Hardy and Kipling. Apart from Yeats, whom I will look at in a later chapter, these are the two most important figures as the century begins. They have much in common, such as an interest in ballad and song forms, in what Kipling calls the 'uncounted folk', and in vernacular. But they also represent the poles of dominant versions of national identity in 1900: Hardy, whose provincial, bucolic poetry looks to the past and laments the erosion of its traditions, proffers an ambivalent contemporary national identity that is the opposite of Kipling's almost devout imperial vision (though Kipling was to locate Englishness in Sussex nearly as much as Hardy found it in Wessex). Which is perhaps why Hardy appears to talk of individuated characters whereas Kipling utilises composite or representative figures. Kipling, far and away the most popular and successful writer of his day, is still often marginalised as a poet in academic circles because of his association with the Empire, which too frequently confines him to academic work within colonial studies. Orwell's comment from 1942 has now applied for twice as long: 'During five literary generations every enlightened person has despised him, and at the end of that time nine tenths of those enlightened persons are forgotten and Kipling is in a sense still there' (Orwell 1965: 45). As Auden once wrote, 'time' has indeed 'Pardoned Kipling and his views', such that, in 1995, Kipling's 'If' was voted favourite poem in a BBC national poll.[9] For the majority of the poets I will discuss in the next chapter, Kipling is the genius of contemporary literature and provides the benchmark against which their work is judged. Though he is a far more versatile writer than those who followed him, Kipling's robust rhythms and sing-song lyrics become for many poets the models for their verse, as do his frequent themes of imperialism and national identity. By contrast, it is often argued, at greatest length by Donald Davie in his book *Thomas Hardy and British Poetry* (1973), that Hardy is the key writer at the turn of the century who links the English poetry of the past found in the work of Wordsworth and Tennyson, to the

supposed mainstream of twentieth-century poetry running through
Edward Thomas, W.H. Auden, and Philip Larkin. In this narrative, the
innovations and experiments of 1920s modernism are not central to
English poetry – or an *English* modernism – but European diversions
instigated by the Americans Pound and Eliot (even if Hardy 'showed the
way for the imagists').[10] Though Hardy didn't start publishing poetry
until 1898, after his last, ill-received novel *Jude the Obscure*, he had been
writing it for many years. His influence as a poet is most strongly felt
after 1910. For some he is a nature poet, for others he is a writer of the
machine age; he is best known for the love poems of 1912–13 he wrote
after the death of his estranged wife, Emma.

Though they are rarely discussed in overviews of these periods, both
Kipling and Hardy were to continue writing poetry well into the
interwar years, Kipling into the mid-1930s.[11] Neither was impressed by
the changes twentieth-century 'progress' wrought. Hardy, looking back
on the previous war, delivered this short bitter response to Christian
hypocrisy at 'Christmas: 1924':

> 'Peace upon earth!' was said. We sing it,
> And pay a million priests to bring it.
> After two thousand years of mass
> We've got as far as poison-gas.

In 1932, Kipling wrote one prophetic poem, 'The Storm Cone', antici-
pating the coming wars:

> Stand by! The lull 'twixt blast and blast
> Signals the storm is near, not past;
> And worse than present jeopardy
> May our forlorn to-morrow be.

Each with a volume of collected poems that stretches to a thousand
pages, these prolific writers straddle the century's threshold, and are
Victorians in one sense, modernists in another.[12] They are also poets of
World War I.[13] But Hardy and Kipling were established writers by
1900. Both were to have poor inheritors and imitators in the ensuing
decade. The sense of community in Hardy and the sense of commonwealth in Kipling become unpleasant celebrations of the English 'race',
its glorious history and supreme achievements. Hardy's individuals and
Kipling's representatives become 'the people' and 'the nation', abstract
ideals in which everyone can share but about whom, because of their
artificial, conglomerate nature, nothing particular can be said. The

emblem of this prewar period, blithely heading for social revolution or international war, seems to be the *Titanic*, full of Edwardian confidence but bound for disaster. Hardy's poem on the loss of the ship, 'The Convergence of the Twain', expresses this well:

> And as the smart ship grew
> In stature, grace, and hue,
> In shadowy silent distance grew the Iceberg too.
>
> Alien they seemed to be:
> No mortal eye could see
> The intimate welding of their later history.

In the majority of literary histories, the hiatus in literary development early in the century is thought to have been challenged by the war poets and ended by the modernists. In his book, *Poetry as Discourse*, Antony Easthope (1983) claims that modernist poetry subverts traditional ways of reading poetry by eschewing use of the iamb. The argument runs that the iambic pentameter (think of Shakespeare's sonnets) has contributed to the notion of a speaking voice in poetry, which has led to the habitual identification of readers with the actual or implied 'I' of poems. Modernist poetry's emphasis on the signifier over the signified – on what words connote rather than denote – has disrupted this kind of identification, causing the reader to concentrate on form and dissonance rather than emotion and self-expression. Eliot famously wrote, contra Wordsworth, 'Poetry is not a turning loose of emotion, but an escape from emotion; it is not the expression of personality, but an escape from personality' (Eliot 1972: 76). Easthope's theory is a variation on arguments put forward by formalists and Marxists early in the century, such as Victor Shklovsky and Bertolt Brecht, that the purpose of art is to make strange or to defamiliarise: only by distancing the reader from the objects and situations presented can literary techniques make people change their perceptions, and this is taken to be the chief purpose of art.[14] Along similar lines, Gary Day offers modern poetry, with its complexities and alternative narrative forms, as a subversive force (Day 1993: 8–9). He argues that, because of the mass media and its drive to create consumers, language has become increasingly institutionalised in the twentieth century, and that poetry has been able to counter this trend. Again, Day's argument actually resembles those of the modernists, such as Yeats and Eliot, that modern Western civilisation (or, as they would term it, democracy) has led to a devaluation of art and language. Eliot put it thus in *The Egoist* in 1918:

What we want is to disturb and alarm the public.... [T]he intelligence of a nation must go on developing, or it will deteriorate.... That the forces of deterioration are a large crawling mass, and the forces of development half a dozen men.

As Stan Smith comments, citing this passage, the modernists thought: 'Democracy is the source of linguistic corruption, and therefore of social decay' (Smith 1983: 5). For Eliot, poetry was to be an antidote to this poison, but for the purposes of the present book, I would like simply to underline the way in which once more links are being forged between poetry and society.

I began this introduction by saying that critical practice involves a 'habit of reading'. To end, I would like to explain this a little more fully. All writing, and poetry especially so, is polysemic: it 'means' many different things. A poem exists in two senses at least: as an isolated collection of words, irrespective of any social context or any reader, and as the set of interpretations that are made of it. It is only in the latter sense however that the poem reaches us and is discussed by us – in *our* context, not in isolation. The American reader-response critic Stanley Fish coined the term 'interpretive community' to suggest the way in which a similarly educated group of people will have in common particular ideas and ways of reading texts, together with shared conscious beliefs and unconscious assumptions. Certain interpretations will gain currency within such a community and texts will therefore not generate meanings for them so much as fit into their conceptual models. In other words, texts come to have meanings within, and only within, contexts. The contexts for poetry in this book are history and society, and it is written with the conviction that this dimension to the study of poetry has been comparatively neglected, while such approaches to the novel have proliferated. This is in part for the reasons discussed at the start of this chapter, but perceptions of poetry's isolation and ahistorical condition are not conclusive, merely current habits of reading. To relate poetry to history is an alternative approach to interpretation, but it is also a dangerous enterprise, and we need to sound a note of caution:

The notion of a direct, spontaneous relation between text and history, then, belongs to a naive empiricism which is to be discarded.... The text can no more be conceived as directly denoting a real history than the meaning of a word can be imagined as an object correlated with it. Language, among other things, certainly denotes objects; but it does not do so in

11

some simple relationship, as though word and object stood adjacent, as two poles awaiting the electric current of inter-connection.

(Eagleton 1976a: 70)

This book provides a starting point for reading twentieth-century British poetry alongside history, but readers are also encouraged further to problematise and interrogate both the complexities of language and the categories of literature and history themselves.[15]

1

'UNION JACKS IN EVERY PART'

Prewar and Georgian poetry

The heaven that fills an English heart,
Is Union Jacks in every part.
The Irish heaven is heaven of old,
When Satan cracked skulls manifold.
The Scotsman has his heaven to come –
To argue his Creator dumb.
The Welshman's heaven is singing airs –
No matter who feels sick and swears.

(W.H. Davies, 'Heaven', in Reeves 1962: 35)

Introduction

This book builds a narrative of twentieth-century history and poetry
that is broadly chronological and necessarily selective. The intention is
to focus on poetry in the glare of the events of the century, rather than
in the light of aesthetic judgement, formal changes, and biographies of
individual poets, though these will also be touched on. The broad
sketch that I want to make in this first chapter is bounded by the
accession of Edward VII at the start of the century and the early years
of the reign of George V from 1910 up to World War I.

When Queen Victoria died in 1901, England was fascinated with its
own national identity, as though the combination of the end of a
century, the last years of a sixty-year reign, the Boer War and increased
Imperial activity prompted a renewed interest in the country's role in
the world. Many writers saw a significance in the coincidence of the
death of the monarch and of the century. H.G. Wells wrote that
'Queen Victoria sat on England like a great paper-weight and that after
her death things blew about all over the place' (Millard 1991: 2).
According to Yeats's idiosyncratic view, 'in 1900 everybody got down

off his stilts; nobody drank absinthe with his black coffee; nobody went mad; nobody committed suicide; nobody joined the Catholic church.... Victorianism had been defeated' (Yeats 1936b: xi–xii). For others, there was 'scientific' cause in the 1890s to show concern over national identity: following decades of mass migrancy to the cities, theories of social degeneration argued that the English yeoman stock was adapting downwards to the unhealthy conditions of the metropolis.

With respect to poetry, the turn of the century was also characterised by pronouncements on national destiny. There appeared W.E. Henley's *For England's Sake* in 1900, William Watson's *For England* in 1904, and Laurence Binyon's *England and Other Poems* in 1909, the year C.F.G. Masterman published his famous social account of *The Condition of England* (Millard 1991: 27). But why was there this outburst of heritage culture and national self-scrutiny? Apart from internal catalysts to change, this was a time of Imperial pride but also uncertainty, as the expanding Empire was becoming a financial burden and the Boer War (1899–1902) proved that, contrary to popular belief, the British could be outfought. The opening decades of the century were also a period of state expansion as legislation affecting poverty, unemployment, and the vote contributed to the idea that people could and should be administered, managed, and policed. This was in several respects a working through of the late nineteenth-century interest in Social Darwinism, the theory that cultures and civilisations might actually develop in ways that parallel the evolution of species, such that the most successful peoples would be those best adapted to changing conditions.

Literature from 1900 to 1914 was concerned with similar issues of social identity and national pride: and it is these that cause it to stand out as a particular period. Samuel Hynes argues that 'the time between the turn of the century and the First World War does seem to have the qualities that make a literary period' including 'a consciousness of its own separateness from what went before and what followed, and a body of literature that expresses that consciousness' (Hynes 1972: 1). Commonly, that body of literature would be discussed in terms of drama and particularly fiction. This was the time of Barrie's *Peter Pan* and Grahame's *The Wind in the Willows*, of E.M. Forster's *Howards End*, Kipling's *Puck of Pook's Hill*, and H.G. Wells's condition-of-England novels such as *The History of Mr. Polly* and *Tono-Bungay*. In all these works the concrete encroachments of the cities are contrasted with an endangered but perennial, idyllic rural England. This national sense of threat and loss is also there in poetry, where the change is perhaps best seen in terms of the death of certain figures. Although other well-established writers were to live well into the twentieth century, Matthew Arnold had died in 1888, Robert Browning in 1889, and Tennyson in 1892. Dante and Christina Rossetti were also both dead by 1894. A new vanguard was expected to emerge at this momentous point in history and in literature, yet the enormously popular poets that came to the fore were those who merely wished to celebrate the past and their own relation to it. The poets of Edward's reign from 1901 to 1910 were deeply conscious of all that had gone before them; concerned with the veneration of an existing order, their poetry was for the most part patriotic, conservative, imperialistic, and imitative.

As an example, there is Alfred Austin, a prominent Tory journalist who stood twice for Parliament and was Poet Laureate from 1896 to 1913. In 1898 he published his first collection in this capacity, *Songs of England*, to follow up his most successful volume, *The Garden that I Love*, published four years earlier. However, he was treated with scant respect even by many of his contemporaries and posterity has little to say about him (and Robert Bridges, his successor to the Laureateship, though a much better poet, is far more gratefully remembered for bringing the writing of Gerard Manley Hopkins to light than for his own poetry). One of Austin's poems is simply entitled 'Who would not die for England!':

> This great thought,
> Through centuries of Glory handed down
> By storied vault in monumental fane,
> And homeless grave in lone barbaric lands,
> Homeless but not forgotten, so can thrill
> With its imperious call the hearts of men,
>
> That suddenly from dwarf ignoble lives
> They rise to heights of nobleness, and spurn
> The languid couch of safety, to embrace
> Duty and Death that evermore were twin.

John Lucas describes Austin as simply 'a ridiculously bad poet'. His other poems have titles such as 'In Praise of England', 'On Returning to England', and 'Why England is Conservative'. In *Songs of England*, Austin offers an 'Explanatory' note on what he means by his key term:

> by 'England', for which no other appellation equally compre-hensive and convenient has yet been discovered, it is

intended to indicate not only Great Britain and Ireland, but Canada, Australia, South Africa, India, and every spot on earth where men feel an instantaneous thrill of imperial kinship at the very sound of the Name ['Victoria'].

(Millard 1991: 28)

Austin here can be said to be a part of the late nineteenth-century Imperialist drive to spread the English 'race' to the four corners of the globe, as argued in J.R. Seeley's *The Expansion of England* (1883) and Charles Dilke's *Problems of Greater Britain* (1890). For Seeley, who wished to see a commercial union of English-speakers across the world with London as its hub, the purpose of history was very similar to that of poetry for Austin: to inspire and proselytise as well as teach. Seeley explained that:

> It is a favourite maxim of mine that history, while it should be scientific in its method, should pursue a practical object. That is, it should not merely gratify the reader's curiosity about the past, but modify his view of the present and his forecast of the future. Now if this maxim be sound, the history of England ought to...exhibit the general tendency of English affairs in such a way as to set us thinking about the future and divining the destiny which is reserved for us.
>
> (Seeley 1883: 1)

Yet, the patriotic fervour of Seeley and Austin did not monopolise intellectual debate. Against such a vision we need to place a rival view: that of the Decadent poets of the 1890s, such as Ernest Dowson and Arthur Symons. The emphasis of these London avant-garde aesthetes, most widely celebrated in the work of Oscar Wilde, was on style and sensation – not on the meaning of experiences but their intensity and sweetness. It is the Decadents who in the face of nationalist, masculinist, and collectivist discourses championed the values of the individual and offered a challenge to the dominant sexual and social attitudes of the time, influencing the internationalism and experimentation of modernism. The Decadents proposed the kind of 'art for art's sake' revolution that might have led to significant changes in British aesthetics similar to the many contemporary advances in science and engineering. In the arts, despite the efforts of Jacob Epstein, T.S. Eliot, Ezra Pound, Wyndham Lewis, and D.H. Lawrence, the force of modernism would not be greatly felt in Britain until after the war. Not until then, as the critic F.R. Leavis argued in his book

New Bearings in English Poetry (1932), could it be said that in Britain 'the modern's perception of rhythm has been affected by the internal combustion engine' (Leavis 1972: 24). Meanwhile, Kafka was writing *The Trial* and Proust *In Remembrance of Things Past*. Baudelaire, Mallarmé, Verlaine and Rimbaud had already transformed French poetry. In fine art, Picasso, Braque, Duchamp and others were over-turning the fundamental principles of representation and perspective. The first London post-impressionist exhibition stunned the English in 1910, while in Paris two years later there was already the first Futurist exhibition. Schoenberg's first atonal work was produced in 1909 and Stravinsky's *Rite of Spring* was performed four years later.

Britain and British literature seemed preoccupied with the past in comparison with most of the rest of Europe. Samuel Hynes charac-terises the beginning of the Edwardian period in terms of sombre moods, melancholy and nostalgia: the end of a century, the death of a monarch whose predecessor few were old enough to remember, the culmination of an economic and social revolution of living patterns. The Edwardians, he says, were conscious of living in a period of transi-tion, of having left late Romantic Victorian poetry behind but of having travelled nowhere new. The century had started inauspiciously, leaving T.S. Eliot to conclude:

> In the first decade of the century the situation was unusual. I cannot think of a single living poet, either in England or America, then at the height of his powers, whose work was capable of pointing the way to a young poet conscious of the desire for a new idiom.
>
> (Hynes 1972: 9)

Another country

I'd like now to consider some of the social and political aspects of turn-of-the century Britain that are refracted, often unintentionally or by omission, through the poetry of the time: urbanisation, gender, educa-tion, and empire.[1] In 1890, 62 per cent of the population of England and Wales lived in cities, compared with 20 per cent in 1800. No other European power had experienced anything like this shift in population: in Germany the figure was still only 28 per cent, in France only 26 per cent (Hobsbawm 1987: 343). Yet this urban relocation was synchronous with an idealisation of country life especially common in an English poetry which was reluctant to see the city as an appropriate subject. Raymond Williams says that from about 1880 there was:

> a marked development of the idea of England as 'home', in that special sense in which home is a memory and an ideal. Some of these images of 'home' are of central London.... But many are of an ideal of rural England: its green peace contrasted with the tropical or arid places of actual work; its sense of belonging, of community, idealised by contrast with the tensions of colonial rule and the isolated alien settlement. The birds and trees and rivers of England; the natives speaking, more or less, one's own language: these were the terms of many imagined and actual settlements. The country, now, was a place to retire to.
>
> (Williams 1973: 281–2)

Alongside the persistent cult of the bucolic, domestic, and homely in the Edwardian era, the prewar years contained many radical changes in political and working life, and in science. There was the foundation of the Labour Party and of Sinn Fein, the end of the Boer War, and the start of the suffragette campaigns after the founding of the Women's Social and Political Union by Emmeline Pankhurst in 1903. In Britain there was considerable labour unrest while the launch of the Model T Ford in America inaugurated the era of the production line. The first air flight of the Wright brothers took place in 1903 and the first flight of the English Channel by Blériot in 1909. Technology was no longer affecting just industry, distribution, and agriculture but also the home, private travel, and entertainment, such that art would have to readjust to the perspectives offered, in particular, by the camera and the motor car. In the last dozen years of the nineteenth century, machines which would revolutionise the twentieth century had been invented: the Kodak camera (1888), the electric motor (1888), the diesel engine (1892), the Ford motor car (1893), the gramophone (1894), Marconi's radio (1895), Lumières' cinematograph (1895), and X-ray machines (1895). Powered flight, sound recordings, and the discovery of radium were soon to follow. Domestic appliances such as electric kettles, telephones, electric irons, and refrigerators were available, though too expensive for all but the richest households. Theoretical science was also revolutionised in this period, defined by Planck's introduction of quantum theory in 1900 and Einstein's unveiling of his General Theory of Relativity in 1916. In cultural terms, this was the period in which it could be said, following the push for ever more trade markets, that the era of global knowledge had arrived. Peary reached the North

Pole in 1909, while Amundsen made it to the South in 1911. The invention of the electric telegraph meant that communication across the planet could take place within hours. The five-fold expansion to a million kilometres of the world's railways between 1870 and 1914, and the doubling of merchant shipping, brought increased trade and tourists into every major city.

Such changes also affected both working life and gender roles. In Britain, in the 1880s and 1890s, approximately 83 per cent of all males over the age of ten were in recognised paid employment, compared with 34 per cent of females. The change in living and employment patterns over the nineteenth century meant that 'work' in the twentieth century was predominantly both outside the home and fixed, in terms of place and hours. The household income was now generally earned by specific persons who went 'out' to work. In many ways, this reinforced traditional pay differentials as it was assumed that a man was earning for a family, while a woman was earning only for herself. Women worked in only a few professions, usually in the food and textile industries. On the other hand, if the term 'employment' is used in its wider sense then the number of women working was far higher – they worked as domestic servants (10 per cent of the entire population in 1900), landladies, or laundresses. The effect of this was, in Eric Hobsbawm's words, a masculinisation of business and of what economics considered as 'labour' (Hobsbawm 1987: 198–9). A similar case obtained in politics, as the widening of the vote, in terms of socio-economic position, meant that women were now specifically instead of generally excluded. Such masculinisation is also found in literature, which was increasingly perceived as a profession, and therefore outside of women's domestic sphere, as will be discussed below.

As for poetry, the combination of increased state education following the 1902 Education Act and the many assertions of the importance of national culture meant that literature was beginning to be seen as a serious academic discipline, one that had to be assessed and regularised. One of the reasons why it hadn't been appraised in this fashion before was that literary study had been considered suitable for women and not for men. At the turn of the century, however, it was increasingly thought that instead of being an escapist amusement, literature could teach codes of behaviour and define national identity. Consequently, 'the world of letters' became colonised by various commercial and didactic interests. For example, in addition to the appearance of the *Oxford Book of English Verse* in 1900, the first decade of the new century saw the establishment of the *Times Literary Supplement*, the Oxford University Press series of World's Classics, and the Everyman imprint, to bring literary masterpieces to the mass of the population. The Nobel Prize for Literature was founded in 1901, and in the year it was won by Kipling, 1907, the English Association was created 'to explain and promote the essential role played by the study of English in the national culture' (Trodd 1991: 2). The Association was led by Henry Newbolt, the English Edwardian poet I will discuss shortly.

This growing emphasis on a masculine national culture could be said to have culminated in the setting up in 1910 of the Academic Committee: a coterie of male writers gathered together with the aim of establishing all that was best and most important in English letters. It included Hardy, Yeats, and Joseph Conrad, and at times constituted a dining and debating club which was to a degree set upon establishing a virile, manly English literature. One of their conclusions was that Victorian literature had been too feminine and moralistic, and that writers such as George Eliot, whose reputation has never been lower, had held back the English novel in comparison with its European equivalents. Much of this can be easily read as a reaction to the rise of the suffragette movement and its equivalent in writing, the New Woman, against whom Kipling wrote 'The Female of the Species' in 1911, asserting that women 'may not govern': 'She can bring no more to living than the powers that make her great / As the Mother of the Infant and the Mistress of the Mate.' Yet women, whose protests against inequality culminated in that same year in riots, were able to attack government instead. In 1914, the slicing of Velasquez's painting 'Venus at Her Mirror' in London's National Gallery by a militant suffragette called Mary Richardson, caused museums up and down the country to be temporarily closed. While it was clearly an attack on certain male depictions of women, it was also a protest against the government's treatment of Emmeline Pankhurst.

The fight for the vote by women up to 1918 is a crucial social and cultural aspect to the period, though it is the kind of political dissent omitted from contemporary poetry; another is the growing opposition between labour and capital (even in 1913 one per cent of the population owned two-thirds of the wealth). Strong unions were behind the miners' and dockers' strikes of 1912, and in the following years of the decade union memberships were to double, with TUC affiliation rising from 2.2 million in 1913 to 6.5 million in 1920. Given the continued nationalist agitation for independence in Ireland, and the campaigns in Ulster against Home Rule, some critics have seen the prewar period as one of mounting social disorder and political confrontation which, but for the war, would have led to revolution. It has even been said that a general strike was planned for the month war was declared.[2]

The main political interests used to mask this internal division, British Imperialism and national identity, also excluded women – as late as 1938 Virginia Woolf was to argue in *Three Guineas* that women were still positioned outside a masculine patriotism that had appropriated English identity. While Imperialism, the dominant political creed since the 1890s, was synonymous with masculinity, British women were for Woolf part of an 'Outsiders' Society', for which there were no 'foreigners' since any woman would become a 'foreigner' if she married one (Woolf 1952: 193–7). For the ruling elite of the European powers, by contrast, the world was divided between the nation, its empire, and its foreign rivals. Eric Hobsbawm calls the period 1875–1914 the 'Age of Empire', partly because of the extraordinary number of rulers who, using a title almost unknown a century later, named themselves 'Emperor', including those of Germany, Austria, Russia, Turkey, and Britain. By World War I:

> Europe held a grand total of roughly 85 per cent of the world as colonies, protectorates, dependencies, dominions and commonwealths.... And in Europe itself at the end of the nineteenth century, scarcely a corner of life was untouched by the facts of empire; the economies were hungry for overseas markets, raw materials, cheap labour, and hugely profitable land, and defence and foreign-policy establishments were more and more committed to the maintenance of vast tracts of distant territory and large numbers of subjugated peoples.
>
> (Said 1993: 6–7)

To both solemnize and celebrate this position in the world, the British had established an annual 'Empire Day' in 1902. This is perhaps the best example of how, as Raymond Williams writes, at the turn of the century, 'the vision of Englishness itself changes': not only is it masculinised, standardised, and institutionalised, 'whereas earlier it is really internal to England, in the 1880–1920 period it is far more defined in terms of an external imperial role' (Williams 1979: 263). Particularly in the Edwardian period, poetry was also caught up in the drive to define Englishness by looking to the rural past, and to position that essence at the centre of an imperial mythology. Just as organisations such as the Academic Committee seemed to be opposing the suffragette movement by excluding women from the front ranks of literature, this pastoral and nationalist vision can be seen as part of a repression of the social upheavals of the time: an attempt in poetry to transcend the political by promoting values of the past (before industrial conflict), the countryside (opposed to the strife of the cities), and the Empire, far away.

Edwardian England, Edwardian poetry

The dominant idea of an agricultural England persisted in the new century in spite of, or perhaps because of, the mass migration to the cities. The country was to be preserved by the National Trust, created in 1895, and celebrated in *Country Life*, founded in 1897. It was sustained in Vaughan Williams's blend of Elizabethan and traditional English folk songs, in mock Tudor village architecture, and in music-hall Romanticism.[3] This was an England also found in poetic attempts to create a modern national mythology. For example, there is this rallying-cry in W.E. Henley's 'A New Song to an Old Tune' from *For England's Sake: Verses and songs in time of war*, 1900:

> Sons of Shannon, Tamar, Trent,
> Men of the Lothians, men of Kent,
> Essex, Wessex, shore and shire,
> Mates of the net, the mine, the fire,
> Lads of desk and wheel and loom,
> Noble and trader, squire and groom,
> Come where the bugles of England play,
> *Over the hills and far away*!

Henley's attempt at an all-inclusive but masculine Englishness is typical of much contemporary poetry in that it is traditional, bellicose, and expansionist – it attempts to transcend class divisions by appealing to all *men* to participate in national celebration. Despite its crudeness, it captures the mood of the time and is similar to the rhetoric of pro-Imperial newspapers such as the *Daily Mail* and the *Daily Express*, both founded at the turn of the century. The Edwardian period is generally seen as one that produced worthwhile fiction and drama, much of which reflected the changing political scene,[4] but worse than indifferent poetry which was hackneyed, sentimental, and blindly patriotic. Robert Conquest speaks damningly of 'the deplorable state of English poetry in the first decade of this century' (Millard 1991: 5). Despite the political changes, the decade is often characterised as a time of sunshine and progress before crisis, and poetry especially suffered from a sense of complacency. Writing about the Georgian poets who were to follow in 1911, one critic maintains:

However nostalgically one may look back on the uncompli-
cated Edwardian days of the bicycle and bloomers, feminism,
Fabian socialism, and ta-ra-ra-boom-de-ay, surely one cannot
claim that the age produced, with one or two obvious exceptions, any but mediocre verse. In the history of English poetry
the Edwardian age appears as a hiatus.

(Ross 1967: 29–30)

Sir Henry Newbolt, an Imperialist Liberal who later wrote several
books about England's military victories, represents much of what both
the Georgians and the war poets were to come to react against.
Newbolt was educated at Clifton, one of the two schools that sent the
largest number of pupils on to military training at Sandhurst and
Woolwich. He wrote many poems about the school and forged his
patriotic ideals there. Oxford came as a disappointment, lacking as it
did the allegiances and loyalties of School and House. Newbolt was a
lawyer until his literary success at the turn of the century meant he
could devote his time to writing, and in 1900 he founded *The Monthly
Review*. An influential figure, he was made President of the English
Association in 1907, a Professor of Poetry by the Royal Society of
Literature in 1911, and a Knight in 1915. One of his most famous
poems is 'The Vigil':

England! where the sacred flame
　Burns before the inmost shrine,
Where the lips that love thy name
　Consecrate their hopes and thine,
Where the banners of thy dead
Weave their shadows overhead,
Watch beside thine arms tonight,
Pray that God defend the Right.

This poem spans our period very well because, although published in
1898, it became nationally famous in 1914, when Newbolt wrote that
'The Vigil is being quoted, sung, recited and reprinted from one end of
the country to another, and I have had letters of thanks by every post'
(Winterbottom 1986: 66).

There is scarcely a poem of Newbolt's in which 'England' does not
appear – it becomes almost an incantation: 'The certainty with which
he can rely upon "England" is as unquestioning as the selfless sacrifices
of soldiers such as Younghusband and Haig. "England" is the talisman
of Newbolt's poetry, as are the names of her national figures' (Millard

1991: 26). He is therefore, like other contemporary poets, nostalgic for an England past; his poetry seeks authority and expresses a desire to submit to it. His 'England' is constructed from the usual rota of place names and heroes, from national qualities and characteristics: 'a race high-handed, strong of heart, / Sea-rovers, conquerors, builders in the waste' ('The Non-Combatant' in *The Island Race* (Newbolt 1898)).

Newbolt, born in 1862, did not publish a book of poetry until 1897, when *Admirals All, and Other Verses* introduced a sub-Tennysonian brand of heroic, historical, and partly hysterical narrative poems. Initial fame came with a Kiplingesque ballad called 'Drake's Drum', which set the standard and tone of his future paeans and eulogies. Newbolt's *Collected Poems 1897–1907*, dedicated to Thomas Hardy, has a portrait of Sir Francis Drake as a frontispiece, partly because Newbolt viewed Drake as a hero of Arthurian proportions whose spirit would come to the rescue whenever England was threatened. 'Vitaï Lampada', his most famous poem, and 'The Vigil' come from *The Island Race* of 1898. The first takes its title, meaning 'torches of life', from a reference in Lucretius to Greek relay races in which a lighted torch was passed from runner to runner (remembered now in the carrying of a torch to the opening ceremony of the Olympic Games). It is a short, episodic narrative poem about handing on public-schoolboy ethics to the Empire, and has the famous juvenile refrain 'Play up! play up! and play the game!'. The second, 'The Vigil', maintains England's need to be ceremonially watchful for the 'Right' of God and country while at war – not that Newbolt had any experience of war, at a time when, immediately before the Boer War, Britain still championed the 'Pax Britannica' as a lasting peace that its Imperial might would ensure. Throughout his poetry, Newbolt is trying to express a national vision, but it is of a particular, idealised, and nostalgic Englishness. The very need for its assertion suggests the threats posed by women, the working class, and war.

For Newbolt, the English are the imperial race, ambassadors from a small island who bear their Englishness 'through life like a torch in flame' ('Vitaï Lampada'). It is important but hard for us today to grasp the enthusiasm for such a writer, other than for his ballads' simplicity, jolliness, and optimism. His first slim book of poetry was reprinted twenty times in its first twelve months of publication late in 1897, and this may have been helped by its capturing of a national mood in the wake of Queen Victoria's Diamond Jubilee celebrations that year. When *The Island Race* came out the following year, Newbolt became a literary sensation, and his poetry was quoted in parliament, included in sermons, and memorised by people such as Leslie Stephen, Virginia

Woolf's father and editor of the *Dictionary of National Biography* (Winterbottom 1986: 45). Newbolt himself commented on the philosophy behind 'Vitaï Lampada':

> It was a Roman rule, peculiarly fitted to the needs of the English schoolboy…demanding of us the virtues of leadership, courage and independence; the sacrifice of selfish interests to the ideal of fellowship and the future of the race. In response we gave enthusiastically but we gave something rather different: we set up a 'good form', a standard of our own. 'To be in all things decent, orderly, self-mastering: in action to follow up the coolest common sense with the most unflinching endurance: in public affairs to be devoted as a matter of course.'
>
> (Newbolt 1932: 65)

A key phrase here is 'the future of the race', and Newbolt expressed many of the common national aspirations of the Edwardian years, just as Kipling, who wrote speeches for Edward VII, expressed those of the Imperial years. Employing the popular term that was associated with this kind of patriotic fervour, John Lucas states baldly that Newbolt was wedded to 'an especially nasty kind of Imperialistic jingoism' (Lucas 1986: 61). And in many ways, the best comparisons with his verse come not from poetry books but lyric sheets and so I want to end this section by mentioning the importance of the music hall, an uncompromisingly cheap and cheerful form of Edwardian entertainment which, after World War I, was to give way to 'variety' and American music (Morton 1993). In comparison with poetry, the music hall provided a communal kind of participatory patriotism which provoked sentiments that lasted long after the show, as tunes were whistled, lyrics sung, and sheet music bought. Jingoism arose as a term from G.W. Hunt's song 'By Jingo': 'We don't want to fight, but, by Jingo, if we do, we've got the men, we've got the ships, we've got the money, too'. This is a world like Newbolt's in which 'plain-speaking' is valued, and in which the Imperial race, having learned the lessons of Dilke's 'Greater Britain' and of Lord Roseberry's 'Commonwealth' (first mooted in 1885), is defined by its common language, found in music-hall songs like 'It's the English Speaking Race Against the World':

We're brothers of the self same race
speakers of the self same tongue
With the same brave hearts that feel no fears

from fighting for a thousand years
Folks say what will the British do?
Will she rest with banners furled?
No No No
When we go once again to meet the foe
It's the English speaking race against the world.

The identification of enemies elsewhere undoubtedly helped to paper over the cracks in national unity created by myriad social threats to traditional power. Challenges of class and gender are noticeably repressed in the lyrics of the late Victorian and Edwardian periods, but improvements in education were soon to be compounded as weapons against the political and literary establishments when all social groups would be required to fight an Imperialists' war that would signal the beginning of the decline of the old order.

The Georgians: between Edwardianism and modernism

Perhaps oddly, given the Edwardian poetry it replaced, the expression 'Georgian poetry' has almost become a term of abuse. To be a Georgian poet is to be a bad poet in nearly all critical commentary since the 1930s, even though in the 1910s and 1920s they were enormously popular and praised by such independent-minded critics as D.H. Lawrence. It is the canonization of modernism that has made the Georgians appear so conservative and unoriginal. As Kenneth Millard notes, 'The word "Georgian" remains in use as an often arbitrary designation for a kind of insipid rural verse' (Millard 1991: 10). When critics want to recommend an early twentieth-century poet they often feel obliged to begin by arguing that he or she is not a Georgian, despite any appearances to the contrary. The Georgians are popularly thought to have been interested in little more than flora and fauna, to have reproduced the worst aspects of Victorian verse, and to have written no experimental poetry at all, but to have used traditional, often balladic, forms with simple diction, straightforward syntax, and conventional metre. Also noting that Englishness in most of its varieties was largely about the countryside of the south, Linda Williams writes: 'Georgianism perhaps epitomizes the popular notion of English poetry – parochial, solid and unironic, celebrating English rural life, particularly the home counties variety' (Williams 1992: 65).

Like most literary labels, 'Georgian poetry' is an imprecise term. It includes such well-remembered poets as Walter de la Mare,

W.H. Davies (also author of *Autobiography of a Super-Tramp*, 1907), and John Masefield, but also some of the work of more famous names such as Robert Graves, Rupert Brooke, Siegfried Sassoon, and D.H. Lawrence himself. In one sense it could be said that the term refers to the poets, such as those mentioned above, published in Edward Marsh's five anthologies of *Georgian Poetry* from 1912 to 1922. Though sales of the last anthology were comparatively poor, the first four collections each sold in excess of 15,000 copies, a remarkable achievement for books of contemporary poetry. The first volume went into six editions in its initial seven months. Marsh, educated at Westminster and Cambridge, was a prominent civil servant and Parliamentary Private Secretary to Winston Churchill, then First Lord of the Admiralty. Though strictly an 'amateur' who believed a poem's chief qualities should be 'intelligibility, music and raciness', he argued that new young poets like Masefield and Brooke, whom he thought were being ignored, constituted 'another "Georgian period" which may take rank in due time with the several great poetic ages of the past'.[5] Marsh's preface claimed that with these poets, English poetry was 'again putting on a new strength and beauty'. Many critics, including the reviewer in the *Times Literary Supplement* in February 1913, agreed.[6] On the other hand, both Wilfred Owen and Edward Thomas thought of themselves as akin to the Georgians, and the group can be said to have had no common agenda or programme. However, it could be argued that they shared an ideology. For example, Bernard Bergonzi says that the Georgians' outlook was 'essentially, a little-Englander's vision, as opposed to Kipling's interest in a Greater Britain, an England beyond the seas' (Bergonzi 1973: 148).

The Georgians were concerned with England in terms of nature and the countryside but, unlike Newbolt, William Watson, or Alfred Noyes, not with the English as a nation or a 'race'. Even Rupert Brooke's war sonnets describe not English people but 'A dust whom England bore', 'English air', 'thoughts by England given' and 'an English heaven' (all from 'The Soldier'). Harold Monro, owner of the influential Poetry Bookshop, publisher of *Georgian Poetry* and founding editor of the *Poetry Review*, decided that

> poetry is far more native [than thought] to the national genius. We have a strong capacity for enthusiasm; we have a calm obstinate persistence, and there is no one so inflexible as an Englishman who has finally set his eyes towards Beauty.
>
> (Hynes 1972: 99)

This is a southern, upper-middle-class vision and it is also a male one. Like other prewar literary enterprises, the Georgian anthologies excluded women. The first to be proposed for inclusion, Charlotte Mew, was left out by Marsh from the third collection, despite Monro's recommendations. In retrospect, Mew now seems one of the most interesting of the 'Georgian' poets, which was at least recognised by Hardy, who described her as 'the greatest poetess I have come across lately' (Trodd 1991: 95).

A collection of seventeen of Mew's poems, *The Farmer's Bride*, was issued in 1916 by Monro's Poetry Bookshop. The poems focus on lost love and emotional denial, quite possibly because Mew was fearful of the hereditary mental instability in her family, or because she was caught between her sense of propriety and her lesbianism (her most well-known poem, 'The Farmer's Bride', ends with a man's over-powering desire for his newly returned runaway wife, who sleeps not with him but in their attic: 'The soft young down of her, the brown, / The brown of her – her eyes, her hair, her hair!'). Mew renounced marriage and children, and her poems deal not with family life or with the traditional subjects of the Georgians but with pedlars, changelings, and asylums.[7] Her longest and best early poem is the contemplative meditation 'Madeleine in Church', in which she experiments with line length and arrangement in a way closer to the modernists than the Georgians. In a general reflection on loss, these lines consider Mary's love for Jesus:

> And through it all, from her, no word,
>   She scarcely saw You, scarcely heard:
> Surely You knew when she so touched You with her hair,
>   Or by the wet cheek lying there,
> And while her perfume clung to You from head to feet all through
>   the day
> That You can change the things for which we care,
> But even You, unless You kill us, not the way.

The poem considers the separation of the physical and the spiritual worlds and the difficulty of faith without revelation; all Mew's poetry is suffused with images of suffering, punishment and denial, reinforcing the general impression that she found Georgianism and the male literary scene intense, sorrowful and, at her suicide in 1927, finally overwhelming. Despite her connection with the Poetry Bookshop, Mew's poems suggest she had little in common with the Georgians.

Robert Graves, who was included in the second Georgian

anthology, has summarised the poets via distinctions that comment on the Victorians, the Edwardians, and the Decadents:

> The Georgians' general recommendations were the discarding of archaistic diction such as 'thee' and 'thou' and 'flowerer' and 'whene'er' and of poetical constructions such as 'winter drear' and 'host on armed host' and of pomposities generally. It was also understood that, in reaction to Victorianism, their verse should avoid all formally religious, philosophic or improving themes; and all sad, wicked, cafe-table themes in reaction to the 'nineties'. Georgian poetry was to be English but not aggressively imperialistic; pantheistic rather than atheistic; and as simple as a child's reading book.
>
> (Walter 1995: 19)

It has been argued that the Georgian movement had three phases (Ross 1967). The poets of the first Marsh volume, including Lascelles Abercrombie, Gordon Bottomley and Wilfred Gibson, were moderately radical, particularly Brooke (in his language and imagery). The second phase admitted some of the war poets, such as Graves and Sassoon, while the third contained 'Neo-Georgians' such as J.C. Squire, Edward Shanks, and John Freeman. Over this ten-year period, the Georgians changed from innovatory, affirmative minor rebels to reactionary and sentimental escapists.

Considering the early rather than the late Georgians and by turning aside from the more famous poems, George Walter answers the charge that the Georgians ignored contemporary history and reality. He notes that W.H. Davies wrote one poem included in the first Georgian anthology about a Thames-side tramp, 'The Head of Rags', and one in the second anthology about the death of a prostitute, 'The Bird of Paradise' (Walter 1995). Wilfred Gibson has a similarly unsentimental poem about a flower-seller, 'Geraniums', in the first collection. Such examples have been termed 'Georgian realism' and were acknowledged by contemporary reviewers but seldom since, because even a poet such as Davies produced Georgian clichés (e.g. see the poem 'Sheep'). For Gary Day, returning to the discussion of our introductory chapter, because of the shift from an individualist to a collectivist state, the Georgians exhibited a crisis of subjectivity. This meant they seldom used human relationships as a subject and wrote awkwardly about nature, making it exotic, mystifying, or dangerous. Similarly, their liking for multiple adjectives, expressing a need to personalise and qualify, could be seen as a symptom of their concern with self-expression and individuality (Day 1993). These are traits epitomised by the life and work of Rupert Brooke, a writer at whom, somewhat ironically given his later reception and popular image, accusations of brutality and coarseness were levelled when the Georgians published their first collection.

Rupert Brooke

On 26 April 1915, three days after one of his untrained sub-lieutenants died of blood-poisoning on the way to Gallipoli, Winston Churchill wrote an obituary in *The Times*:

> [Rupert Brooke] expected to die; he was willing to die for the dear old England whose beauty and majesty he knew; and he advanced towards the brink in perfect serenity, with absolute conviction of the rightness of his country's cause and a heart devoid of hate for fellow-men.
>
> (Hibberd 1981: 38)

The mythologising of Brooke as the quintessentially noble, youthful, and beautiful poet was at its height. The photograph for his 1915 *Poems*, of a bare-shouldered Brooke in profile, has been described by his biographer as 'a visual image that met the needs of a nation at a time of crisis' (Hassall 1972: 390). While the Brooke myth was to endure, esteem for his poetry was not to last long after the war and his reputation collapsed in the 1930s under the criticisms of left-wing poets. He is the most representative Georgian poet and so worth considering in some detail.

Brooke was born at Rugby, where his father was a schoolmaster, on 3 August 1887. At school a Decadent and at university a Fabian, he travelled extensively after leaving Cambridge and much of his best poetry was written during this world tour. Considered a golden youth, Brooke was full of the energy and hopes of his time. A cricketer and footballer, an actor and a scholar, he divided his time after university between literary circles in London and Cambridge. In a fit of enthusiasm, Brooke nearly wrote the entire first Georgian 'anthology' himself. In an anecdote that sounds like an excerpt from a *Boy's Own* adventure, Marsh writes about the organising of this initial collection:

> There was a general feeling among the younger poets that modern English poetry was very good, and sadly neglected by readers. Rupert announced one evening, sitting half-undressed

on his bed, that he had conceived a brilliant scheme. He would write a book of poetry, and publish it as a selection from the works of twelve different writers, six men and six women, all with the most convincing pseudonyms....It occurred to me that as we both believed there were at least twelve flesh-and-blood poets whose work, if properly thrust under the public's nose, had a good chance of producing the effect desired, it would be simpler to use the material which was ready to hand. Next day (September 20th it was) we dined in my rooms...and started the plan of the book which was published in December under the name of *Georgian Poetry, 1911–12*.[8]

Such a story indicates Brooke's energy and also his self-confidence, which alternated with periods of crisis and despondency. He was an enthusiast, an aesthete, and an adventurer motivated by boyish ideals but prone to bouts of despair. In a typical fit of eagerness and escapism, Brooke set off on a year-long world tour in May 1913, calling at Vancouver, Fiji, Samoa, New Zealand, and Honolulu amongst other places. From Tahiti, the subject of one of Brooke's best poems, the satirical 'Tiare Tahiti', he wrote:

Everyone has a white flower behind their ear. Mamua has given me one. Do you know the significance of a white flower worn over the ear? A white flower over the right ear means 'I am looking for a sweetheart.' And a white flower over the left ear means 'I have found a sweetheart.' And a white flower over each ear means 'I have one sweetheart, and am looking for another.' A white flower over each ear, my dear, is dreadfully the most fashionable way of adorning yourself in Tahiti.

(Marsh 1942: 107)

The anecdote and the mannered, foppish attitude indicate Brooke's major themes: the search for love and fashionability, the discovery of loss and betrayal. Brooke was obsessed with nakedness, physical perfection, and the body, although his poetry rejects romantic love (Knight 1971). He attempted to introduce realism in opposition to a vogue for 'prettiness', but had little to say. Hynes calls Brooke

a lyric poet of Youth, Love and Death, who developed from a Late Decadent to an Early Georgian. Most of [his] poems are hard going now...because they are uniformly and conventionally

31

dull; they are poems that might have been written by...a committee of Georgians.

(Hynes 1972: 145)

Yet some of Brooke's poems were considered ugly, crude, and indecorous on publication (Hassall 1972: 366–7). For example, there is the bitterness of 'Jealousy':

When all that's fine in man is at an end,
And you, that loved young life and clean, must tend
A foul sick fumbling dribbling body and old,
When his rare lips hang flabby and can't hold
Slobber, and you're enduring that worst thing,
Senility's queasy furtive love-making,
And searching those dear eyes for human meaning,
Propping the bald and helpless head, and cleaning
A scrap that life's flung by, and love's forgotten, –
Then you'll be tired; and passion dead and rotten;
And he'll be dirty, dirty!

Kenneth Millard thinks that 'Jealousy' has to be read in 'the context of a clash with both an elevated conception of love and the refined language which commonly expresses it'. It is a kind of reaction also found in the anti-love poems 'Lust' and 'Dead Men's Love'. In the latter, Brooke undermines the couple's desire to find self-love through another: 'in the other's eyes, to see / Each his own tiny face'; which leads to 'The emptiness of eyes'. Brooke's humour, sometimes playful, sometimes acerbic, is often undervalued or overlooked, but it is best to see his most famous poem, 'The Old Vicarage, Grantchester', as a satire on the earnestness of poems such as Robert Browning's 'Home Thoughts from Abroad'. 'Granchester' presents a comically narrow view of the world, whose bathos is summed up in the couplet: 'God! I will pack, and take a train, / And get me to England once again'. Brooke intended to call 'The Old Vicarage, Grantchester' by the title 'The Sentimental Exile' but Edward Marsh chose the final name and so this rather tongue-in-cheek parody has more often been read as a solemn evocation of England's rural 'honey and tea' continuity. In addition to such pastiches of Edwardian poetry, Brooke also mocked both the poetic image of idealised love (as in 'Sonnet Reversed') and the way in which 'noble humanistic aspirations are confronted by a disgusted fascination with man's basic animal nature' (Millard 1991: 165–7).

Brooke suffered a nervous breakdown while in Germany between

32

1911–12, the time of writing 'Grantchester' but also of the more problematic anti-love poems which reify and dismember their human subjects. This collapse can be ascribed to various sexual problems, and Brooke's loss of faith in relationships, expressed in poems such as 'The Busy Heart', has been attributed to the promiscuous bohemianism of the famous Bloomsbury Group with whom he was involved.

Through analyses of his use of satire and bitterness, we can locate Brooke away from the accusations of extreme dilettantism levelled at him. However, he is still typical of most Georgians in his avoidance of contemporary issues:

> The conventional image of Brooke as an indulgently romantic young socialite hopelessly ill-equipped to cope with the ugly realities of Edwardian social and political issues (women's suffrage, the new left, Irish home rule, the end of Empire) cannot be entirely refuted.
>
> (Millard 1991: 170)

It has also been said that from his different position, Brooke was similar to Newbolt in wanting to remain youthful and boyish, and this undoubtedly suffused his poetry as his life was driven by personal and sexual disappointments. Sex and overt sexuality served only to destabilise his earlier innocent friendships. Hynes summarises Brooke as 'immature (his favourite play was *Peter Pan*), provincial, puritanical, frightened by sex and harassed by a tyrannical mother who could end a typical letter, "Why are you so unsatisfactory?"' (Hynes 1972: 151). In this, Brooke still seems to be emblematic of his age, not just because of his enthusiasm and youthful confidence, but because his precocity overlaid fears and neuroses, to do with women, adulthood, and the realities of the everyday world, amounting to a life of promise undercut by breakdowns and the threat of change.

Edward Thomas

A very different poet of the time, and probably the most accomplished of the 'Georgians' even though he was repeatedly excluded from Marsh's anthologies, was Edward Thomas. Thomas is sometimes discussed as a war poet, sometimes as a Georgian, and sometimes as neither.[9] In many accounts, he is the *Welsh* poet who stands between Hardy and Auden, bridging the gap in *English* poetry introduced by the *Franco-American* modernism of Pound and Eliot. (Stan Smith persuasively characterises Thomas as a socialist poet caught between his affinity for the south of England and his Welsh ancestry (Smith 1986: 13ff.)). Thomas was friends with several of the anthologised Georgians and his style has often been associated with theirs – James Reeves's 1962 collection of *Georgian Poetry* includes several poems by Thomas, and by others not included by Marsh such as A.E. Housman, who declined inclusion, and Charles Sorley. Thomas has also been grouped with authors such as Brooke, Lascelles Abercrombie, and Robert Frost as the Dymock poets who gathered in Gloucestershire in 1914. Among them was one of the few recognised female poets of the period, Eleanor Farjeon. Her fine poem 'Easter Monday', included in the volume of women's World War I poetry discussed in the next chapter, *Scars Upon My Heart*, is a eulogy to her lover, the recently killed Thomas.

Born in 1878 in London, Thomas studied history at Oxford, where he married. Most of his life was spent in the south of England and he lived in Hampshire from 1906. He decided to live by his writing even though it paid poorly and consigned him to a life of drudgery. In the eighteen years from 1897 to 1915 he wrote thirty books, none of them poetry. Thomas did not even begin writing verse until his mid-thirties, under the encouragement of Robert Frost, and in 1917 he died without ever having published poetry under his own name. His last poem was written before he embarked for France, but he had enlisted in the Artists' Rifles eighteen months earlier – all his poetry was written between November 1914 and January 1917, the month before he left for the front line.

Thomas declared:

> The worst of the poetry being written today is that it is too deliberately, and not inevitably English. It is for an audience: there is more in it of the shouting of the rhetorician, reciter, or politician than of the talk of friends and lovers.
>
> (Silkin 1987: 87)

With regard to the poets I have looked at in this chapter, Thomas was unimpressed. He said of Newbolt: 'all his verse might be described as an elaborate corollary to "Rule Britannia" '.[10] He also mocked Brooke in a poem called 'No One Cares Less than I': 'No one cares less than I, / Nobody knows but God, / Whether I am destined to lie / Under a foreign clod'. However, he admired the way the younger Georgians brought out 'the modern love of the simple and primitive, as seen in children, peasants, savages, early men, animals, and Nature in general'.[11]

Thomas is another writer preoccupied with the countryside, but he is not a pastoral poet. His early prose works catered for the kind of heritage market we have already identified, but if his view of England is sometimes romanticised it has little in common with the mythologising gestures of other contemporary writers. His verse is written from firsthand experience, and much of it deals with the paths, woods, and hedgerows that he loved, as do many of his books, such as the essays in *The Heart of England* (1906), a series of unadorned descriptive accounts of the passing scenery on peaceful country walks. His is simple poetry but it is not simplistic; it is understated, contemplative, and reverential. His most famous poem, 'As the Team's Head-Brass', contains Thomas's common themes of nature, love, rural tradition, and the threat posed by changes such as the war. The decline of Britain's rural way of life (partly due to wheat and refrigerated meat arriving from America) is apparent in several of his poems, many of which stress continuity but imply a deep melancholy and alienation too. This is at a time when not 62 per cent as in 1890 but 80 per cent of the population of England and Wales were living in urban districts.

Edna Longley argues that the long poem 'Lob' shows Thomas's importance as a bridge between the Romantics and Moderns: 'It celebrates a spirit that has historically informed and interconnected the countryside, character, folklore, language, and literature of England' (Longley 1986: 47):

He is English as this gate, these flowers, this mire.
And when at eight years old Lob-lie-by-the-fire
Came in my books, this was the man I saw.
He has been in England as long as dove and daw,
Calling the wild cherry tree the merry tree,
The rose campion Bridget-in-her-bravery;
And in a tender mood he, as I guess,
Christened one flower Love-in-idleness,
And while he walked from Exeter to Leeds
One April called all cuckoo-flowers Milkmaids.

But Raymond Williams says the poem offers

the casual figure of a dream of England, in which rural labour and rural revolt, foreign wars and internal dynastic wars, history, legend, and literature, are indiscriminately enfolded into a single emotional gesture. Lob or Lud, immemorial

peasant or yeoman or labourer: the figure was now fixed and
its name was Old England.

(Williams 1973: 258)

'Lob' presents a familiar view of England that can be found in
numerous other poets such as Hardy, Clare, and Wordsworth, but this
is very different from the celebrations of privilege and elite institutions
found in the work of Thomas's contemporaries. Thomas expresses a
love for the country, its woods, and its occupations, but not the nation,
its institutions, public buildings, and statespeople.

In general, Georgian poetry is a reaction both to Victorian sentimentalism and to the aesthetic movement of the 1890s. One critic
argues that it 'sought to strike a new and energetic note of patriotism'
because it was 'essentially retrospective, drawing for its images on an
imagined English countryside of the past containing the predictable
landmarks, "country cottages, old furniture, moss-covered barns, rose-
scented lanes, apple and cherry-orchards"' (John Williams 1987: 13).
However, Thomas cannot be said to be a patriotic poet. He is specific
in his references and so there is no abstract 'nation' but there is also
no attempt to reduce England to a public school or a country house.
It is a deep love of place and nature that constitutes his motive for
going to war. England 'is all we know and live by, and we trust / She
is good and must endure, loving her so: / And as we love ourselves we
hate her foe' ('This is No Case of Petty Right or Wrong'). There is no
sense of superiority or moral rectitude, only a desire to defend his own
home and his life in the English countryside. Thomas states simply
'Beside my hate for one fat patriot / My hatred for the Kaiser is love
true'.[12] For Thomas, England and the idea of England had been sacrificed for the Empire. Tradition for him lay not, as for Eliot, in books
and intellectual history but in local people and known places; he
once wrote that 'England is a system of vast circumferences circling
around the minute neighbouring points of home' (Thomas 1928:
111). Thomas wanted to make his prose like that of a Surrey peasant
and he sought for idioms that were as close to natural speech as
possible. His interest in folk-song was part of a general approach to
writing through the rhythms and rhymes that were used before poetry
became a (self-)conscious profession. But his vision of a unified rural
England does, for the most part, appear timeless and devoid of social
struggle.

Instead of offering a celebration of the nation, Thomas praises
roads, lanes, and paths as well as ponds, woods, and clouds; but what is
most striking is his love of names. He had a fascination for proper

nouns as concrete, unambiguous references, as in this debate over two names given to one herb in 'Old Man':

Even to one that knows it well, the names
Half decorate, half perplex, the thing it is:
At least, what that is clings not to the names
In spite of time. And yet I like the names.

His poems, because they are obsessed with the referentiality of language, call into question the union of signifier and signified, the ability of names to carry full meaning (in poems such as 'Home', 'Adlestrop', and 'Words'). Also, in 'The Word', 'Women He Liked', and 'I Never Saw that Land Before' there is a sense of symbolic and linguistic failure: 'the name, only the name I hear', 'To name a thing beloved man sometimes fails', and 'I should use, as the trees and birds did, / A language not to be betrayed'. The short statement of the opening line of 'Old Man' asserts the inabilities for Thomas of language, and therefore of poetry: 'Old Man, or Lad's-love, – in the name there's nothing'. Adding to what I have said earlier about the encroachments of the state, Millard argues that Thomas had feelings of isolation and alienation before the war, and that these were in part attributable to his view of the divorce between individual and society (Millard 1991: 126). In this, Thomas expressed some of the social unrest of his time but also pointed towards the disintegration associated with the war and its aftermath. Aside from 'This is No Case of Petty Right or Wrong', Thomas did not himself write much on social or political themes. Before he wrote any poetry himself, he stated in *Maurice Maeterlinck* (1911):

Whatever be the subject, the poem must not depend for its main effect upon anything except the humanity of the reader. It may please for the moment by the aid of some irrelevant and transitory interest – political interest, for example; but, sooner or later, it will be left naked and solitary, and will so be judged, and if it does not create about itself a world of its own it is condemned to endure the death which is its element.

(Longley 1986: 17)

On the one hand, this is an apt comment on the banal, prewar tub-thumping poetry to which Thomas strongly objected; on the other hand, it also explains the appeal of the war poetry that was soon to follow and which has repeatedly been championed precisely for its reintroduction of 'humanity' into poetry which, aside from the work of Thomas and a handful of others, had fallen into sentimentalism and rhetoric.

Conclusion

The war years are dominated in most literary histories by the 'Soldier Poets', and yet another extremely influential style of poetry was emerging in reaction to Edwardian poetry and Georgianism. Imagism was one of many artistic movements which are grouped under the umbrella term of modernism, and it has been argued that it was the only one of these greatly to influence English poetry. Edward Thomas was disapproving of imagists, considering them translators, para-phrasers and even, as he wrote to one Georgian friend, 'imbeciles' (Motion 1980: 118). However, prewar poetry has gained such a poor reputation because the work of Ezra Pound and other imagists and modernists was permanently to change the form and subject matter of English literature at the same time that the war poets were forging changes in diction and sentiment.

Imagism began as a group in Soho led by T.E. Hulme in 1909, and ended with the last anthology published in New England in 1917. The creed of imagism has been expressed in polemical and prescriptive docu-ments, but the poets' emphasis was always on precise and concrete presentation, without excess wordage. They disliked the iamb and abstractions but favoured free verse, accuracy, and scientific principles in poetry. The idea of the 'image', influenced by the Japanese haiku and tanka as well as French symbolist poetry, summed up their preference for concision and compression. As Pound wrote in his Memoir of 1916: 'The image…is a radiant node or cluster; it is…a VORTEX, from which, and through which, and into which, ideas are constantly rushing' (Smith 1983: 3). Richard Aldington, one of the few British imagists, illustrates their principles in his poem 'Sunsets', of the same year:

> The white body of the evening
> Is torn into scarlet,
> Slashed and gouged and seared
> Into crimson,
> And hung ironically
> With garland of mist.
> And the wind
> Blowing over London from Flanders
> Has a bitter taste.

This is also a war poem, but not of the kind we will be examining in the next chapter. Both before and during the war, modernism and also feminism were creeping up on the Georgians. A key example of both is Mina Loy, a radical poet whose involvement with Gertrude Stein and Ezra Pound, modern art and Futurism, free verse and free love, produced poems from 1910 onwards which gained a contemporary notoriety. They were about 'Joyce's Ulysses', 'Brancusi's Golden Bird', 'The Ineffectual Marriage', or 'Parturition' – a poem whose form mimics a woman's contractions in labour. Her characteristic cynical wit and violent imagery in poems such as 'Love Songs' led one of her editors to declare: 'To reduce eroticism to the sty was an outrage, and to do so without verbs, sentence structure, punctuation, even more offensive' (Scott 1990: 233).

Loy's influence on modernism has often been underestimated, as has the role of the feminist movement on changing aesthetics more generally. For instance, it is fundamental to the course of imagism's development that on 15 June 1913, Dora Marsden and Harriet Shaw Weaver produced the first edition of their paper, the *New Freewoman*. They entrusted Ezra Pound with soliciting literary contributions and he duly accepted work from Wyndham Lewis, Robert Frost, William Carlos Williams, Amy Lowell, H.D., Richard Aldington, and other imagists. From the start of 1914, the *New Freewoman* was transformed into *The Egoist*, the famous journal which was to last for a year longer than the war and, after serialising James Joyce's *A Portrait of the Artist as a Young Man* in its first two years, was to introduce as its Assistant Editor, in 1917, an American expatriate called T.S. Eliot (Ross 1967: 60–70). But before the modernist revolution could take hold in Britain, World War I took Georgian poetry in a new direction.

2

'NOT CONCERNED WITH POETRY'

World War I

Introduction

In his poem 'MCMXIV', Philip Larkin suggests that the outbreak of war in 1914 heralded an unprecedented loss of innocence. In this Larkin subscribes to a prelapsarian view which understands British society in 1914 not in terms of its own historical events but in terms of the cataclysm awaiting it. It is a perspective that emphasises the unexpected horror of the war. In 1914, there had been no war involving all the European powers for a hundred years. It had been almost fifty years since any major European power had attacked any similar country. At the turn of the century, when about 1,400 men died each year in British mines, Bernard Shaw had been able to assert in a letter in 1902 that 'There is no certainty that a woman will lose her son if he goes to the front; in fact, the coal-mine and the shunting-yard are more dangerous places than the camp.' By contrast, at some points in the war the average life-expectancy of a new infantry subaltern on the Western Front was three months. In the Edwardian period, war was planned for as a contingency, but was not expected. Armed strength primarily served a civilian purpose and was not only a source of pride but the chief collective embodiment of the power of the nation. To an extent, the military was primarily for display and not intended for use; peace was assumed 'And a great army but a showy thing', as Yeats remarked of the Edwardian period in his poem 'Nineteen Hundred and Nineteen'. Eric Hobsbawm explains that 'It is difficult for anyone born after 1914 to imagine how deeply the belief that a world war could not "really" come was engrained in the fabric of life before the deluge' (Hobsbawm 1987: 302–4).

The most striking aspect to the war is still its scale in comparison with previous conflicts. Britain employed nearly half a million soldiers in the Boer War from 1899 to 1902. Twenty-nine thousand died in the fighting and a further 16,000 from disease. By contrast, over eight and a half million soldiers died in World War I and twenty million were wounded.

The war is generally thought to have been a staging post in English poetry, as it has been in British history. The shift from patriotic to polemical poetry occurs not because of any great literary influence but because of historical exigencies: the self-satisfied poetry of the recent past needed to be broken to cope with the brutal reality of the present. While agreeing that there was this change, Paul Fussell attacks the standard view of war poetry as marking a shift from 'a myth-dominated to a demythologised world'. Instead, he sees a movement almost the other way, 'towards myth, towards a revival of the cultic, the mystical, the sacrificial, the prophetic, the sacramental, and the universally significant. In short, towards fiction.' His description of the most catastrophic event of the war for the British soldiers is both affecting and canonical, and summarises the meaningless carnage that the war poets were to protest against and mythologise:

The Somme affair, destined to be known as the Great Fuck-Up, was the largest engagement fought since the beginnings of civilization.

By the end of June, 1916, Haig's planning was finished and the attack on the Somme was ready. Sensing that this time the German defensive wire must be cut and the German front-line positions obliterated, Haig bombarded the enemy trenches for a full week, firing a million and a half shells from 1,537 guns. At 7:30 on the morning of July 1 the artillery shifted to more distant targets and the attacking waves of eleven divisions climbed out of their trenches on a thirteen-mile front and began walking forward. And by 7:31 the mere six German divisions facing them had carried their machine guns upstairs from the deep dugouts where during bombardment they had harbored safely – and even comfortably – and were hosing the attackers walking toward them in orderly rows or puzzling before the still uncut wire. Out of the 110,000 who attacked, 60,000 were killed or wounded on this one day, the record so far. Over 20,000 lay dead between the lines, and it was days before the wounded in No Man's Land stopped crying out.

The disaster had many causes. Lack of imagination was one: no one imagined that the Germans could have contrived

41

such deep dugouts to hide in while the artillery pulverized the ground overhead, just as no one imagined that the German machine gunners could get up the stairs and mount their guns so fast once the bombardment moved away at precisely 7:30. Another cause was traceable to the class system and the assumption it sanctioned. The regulars of the British staff entertained an implicit contempt for the rapidly trained men of 'Kitchener's Army,' largely recruited among workingmen from the Midlands. The planners assumed that these troops – burdened for the assault with 66 pounds of equipment – were too simple and animal to cross the space between the opposing trenches in any way except in full daylight and aligned in rows or 'waves'. It was felt that the troops would become confused by more subtle tactics like rushing from cover to cover, or assault-firing, or following close upon a continuous creeping barrage.

(Fussell 1975: 12–13)

The range of emotions stimulated by such events, combined with the new experiences at home meant that more people were writing more poetry. A greater number of poems were written during World War I than any other war and *The Times* reported receiving up to a hundred poems a day in August 1915.[1] Another reason for this was the increase in the level of literacy, which I touched on in the last chapter. Nearly 2,500 schools had been set up in England and Wales following the 1870 Elementary Education Act, while Workmen's Institutes and the National Home Reading Union promoted literacy and self-development among adults. The World's Classics and the Everyman Library series made the canon of great literature more affordable. Fussell says that the *Oxford Book of English Verse* 'presides' over World War I (Fussell 1975: 159). On the other hand, most published poetry was written by officers, following the vogue set by the reception granted Rupert Brooke, especially after his death near the beginning of the war. Praising the poetry of soldiers became almost as patriotic a duty as fighting.[2]

Poetry at war

From France, Isaac Rosenberg wrote to Edward Marsh, 'I have been forbidden to send poems home as the censor won't be bothered with going through such rubbish' (Rosenberg 1937: 312). It was not only the officials who expected the war to produce no lasting poetry. Harold Monro argued that 'The sentiment of patriotism has never produced

42

much poetry. Modern warfare will be likely to produce less' (Ross 1967: 163). Henry Newbolt didn't think Owen's 'shell-shocked war poems will move our grandchildren greatly' (Press 1969: 147). In 1914, Edward Thomas wrote of war poetry: 'No other class of poetry vanishes so rapidly, has so little chosen from it for posterity' (Thomas 1914: 25). In terms of English literature, World War I is a notable exception. Thomas also writes that war poems are like hymns: 'they play with common ideas, with words and names which most people have in their heads at the time'. This was also not to be true of the well-known verse of World War I, as it was not true of Thomas's poems, all written after the war began. But it is true of much writing at the start of the war when the Georgians represented the conflict in traditional ways. In August 1914, John Freeman wrote

A common beating is in the air –
The heart of England throbbing everywhere.
And all her roads are nerves of noble thought,
And all her people's brain is but her brain;
And all her history, less her shame,
Is part of her requickened consciousness.
Her courage rises clean again.
('The Stars in their Courses', from *Stone Trees and Other Poems* 1916)

Most of the well-known protest writers, such as Owen and Rosenberg, were not widely recognised or published until after 1918. But they were only the famous names among many soldiers who composed songs, memoirs, and fiction as well as poetry which tried to uncover the lies of the early years. For example, A.G. West, who died at the Somme in 1917, wrote a biting attack on the over-praised boy soldier poets such as Brooke: 'God! How I hate you, you young cheerful men':

God! How I hate you, you young cheerful men,
Whose pious poetry blossoms on your graves
As soon as you are in them, nurtured up
By the salt of your corruption, and the tears
Of mothers, local vicars, college deans
And flanked by prefaces and photographs
From all your minor poet friends – the fools –
Who paint their sentimental elegies
Where sure, no angel treads; and, living, share
The dead's brief immortality.

In some ways the difference between Brooke and the later war poets is described well by Charles Sorley in 1915, after Brooke's death and only shortly before his own:

> He is far too obsessed with his own sacrifice, regarding the going to war of himself (and others) as a highly intense, remarkable and sacrificial exploit, whereas it is merely the conduct demanded of him (and others) by the turn of circumstances, where non-compliance with this demand would have made life intolerable.[3]

It is, I think, useful to consider why the other famous war poets went to fight. Wilfred Owen was without a career and at a loss as to what to do with his life, such that, with little immediate hope of being a published poet, he joined the army. Edward Thomas went to war not for the English but for 'This England', having realised that he loved the southern countryside enough to fight for it (Thomas 1928). Sassoon, after education at Marlborough and Cambridge, had established himself as a poet by 1914. He joined up on the first day of the war, was awarded the Military Cross in 1916, suffered many wounds and a breakdown, and was known as 'Mad Jack' because of his courage. The portrait of George Sherston in Sassoon's largely autobiographical *Memoirs of a Fox-hunting Man* (1928) suggests that Sassoon went to the war almost blithely. It is probably only with 'They' that he began to express disillusionment in his poetry. Viewing the conflict from outside the officer class, Isaac Rosenberg was the least willing recruit and declared that nothing could justify war (Sisson 1981: 87). While on training he complained of the 'brutal militaristic bullying meanness' with which duties were thrust on ordinary soldiers (Ross 1967: 171).

Inevitably, at the start of the war most poetry was still a blend of the pomposity of Newbolt and the high-flown sentiments of Victorian verse. J.C. Squire complained in the first month that poets

> start with a ready-made set of conceptions, of phrases, of words, and of rhymes, and turn out their works on a formula. Put England down as 'knightly', state her honour to be 'inviolate' and her spirit 'invulnerable'...summon the spirit of Drake and Grenville...and that's the formula for a poem.
>
> (Ross 1967: 163)

The war was seen as a game and a competition: an opportunity to win glory and play one's part for the Empire. Consequently, Newbolt's comparison of cricket and war in 'Vitaï Lampada' was parodied by Siegfried Sassoon in several of his poems, such as 'Dreamers' ('Dreaming of things they did with balls and bats') and 'A Subaltern' ('twenty runs to make, and the last man in'). Similarly sceptical in his own way, Thomas Hardy had already expressed his characteristically tangential view of war in 1902 in 'The Man He Killed', a poem which seems to anticipate the later realisations of World War I soldiers that they were fighting their own class in a war of others' making. (Kipling was capable of many different responses but his dominant war theme appeared to be 'Who dies if England live?'.)

Philip Hobsbaum concluded in 1961 that English poetry in the twentieth century had suffered four atrocious strokes of luck:

> First of all, that the wrong emphasis should have been placed on the work of the one great Victorian who could have had a useful influence – I mean Hardy. Secondly, that the Georgians, for the most part, should have chosen to regard tradition as a resting-place rather than a spring-board. Third, that three of the poets who *were* developing an essentially English modernity should have been killed in the war [Owen, Thomas, and Rosenberg] – their publication, too, was a delayed and incomplete one. And, lastly, that Eliot and Pound should have chosen to start an essentially American revolution in verse technique over here rather than in the United States, and so filled the gap which the death of the war poets left with an alien product whose influence has been a bad one. Of these points, the third is undoubtedly the most important.
>
> (Hobsbaum 1961: 218)

Many critics would agree that Owen, Thomas, and Rosenberg were the finest poets to be writing during the war. Along with Sassoon, Edmund Blunden, Ivor Gurney, Charles Sorley, and Rupert Brooke they are certainly the most discussed. Of these, only Rosenberg and Gurney were not officers. Sorley also died in the war and Gurney spent the majority of the rest of his life in mental hospitals. All were under thirty, and all but Rosenberg (who is there in Marsh's 1916–17 Georgian anthology) are also included in James Reeves's 1962 anthology of *Georgian* poets. With very few exceptions, this is what the war poets were.

Perhaps to a greater extent than any others, the Soldier Poets, as they were known, have been treated as a group despite never having

45

constituted any kind of movement. It is also curious how often they are considered not to be poets at all, but to be amateurish, 'bad at rhyme', or simply polemical. Hugh Massingham, writing in 1917, commented favourably that Sassoon was writing not poetry but epigrams in verse, the most suitable style for the rage and scorn he felt (Massingham 1917 and Murry 1918). John Middleton Murry similarly thought that Sassoon's verses were not poetry, because they expressed little except pain, as in 'Counter-Attack':

> The place was rotten with dead; green clumsy legs
> High-booted, sprawled and grovelled along the saps
> And trunks, face downward, in the sucking mud,
> Wallowed like trodden sand-bags loosely filled;
> And naked sodden buttocks, mats of hair,
> Bulged, clotted heads slept in the plastering slime.

As late as 1964, Donald Davie defended Owen and Rosenberg on the grounds not of their poetry but their significance to the country that fought the war:

> for the British reader [Rosenberg's 'Dead Man's Dump' and Owen's 'Greater Love'] are not poems at all, but something less than that and more; they are first-hand and faithful witnesses to a moment in the national destiny...as high-water marks in the national psychology.
>
> (Davie 1964: 110)

If, however, we want to look for a way of beginning to consider differences between the war poets, Jon Silkin, in his important study *Out of Battle*, divides them into four 'stages of consciousness': patriotism (e.g. Brooke); anger and protest against the war (e.g. Sassoon); compassion (e.g. Owen); and desire for social change (e.g. Rosenberg) (Silkin 1987: 26–30).

By the time of World War I, to fight for England was a patriotic duty and even a privilege. The representation of soldiering had shifted from images of mercenaries to ordinary 'Tommies', made popular after Kipling's Tommy Atkins in the *Barrack-Room Ballads*. Many soldiers' songs were published in *Tommy's Tunes* (1917) and *More Tommy's Tunes* (1918). 'Tunes' were produced by the subalterns ('Out clump the clumsy Tommies by platoons, / Trying to keep in step with rag-time tunes': Owen, 'The Calls'), but their superiors wrote 'poetry'. The officer class was epitomised by Brooke, a soldier who died of blood-poisoning on St George's Day, on his way to fight. 'The Soldier', from his war sonnets entitled *1914*, was quoted by the Dean of St Paul's on Easter Sunday 1915 and printed in *The Times* on 5 April. The first sonnet, 'Peace', is equally grandiose and patriotic in its gratitude for the war. In its pity for those who will not be fighting for England, the octave is reminiscent of the St Crispin's day speech in Shakespeare's *Henry V*:

> Now, God be thanked Who has matched us with His hour,
> And caught our youth, and wakened us from sleeping,
> With hand made sure, clear eye, and sharpened power,
> To turn, as swimmers into cleanness leaping,
> Glad from a world grown old and cold and weary,
> Leave the sick hearts that honour could not move,
> And half-men, and their dirty songs and dreary,
> And all the little emptiness of love!

When war broke out, Siegfried Sassoon, born in 1886 to rich parents and educated at Marlborough and Cambridge, was even keener to fight than Rupert Brooke. It took the extremities of war to mobilise his political radicalism; in peace, as evidenced by his fox-hunting memoirs, he had said little against class inequalities and shown little interest in ideas. His early war poetry is conventional but his later work seems to adopt the direct propagandist approach of the authorities, which culminated in the creation of Lord Beaverbrook's Ministry of Information in January 1918 – a government body in which Sassoon was offered a job but replied 'he had no qualifications for War Propaganda except that he had been wounded in the head.'[4] In these later poems, it was probably Sassoon's own amazement at what he found in the war that became his main theme. Much of his poetry after 1916 is aimed at unsettling the civilian complacency that he himself would have had. For example, there are these lines in 'They', in response to a sermon preaching that a just and holy war 'changes' men: ' "We're none of us the same!" the boys reply. / "For George lost both his legs; and Bill's stone blind" '. Similarly, 'Base Details' attacks the remoteness of majors and generals: 'And when the war is done and youth stone dead / I'd toddle home and die – in bed.' Of the war poets, it is Sassoon who is most likely to use the kind of vernacular that would have been heard in the trenches: 'Oh Jesu, make it stop!' ('Attack') and ' "O Christ, they're coming at us!" ' ('Counter-Attack'). His protest poems are simple in form and in imagery – their force comes from their bitterness and their satirical barbs.

Sassoon was changed by his war experiences at the Somme and else-where but also by the arguments he heard at home from the pacifist friends of Lady Ottoline Morrell. Of these, Bertrand Russell was the most prominent intellectual to argue against the war. He influenced Sassoon, who had in every way lost his belief in the war and quit his commission in 1917 by composing an indictment of the war leaders which he sent to his commanding officer and also made public. After the Conscription Act of 1916, Russell set up the No-Conscription Fellowship (NCF) for conscientious objectors. As a consequence of his views, or rather their publication in Britain and the US, he was dismissed from his post at Cambridge and imprisoned for six months under the Defence of the Realm Act.

For Sassoon it was above all the 'old lie', epitomised by Brooke's poetry, that war was noble and dying for one's country an honour, that had to be destroyed. This is quite different from Wilfred Owen. Sassoon wanted to shock and cajole people into action whereas Owen tried to elicit sympathy and understanding. Born in Shropshire in 1893, the son of a minor railway official and a devoted mother with literary leanings, Owen died one week before Armistice, machine-gunned at the age of 25 on 4 November.

Owen's work was largely unpublished until 1920 (the amount of antiwar poetry published during the war is often exaggerated) and only came to the fore in the 1930s when poets interested in writing political verse, such as Auden and Spender, saw in him a precursor. Only four poems were published in his lifetime and it was Edith Sitwell, in her *Wheels* magazine, which supported the modernists against the Georgians, who first brought him to public attention in 1919. In contrast with this favourable recognition, Yeats called Owen 'all blood, dirt, and sucked sugar stick' (Yeats 1936a: 80). Yeats thought that the 'passive suffering' of the war was not a suit-able subject for (great) poetry, and in this he found agreement from Edward Thomas who believed that public events were not the raw material of verse.

Unlike Sassoon, Owen often uses rhetorical questions, poignant descriptions, and literary and religious allusions. For example, he sets up quite explicitly the generation gap, in terms of Abraham and Isaac, between those fighting and those who sent them to fight: 'But the old man would not so, but slew his son, / And half the seed of Europe, one by one' ('The Parable of the Old Man and the Young'). He also felt that he himself as an officer was leading men to slaughter: 'What passing-bells for those who die as cattle?' ('Anthem for Doomed Youth'). Owen compares soldiers to Christ in his poems and letters, evidently seeing himself as both witness to the suffering of his men and also their crucifier.

Technically, Owen was also a stage on from Sassoon. Owen is perhaps the first poet consistently to use half-rhyme (where the final consonants rhyme but not the final vowel, as in 'good/blood') and pararhyme (like half-rhyme, but with additional rhyming consonants, as in 'groves/grieves'). Dominic Hibberd comments that 'The use of half- and pararhyme to describe war is particularly apt, since they produce an effect of dissonance and failure: we expect the rhyme to be completed and it is not' (Hibberd 1973: 34). By contrast a contemporary reviewer in the *Times Literary Supplement* in 1921 asked whether they could be said to be rhymes at all (De Selincourt 1921: 59). Owen's technique can be best appreciated in 'Strange Meeting' where his experiments with rhyme are combined with vowel and consonant patterns:

> It seemed that out of battle I escaped
> Down some profound dull tunnel, long since scooped
> Through granites which titanic wars had groined.
> Yet also there encumbered sleepers groaned,
> Too fast in thought or death to be bestirred.

Owen and Sassoon met at the Craiglockhart hospital for 'shell-shocked' soldiers near Edinburgh and Owen tentatively approached Sassoon for advice on his poetry. Though he proved to be far more accomplished than his mentor, Owen wrote none of his major war poems prior to this meeting with Sassoon in August 1917. Subsequently his themes are the breaking of bodies and minds, in poems that see soldiers as wretches, ghosts, and sleepers. While Owen conveys the effects of gas-attacks ('Dulce et Decorum Est') or extreme cold ('Exposure') or physical loss ('Disabled'), he also describes the cumulative impact of trench life. Probably his best writing to deal with the effect on the mind of war is 'Mental Cases':

> Who are these? Why sit they here in twilight?
> Wherefore rock they, purgatorial shadows,
> Drooping tongues from jaws that slob their relish,
> Baring teeth that leer like skulls' teeth wicked?
>
> ...
>
> Always they must see these things and hear them,
> Batter of guns and shatter of flying muscles,

Carnage incomparable, and human squander,
Rucked too thick for these men's extrication.

Therefore still their eyeballs shrink tormented
Back into their brains, because on their sense
Sunlight seems a blood-smear, night comes blood-black;
Dawn breaks open like a wound that bleeds afresh.

Like Owen, many other writers dealt with what Sassoon in 'Does it Matter?' calls 'dreams from the pit', but the poet who best conveys the effect of war on the mind is Ivor Gurney, especially in his images of 'Strange Hells'. Gurney, who suffered a breakdown in 1918 and was held in the City of London Mental Hospital from 1922, writes in broken rhythms and an unusual syntax which, like Owen's extensive use of pararhyme, suggest the dislocations of war, particularly with regard to the mind's inability to make coherent sense of extreme experience.

'Shell-shock', as it came to be known, was the major challenge to British psychiatry in the 1920s. Coined by C.S. Myers in 1915, the word's popularity with doctors may well have something to do with its manly sound in contrast to the identical term 'hysteria'. Shell-shock was

a condition of alternate moods of apathy and high excite-ment, with very quick reaction to sudden emergencies but no capacity for concentrated thinking.... Its effects pass off very gradually. In most cases the blood was not running pure again for four or five years; and in many cases men who had managed to avoid a nervous breakdown during the war had collapsed badly in 1921 or 1922.

(Dowling 1991: 87)

By the end of 1918, some 80,000 cases of shell-shock had been treated by army doctors, and in the twenties there were 114,000 applications for pensions related to war trauma (the war office committee that investigated shell-shock in 1922 was reluctant to admit the term at all because it suggested that war rather than a weakness in the men was responsible for the breakdowns). And by 1932, of veterans receiving disability pensions 36 per cent were psychiatric casualties. Initial reac-tions of military doctors were extreme – for example, it was suggested that in war time if no actual physical injury could be detected then the individual should be shot. Shell-shock was for many indistinguishable from cowardice or disobeying orders (see Gurney's poem 'On Somme'). However, doctors gradually began to draw on Freud's ideas of neurosis and the unconscious, and it was partly because of shell-shock that Freudian analysis gained acceptability in England.

Where Sassoon expresses indignation and bitterness, Owen appears more emotionally involved. He is neither satirical or polemical but his poems document the futility of war, the sense of waste: 'Red lips are not so red / As the stained stones kissed by the English dead' ('Greater Love'). In Silkin's four-part schematic, it took another kind of war poetry to argue and look for change.

Isaac Rosenberg, who grew up in poverty in London's East End from the age of seven, was a Jew of Lithuanian-Latvian origin (Sassoon's father was also Jewish – the first in his family to marry outside the faith). He attended the Slade Art School from 1911 to 1914 and joined the King's Own Royal Lancaster Regiment in 1915. The war arguably had little effect on his poetry in terms of style or tone, and it is likely that his class and ethnic background are more important influences. His poetry uses juxtaposed and odd images, such as the rat in 'Break of Day in the Trenches' or the insects of 'Louse Hunting', to convey complexity and ambivalence. He is not as romantic or appalled as Owen, and, as might be expected of a painter, his poetry is very visual: 'A man's brains splattered on / A stretcher-bearer's face; / His shook shoulders slipped their load, / But when they bent to look again / The drowning soul was sunk too deep / For human tenderness' ('Dead Man's Dump').

Rosenberg is acutely aware of prejudice, in terms of class and ethnicity: 'The blonde, the bronze, the ruddy, / With the same heaving blood, / Keep tide to the moon of Moses. / Then why do they sneer at me?' ('The Jew'). In addition to a concern with British social differences there is also in his poetry an understanding of the absurdities of forced national distinctions made by the war: 'Droll rat, they would shoot you if they knew / Your cosmopolitan sympathies. / Now you have touched this English hand / You will do the same to a German' ('Break of Day in the Trenches'). It is also because of his status as infantryman not officer that Rosenberg brought different perspectives to conditions in the trenches (Cohen 1975: 126–7). For example, he developed images of war in relation to the constant battles he fought with lice. 'The Immortals' pictures an eternal personal struggle between good and evil in which not Germans but the lice Rosenberg has continually to kill return to torment him: 'I killed till all my strength was gone. / And still they rose to torture me'. And in 'Break of Day in the Trenches' he imagines the battleground through the eyes of one of the omnipresent black rats. These scavengers were described thus by one officer at Ypres:

> They have eaten nearly everything in the mess, including the table-cloth and the operations orders! We borrowed a large cat and shut it up at night to exterminate them, and found the place empty next morning. The rats must have eaten it up, bones, fur, and all, and dragged it to their holes.
>
> (Fussell 1975: 49)

Rosenberg, who described the war as 'A burnt space through ripe fields, / A fair mouth's broken tooth' ('August 1914'), envisioned the fighting in terms of mythic desires and doomed struggles. He thought his finest poem was 'Daughters of War', in which he strives

> to get that sense of inexorableness the human (or inhuman) side of this war has. It even penetrates behind human life for the 'Amazon' who speaks in the second part of the poem is imagined to be without her lover yet, while all her sisters have theirs, the released spirits of the slain earth men.[5]

The immortal Amazons dance while they wait for their lovers who will only come to them after death in battle: 'Frail hands gleam up through the human quagmire, and lips of ash / Seem to wail, as in sad faded paintings / Far-sunken and strange.' It is to this poem of loss and desire, love and death, that the more famous 'Dead Man's Dump' forms a companion piece. Here, Rosenberg envisions the dead soldiers returning to the earth from which the Amazons may raise them:

> The wheels lurched over sprawled dead
> But pained them not, though their bones crunched,
> Their shut mouths made no moan,
> They lie there huddled, friend and foeman,
> Man born of man, and born of woman,
> And shells go crying over them
> From night till night and now.

Together the poems range over and blur the differences of living and dying, as well as the pain and longing of men's and women's individual and collective suffering. By simultaneously looking to images of mortality and immortality, Rosenberg points to the end of the war and the kinds of death and rebirth envisaged in Eliot's postwar analysis in

The Waste Land, which I will discuss in the next chapter. The poems also have in common a fascination with differences of gender and desire: the sexual drive that leads to the regeneration opposing war's annihilation, but which also divides as much as it unites men and women.

Gender and sexuality

While the American novelist Marie Von Vorst was awed by the enthusiasm with which the English in London greeted the war, Ruth Adam writes of women:

> There was nothing for them to do while the men queued outside the recruiting offices and drilled in the square and marched about the countryside singing ribald men-only versions of patriotic songs. There was no exhilaration, no sense of starting a new and adventurous life for women.
> (Khan 1988: 17 and 139)

However, the sense of new opportunities and new lives is sometimes suggested by the women poets of the war collected in *Scars Upon My Heart*, including Nina MacDonald: 'Girls are doing things / They've never done before, / Go as 'bus conductors, / Drive a car or van, / All the world is topsy-turvy / Since the War began' ('Sing A Song of War-Time').

In her discussion of *Women's Poetry of the First World War*, Nosheen Khan (1988) emphasises the range of responses she finds, from the romantic to the revolted. She divides her book into analyses of verse about the image of war and about life at home and at the front. Two further chapters consider poetry that compares war with religion and nature, while a final discussion focuses on women's grief and suffering. If we consider that the men's poetry of World War I most often read today is concerned with the experience of warfare and the trenches, it could easily be argued that women's poetry has both a wider range of subjects and a larger set of reactions to life during wartime. Some of it, like much early war poetry by men, is mere propaganda, such as Isabel C. Clarke's 'Anniversary of the Great Retreat (1915)': 'O England, sing their fame in song and story, / Who knew Death's victory not Life's defeat.' Others, such as Nora Bomford, protest inequalities: 'Why should men face the dark while women stay / To live and laugh and meet the sun each day' ('Drafts'). However, the dominant image, often portrayed enthusiastically but sometimes pejoratively, in poems such as

Madeline Ida Bedford's 'Munition Wages' and Mary Gabrielle Collins's 'Women at Munition Making', is of women experiencing new jobs, social roles, and wages.

While many poets deal with the grief women experienced in the war, several writers speak directly to other women about their relationship to war. Helen Hamilton denounces 'The Jingo-Woman' who, like many suffragettes who followed Emmeline Pankhurst's idea of the 'good war', is a 'dealer in white feathers', such as the speaker in Jessie Pope's poem 'The Call'. Pauline Barrington's 'Education', while alluding to Wordsworth and comparing rows of stitches with lines of soldiers, asks that women do not bring their children up to be fighters:

If the child is father to the man,
Is the toy gun father of the Krupps?
    For Christ's sake think!
    While you sew
    Row after row.

Other women poets imagine the situation of men at war. Mostly, these are more poems of death and the trenches, such as Alice Corbin's 'Fallen' or Sybil Bristowe's 'Over the top'. But some, as with Vera Brittain's 'The Lament of the Demobilised', consider less sensationalist aspects: 'others stayed behind and just got on – / Got on the better since we were away. / And we came home and found / They had achieved, and men revered their names, / But never mentioned ours.' A similar sentiment applies to women's poetry published during the war because it appears in almost no subsequent anthology. For one critic this is because anthologists select poets from a perspective 'predicated upon a canon of "major writers" whose moral and literary development is dependent upon the pressure of war experience on literary sensibility' (Featherstone 1996: 20). Perpetuating the divide between those at the front and those at home, war poetry had been considered to be about combat, and therefore to be experienced and written about only by soldiers. Also, the worth of such poetry has often been judged in terms of its ability to convey a human revulsion to the atrocity of war, such that the responses of those poets, like Edward Thomas, who wrote more subtly, with 'danger and disruption' *behind* their poetry, have been undervalued (Motion 1980: 91–137). C.H. Sisson baldly declares that Thomas's 'whole attitude to war was wrong....The "war poet" must reflect popular sentiment about war' (Sisson 1981: 80). Women's writing has also often been thought to lack this engagement with what is often called the 'reality' of war, and has therefore been deemed superfluous to anthologies, although Janet Montefiore has argued that *Scars Upon My Heart* simply contains bad poetry suffused with chauvinist ideologies and literary clichés.[6]

So, in many accounts, the poet is seen as expressing the truth, from the trenches, in opposition to the propaganda of the war machine.[7] This emphasis on the front line has led to a silence over other wartime experience in poetry. For example, it was of course in World War I that women gained access to many areas of employment – in 1911 only 10 per cent of married women were in paid work. In the war, many more women suddenly found a temporary chance to secure their own jobs and their own decent wage, as Nina MacDonald describes in 'Sing a Song of War-Time': 'Mummie does the house-work, / Can't get any maid, / Gone to make munitions / 'Cause they're better paid.' The gap maintained by Victorian society between private world – female, emotional, domestic – and public world – male, rational, business-social – was being eroded (the Women's Institute was formed in 1915 with the intention of informing and broadening the horizons of the nation's housewives, many of whom received little or no conventional education). However, these jobs – on the land, in factories – were unlikely to inspire poetry of the same intensity as trench warfare, and the 'Soldier Poets' were generally scathing of women, perhaps not least because their homosocial bonding resulted in a resentment of women's new freedoms 'at home'.[8] Owen in 'Disabled' and 'Apologia pro Poemate Meo', Sassoon in 'Glory of Women', and Rosenberg in 'Daughters of War' are hostile towards the women who encourage men to go to war (as in Jessie Pope's 'The Call'), but this also seems to spill over into a general dislike – first, of all women, and second, of all non-combatants. Against this homogenising gesture, women poets saw their own roles as various: 'reporters, propagandists, interpreters, advocates, satirists, elegists, healers and visionaries' (Khan 1988: 4). More generally, Owen and Sassoon were hostile to civilians who they thought were ignorant of the atrocities and realities of fighting and trench warfare. Sassoon's poetry in particular seems to construct a division between 'Us', who are all those who fight, and 'Them', the generals, civilians, priests, and politicians, who do not. Conversely, Sandra Gilbert has argued that women's war writing contains an unconscious rebellious subtext: their poetry is fuelled not only by a sense of emancipation but also by an anger against and a desire for liberation from prewar male domination (Gilbert and Gubar 1989). Some of that liberation, of course, did come with the end of the war: the vote for women over thirty in 1918, the half-measure of the 1919 Sex Disqualification

Act allowing women's employment by the public services, female undergraduates at Oxbridge, and the right of widows to pensions.

In men's war poetry, much of the prewar emotion over love of country and social duty is transformed into personal feelings: compassion, admiration, desire. This is one of the major forces effecting a change on war poetry. The abstract 'imagined community' of the country is relegated to a position of lesser importance when so many men are brought together and develop concrete attachments to individuals that they meet. The horror of war is thus only one impetus to a new poetry; there is also the camaraderie and friendship of new communities. War brings with it its own kind of expressions of sexuality as the homosocial environment gives rise to alternative expressions of love or desire from those of peacetime (much war poetry contains imagery more commonly found in love poetry, such as eyes, roses, and music (Hibberd 1973: 44)). Owen's 'Apologia pro Poemate Meo' says:

> I have made fellowships –
> Untold of happy lovers in old song.
> For love is not binding of fair lips
> With the soft silk of eyes that look and long,
>
> By Joy, whose ribbon slips, –
> But wound with war's hard wire whose stakes are strong;
> Bound with the bandage of the arm that drips;
> Knit in the webbing of the rifle-thong.

Women are excluded ('except you share with them in hell'). Owen's poem 'Greater Love' begins: 'Red lips are not so red / As the stained stones kissed by the English dead.' Owen also writes of 'blunt bullet-leads / Which long to nuzzle in the hearts of lads.'

Most of Owen's early poetry mixes homoeroticism (especially kissing) with religious iconography (he studied theology and worked for two years as assistant to a vicar near Reading). When Robert Graves met Owen at Craiglockhart military hospital, he decided he was 'an idealistic homosexual with a religious background' (Fussell 1975: 289). Unlike many other poets, Owen hardly ever compares life during wartime with life back home in England. Instead there is an intense identification with either one man/boy/lad or a group. He refers to an enormous number of body parts, their isolation suggesting both the dismemberment of war and the reification of his desire. The emotions he expresses are self-sacrifice, empathy, fellowship, and admiration –

the feelings previous writers had felt for both an ideal 'England' and the English landscape, Owen felt for both individuals and for abstract male human beauty.

With examples in mind such as Robert Nichols's 'Casualty' or Robert Graves's 'Not Dead', Fussell says that that no one can fail to notice in World War I poetry 'the unique physical tenderness, the readiness to admire openly the bodily beauty of young men, the unapologetic recognition that men may be in love with each other' (Fussell 1975: 279–80). The sight of soldiers bathing becomes a 'setpiece scene in almost every memory of the war' according to Fussell (1975: 299). Noting the extreme popularity with the troops of A.E. Housman's A Shropshire Lad (1896), Fussell says that the words 'man', 'boy', and 'lad' each had specific homoerotic resonances: 'men is largely neutral; boys is a little warmer; lads is very warm' (Fussell 1975: 282). He links this to the popularity of the Decadents and aesthetes of the 1890s, especially the Uranians, who included Arthur Symons, Oscar Wilde, Edward Carpenter, and Aleister Crowley:

> a body of enthusiastic pedophiles who since the late eighties had sent forth from Oxford and London a stream of pamphlets, poems, drawings, paintings, and photographic 'art studies' arguing the attractions – and usually the impeccable morality – of boy-love.
>
> (Fussell 1975: 283)

By contrast, Owen famously wrote that he is 'not concerned with Poetry', his subject is 'War, and the Pity of War' (see Sisson 1981: 82). To the aesthetes, a subject was secondary, even unnecessary, to the poetry itself.

Many commentators discuss Owen's regard for the physical beauty of other soldiers, but this is usually rarefied into feelings of pity and admiration, not desire. A fascinating poem in terms of the soldier's negotiation of his own mental and corporeal duality is Edgell Rickword's 'The Soldier Addresses His Body': 'I shall be mad if you get smashed about / we've had good times together, you and I.' As with so much war poetry this is an attempt to bend conventions to new circumstances, such that a poem about the fear of losing another is turned into a split-subject's relationship with his threatened physical self. Ivor Gurney also expresses the tension between traditional subjects of lyric poetry and the destruction of war in 'To His Love'. The poem ends with a request for flowers to conceal 'that red wet Thing' he knows he must forget. Taken in aggregate, such poems accentuate the

degree to which the war, through its creation of new homosocial envi-
ronments at the front line and in the factory, as well as through its
forced separations, impelled men and women to reinscribe gender and
sexual relations.

Conclusion

On the one hand, the importance of prevailing literary styles should
not be underestimated. With dominant models such as Kipling and
Newbolt, there was very little alternative discourse for most poets,
particularly women, to draw upon. There was a tradition of personal
writing, and of sentiment, but in the late Victorian era, an ideal of
patriotic masculine muscular Christianity limited the forms of
expression available. Such views are epitomised in the pre-1914
notion of the individual and the nation at war, expressed by
Newbolt's 'Vitaï Lampada': 'The Gatling's jammed and the colonel
dead, / And the regiment blind with dust and smoke; /...But the
voice of a schoolboy rallies the ranks: / "Play up! play up! and play
the game!"' Newbolt's idea of war as a team game was exemplified
by the common practice of kicking a football ahead of the troops as
they crossed No Man's Land. This began in 1915, the same year
Lord Derby, closing professional soccer down 'for the duration', told
Britain's footballers: 'You have played with one another and against
one another for the Cup; play with one another for England now'
(Parfitt 1990: 33). Poetry, no less than war, was considered a nationalist pursuit in which the poet should be 'writing for England' – for
such reasons, Edward Thomas had held out little hope of good
writing emerging from the trenches.

On the other hand, the canon of war poetry has to an extent
been built around the idea that the mould of poetry was broken,
that conventional forms were overturned, and that the language of
poetry was revised. Undoubtedly, such a change did not happen in
women's poetry (if one can talk of such a grouping): here, the styles
and subject matter are often imitative of what was evidently the
dominant poetry of the time. The war poets, however, found that
the existing uses of language were neither sufficiently sincere or
intense for their purposes: other styles and forms of poetry were
necessary. Arguably, this is because a few writers, such as Owen and
Rosenberg, realised that existing forms were too closely associated
with the propaganda and patrician values to which they were
opposed (Coyle 1995).

Paul Fussell speaks of this change in language as a loss of 'high' diction. After the war, words like 'ejaculation' and 'intercourse' could no longer be used innocently. No longer was warfare 'strife', or one's death one's 'fate', or soldiers' blood, in Rupert Brooke's phrase, 'the red / Sweet wine of youth' (Fussell 1975: 21–3). This alteration in diction was not as sudden or complete a change as has sometimes been suggested, and, famously, W.B. Yeats was to leave Wilfred Owen out of *The Oxford Book of Modern Verse* (along with other war poets) partly because 'he calls poets "bards", a girl a "maid" and talks about "Titanic wars"' (Yeats 1936a: 80). Yeats himself wrote no war poetry as such and explained why in his 'On being asked for a War Poem', where he made it clear that he thought the 'statesman' and not the poet should discuss war. Aside from the imagists such as Richard Aldington, the impact of modernism was not strongly felt by the war poets in the trenches, but its formal and linguistic experimentations are explored in David Jones's superb prose-poem *In Parenthesis*, based on his experiences as a private at the Somme. Published in 1937, it is a complex meditation on a Welsh battalion's journey from the training ground to the battlefield (see Silkin 1987: 315–40):

> Dark-faceted iron oval lobs heavily to fungus-cushioned dank, wobbles under low leaf to lie, near where the heel drew out just now; and tough root-fibres boomerang to top-most green filigree and earth clods flung disturb fresh fragile shoots that brush the sky.

However, what certainly did occur during the war was a change in attitudes towards received ideas of truth, duty, and authority. Consequently, Newbolt was to call Owen and similar poets 'the broken men' who did not know the real heartache undergone by Haig and the other 'Old Men'.[9] Typically, G.K. Chesterton, who was 40 years old when the war started, composed his own comical 'Elegy in a Country Churchyard' to summarise the difference between the war dead and their masters. He concluded that it was a shame for England that the rulers themselves had 'no graves as yet'.

Undoubtedly, one reason why so many 'citizens' signed up to be soldiers at the start of the war was a desire to protect the 'England' I discussed in Chapter 1. On the one hand, this meant defending the country that ruled the largest Empire the world had ever known and had forged throughout the world a *Pax Brittanica*. On the other hand, though most people (over 75 per cent), and therefore most soldiers, lived in urban areas, there had been a link forged between these city dwellers and the land in the Edwardian years. This was a link that could in theory be shared by all, irrespective of class, gender, or country. Which is partly why the burial of Brooke's soldier, making foreign soil forever English, appealed to a large proportion of the nation at the start of the war. It would not have had the same fascination several years later[10], when Ivor Gurney composed this poem:

When I remember plain heroic strength
And shining virtue shown by Ypres pools,
Then read the blither written by knaves for fools
In praise of English soldiers lying at length,
Who purely dream that England shall be made
Gloriously new, free of the old stains
By us, who pay the price that must be paid,
Will freeze all winter over Ypres plains.
Our silly dreams of peace you put aside
And Brotherhood of Man, for you will see
An armed Mistress, braggart of the tide,
Her children slaves, under your mastery.
We'll have a word there too, and forge a knife,
Will cut the cancer threatens England's life.

Written in October 1917, Gurney's 'To the Prussians of England' warns of an equivalent uprising to the Russian Revolution, one that will excise the cancer of poets such as Newbolt and generals such as Haig. Gurney was not alone in this feeling and consequently, while the war had seemed in many ways to bring the nation together, prewar fears of social unrest remained common. In October 1918 Lord Chelmsford wrote to George V: 'We have an educated class here, 95 per cent of whom are inimical to us, and I venture to assert that every student in every university is growing up with a hatred of us' (Bantock 1983: 27).

The interwar years saw massive unemployment, strikes, poverty and the rise of fascism and communism across Europe; in Britain, coalition governments were formed to cope with social and economic difficulties. The war had ended in 1918 but peacetime was to prove no easy alternative for the majority of Europeans. In 1921, T.S. Eliot wrote:

Having only contempt for every existing political party, and profound hatred for democracy, I feel the blackest gloom. Whatever happens will be another step towards the destruction of Europe. The whole of contemporary politics oppresses

me with a continuous physical horror like the feeling of
growing madness in one's brain.[11]

He poured this sense of horror, despair, and dread into *The Waste Land*,
a poem hoping for regeneration but filled with images of destruction.

3

'BIRTH, AND COPULATION, AND DEATH'

The 1920s and T.S. Eliot

> After luncheon he stood on the balcony with a megaphone which had appeared surprisingly among the bric-a-brac of Sebastian's room, and in languishing, sobbing tones recited passages from *The Waste Land* to the sweatered and muffled throng that was on its way to the river.
>
> 'I, Tiresias, have foresuffered all,' he sobbed to them from the Venetian arches.
>
> (Evelyn Waugh, *Brideshead Revisited*)

Introduction

In 1922, over 120 years after the Rosetta Stone's discovery, the Egyptologist Jean-François Champollion finally succeeded in deciphering the inscriptions on the pre-Christian stone slab, written in two languages and three scripts: Greek, Egyptian hieroglyphic and, like Mr Eugenides's French, demotic. In the same year, Hermann Rorschach died. The Swiss psychiatrist had become famous for a psychological test which consisted of ten complex inkblots, the interpretation of which by any individual would suggest her or his character. The coincidence of these two events at first serves only to illustrate the hunger for interpretation in the early twentieth century – in the words of Nietzsche's Zarathustra: 'how could I endure to be a man, if man were not also poet and reader of riddles' – the urge to decode texts, societies, minds and personalities. However, the hermeneutics of the Rosetta Stone and the Rorschach test also help to bring into focus a year in which the two most elusive and enigmatic literary texts of the twentieth century were published. The year 1922, when Marsh's final Georgian anthology appeared (with no poem that mentions the war), was the year that modernism arrived decisively in English poetry with the publication of

T.S. Eliot's *The Waste Land*, as it also did in English fiction with the book publication of James Joyce's *Ulysses*. The Irish expatriate's masterpiece is a compendium of prose styles, classical mythology, and linguistic acrobatics. The American expatriate's poem is a jigsaw of scripts, languages, symbols and hieroglyphs. Neither met with anything like unqualified approval. Joyce's novel was banned for many years in Britain; Eliot's poem widely reviled. Both have alienated readers who find in them a complexity and a dry intellectualism that subjugates narrative, emotion, and lyricism to wordplay, erudition, and formalism.

At the time of writing *The Waste Land* Eliot advocated an 'escape from personal emotions' and a poetry of 'impersonality'. The poem strikes many readers as an impersonal patchwork of cultural rags, one that seems cold and unfeeling in its unsympathetic portrayal of individuals and emotions. Some of this may be put down to Eliot's elitist sensibilities, but much of it is a deliberate attempt to portray what for Eliot was the regimented, mechanical character of early twentieth-century life. The 'individual' was being superseded by the 'citizen', the community by the state, high by mass culture, religion by commercialism, poetry by advertising, the rhythms of the country by those of the city and the suburbs. This is also the final phase of the acute crisis of British government, as liberalism faded before the forces of collectivist organisation and social regulation (Hall and Schwarz 1985). Mass car production reached Britain in 1922, the year the BBC also started its daily broadcasts. Trade union membership was still rising rapidly. On the one hand, service industries were employing more clerks, assistants, and shop staff; on the other hand, the older industries, coal mining, shipbuilding, and cotton, were in decline.

In terms of social and political change, far more stood between the war poets and *The Waste Land* than just the Treaty of Versailles signed at the Paris Peace Conference. In Britain, the Representation of the People Act of 1918 gave the vote to all males over 21 and all females over 30. The Labour Party, which would come to power for the first time in 1924, was a growing force. The Empire was rocked by the Amritsar massacre in 1919, in which a British officer ordered the brutal killing of hundreds of Indian civilians. The emancipated, liberal world that World War I had supposedly been fought for, did not seem to have emerged in the colonies. Imperial fragmentation was most forcefully demonstrated in the Partition of Ireland in 1921. Elsewhere, the Russian revolution of 1917 showed that communism was much more than a theoretical possibility in Europe, while the rise of American economic might marked the eclipse of British international dominance. The League of Nations, without the US, was created to try to ensure the new world peace in 1920 – the same year Hitler founded the Nazi party in Germany. Single perspectives were becoming increasingly untenable philosophically and aesthetically, if not politically. Einstein's Theory of Relativity had been confirmed experimentally in 1919, rocking faith in all kinds of absolutes, to be followed in 1927 by Heisenberg's uncertainty principle, which, because it implied randomness was constructing the universe, would make the physical world seem not more but less comprehensible and also less secure. Such changes in the perception of the physical world were accompanied by alterations in representation. Art had been redirected by works such as Picasso's 'Les Demoiselles d'Avignon' (1907) and Duchamp's 'Nude Descending a Staircase' (1912). A revolution of tone, rhythm and harmony was embarked upon by Stravinsky and Schoenberg, while film was emerging as an alternative form of expression and storytelling, stimulating literary techniques such as montage, flashback, fast-cutting, and rapid dialogue. The influence of Freud, who had previously been promoted by Havelock Ellis, was now only being fully felt in Britain as his work was first translated in 1909 and *The Interpretation of Dreams* in 1913. Other thinkers such as G.E. Moore, Bertrand Russell, Spengler, Bergson, and Wittgenstein were shaking faith in an ordered, knowable Newtonian universe.

Much of this social and philosophical upheaval is apparent in the fractured narrative of *The Waste Land* although it was the form less than the subject matter of the poem that most astonished contemporary readers. Eliot peppers the classical allusions with references to insurance clerks (he worked in a London bank at the time), birth control (clinics had been opened by the Malthusian League and by Marie Stopes in 1921), mental breakdown (Eliot developed the poem while on sickness leave for three months during which he consulted a Swiss psychiatrist), demobilisation, ragtime and gramophones, gashouses and synthetic perfumes, commuters and commerce, cardboard boxes and cigarette ends, motor cars and Brighton holidays. From a contemporary historical perspective Eliot's poem can be said to be about a loss of health: social, spiritual, mental, and physical. Written in the aftermath of the devastation of World War I, and only two years before Britain's first Labour government, it concerns itself with lost social meaning, with the need for spiritual regeneration, with physical collapse (from towers to London bridge), and with mental disintegration (the last line in English concerns Hieronymo's madness). The poem's portrayal of the human body highlights decay and ill-health: carbuncles, rotten teeth, impotency, and dandruff. As Eliot put it in another poem, 'Sweeney

Agonistes', after everything is said the 'facts' of life are simply birth, copulation and death.

This was not the kind of poetry with which the public was familiar. As John Williams writes, despite the interventions of the war poets,

> After the war, with Eliot as yet hardly known, Ezra Pound a figure associated with the avant-garde, and Yeats and Hardy by no means writing, or being read, as 'modernists', the 'new' poetry was still essentially Georgian. Anthologies from this group continued to appear until 1922, and tradition rather than innovation dominated the London literary scene.
>
> (Williams 1987: 28)

At this time, most British people had an enhanced sense of national pride: many thought the country needed new spiritual food after the barbarism of the war; German scholasticism was seen as unpatriotic; the last nail had been hammered into the coffin of ruling-class values and English identity was seen as needing to be resurrected in terms of a shared culture and language. In 1921, the tradition and purpose of literature was the subject of a government report, *The Teaching of English in England*. This evangelising document was produced by Henry Newbolt, one of the poets we discussed in Chapter 1. Newbolt's committee decided that English studies constituted a 'temple' at which 'all should worship' and that university lecturers were 'missionaries' sent to promote social unity and national values through the examples of English literature. Newbolt said that the rise of modern universities delivered 'an ambassador of poetry to every important capital of industrialism in the country' (Newbolt 1995). While literature was seen as a form of religion in the report, poetry was deemed to be setting up embassies in the modern cities – like Newbolt's imperial English poetry, the spirit was essentially expansionist and colonising.

However, while schools still taught Englishness through literature (as a species of propaganda), the universities were forging a new method of literary study centred upon 'analysis'. After the founding of the first modern English degree at Cambridge in 1917, it was in the 1920s that

> English literature as a discipline in higher education shook off much of what had previously been its role (as one aspect of the study of 'national character') and emerged as an autonomous academic domain almost exclusively concerned with the study of its own texts.
>
> (Doyle 1982: 28)

English literature thrived in the universities after World War I, before which it had been seen as a very poor imitation of Classics – especially at Oxford and Cambridge – chiefly useful in its relation to language or history. The most influential group of critics surfaced at Cambridge. These radicals, F.R. and Q.D. Leavis, I.A. Richards, and others, were not sons and daughters of the aristocracy like the prewar professors but the children of tradespeople from the provinces. Over the 1920s, English studies was transformed from an amateurish subject for dilettantes to a highly professional field of enquiry, from an upstart in the academy to the central discipline in the humanities. This metamorphosis was achieved by a close attention to the moral and social values expressed by the language of individual texts, a detailed reading of the specific words used by the poet on every line. Through such rigorous scrutiny, the traditions, sensibilities, emotions, and spirituality of life since Chaucer could be reconstructed to provide a map of English civilisation. The English literary canon, which is still largely intact seventy years later, was assembled in this decade as the criteria of judgement changed from the rather undiscriminating principle of good writing (a direct 'masculine' style) to questions of complexity, seriousness, richness, sensitivity, and organic form. Fine literature no longer promoted simple patriotic feelings but uplifted the reader and placed her or him in the vanguard of civilised manners and morality – a view which persisted until the horrors of Auschwitz revealed to European minds what had been apparent in the colonies for centuries: the compatibility of high culture with the most atrocious brutality. The critical approach taken by this coterie of thinkers was 'practical criticism', which was to evolve into 'New Criticism', a practice of close reading that promoted the minute analysis of a poem (for ambiguity, irony, paradox, and so forth) in isolation from any historical context. The literary work of art becomes divorced from authorial intention, from the reader's private reaction to it, and from social or political events. Instead, the poem stands as an artefact in itself, an enclosed, meaningful, concrete linguistic object to be analysed by the disinterested critic.

For I.A. Richards, whose *Principlies of Literary Criticism* (1924) is a seminal work in the development of English studies, the reading of poetry in the 1920s served a quasi-spiritual purpose. In his 1926 book *Science and Poetry*, Richards argued that with the decline of religion and the ascendancy of science, poetry needed to be studied as the greatest example of imaginative achievement. Richards in certain respects had the same view of the modern world as Eliot, arguing in 'Poetry and Belief' that there is: 'a sense of desolation, of uncertainty, of futility' such that 'the only impulses which seem strong enough to continue unflagging are commonly so crude that, to more finely developed individuals, they hardly seem worth having. Such people cannot live by warmth, food, fighting, drink and sex alone' (Newton 1990: 14). What the world needed was the emotional, spiritual, moral, and intellectual sustenance of poetry. Also, at a time when much of the world was disunited, divided, and war-weary, Richards's *Practical Criticism* (1929) argued that the purpose of literature was to achieve unity, in terms of meaning, the association of thought and feeling, and the relation between form and content. This perspective, largely applied to the texts of literary history, was in stark contrast to other, mainly Marxist, approaches to contemporary modernist literature which will be discussed below. But first I want to say something about the revolutionary literature that for many people Eliot's poem was to come to stand for, and which stimulated the 'modernist' approach of the New Critics.

Modernism, poetry, and Eliot

One working definition of modernism runs as follows:

The starting point of modernism is the crisis of belief that pervades twentieth century western culture: loss of faith, experience of fragmentation and disintegration, and the shattering of cultural symbols and norms. At the centre of this crisis were the new technologies of science, the epistemology of logical positivism, and the relativism of functionalist thought – in short, major aspects of the philosophical perspectives that Freud embodied. The rationalism of science and philosophy attacked the validity of traditional religious and artistic symbols while the growing technology of the industrialised world produced the catastrophes of war on the one hand and the atomisation of human beings on the other. Art produced after the first world war recorded the emotional aspect of this crisis; despair, hopelessness, paralysis, angst, and a sense of meaninglessness, chaos and the fragmentation of material reality. In a variety of ways suited to their own religious, literary, mythological, occult, political, or existentialist perspectives, artists emerged from the paralysis of absolute despair to an active search for meaning. The search for order and pattern began in its own negation, in the overwhelming sense of disorder and fragmentation caused by the modern

materialist world. The artist as seer would attempt to create
what the culture could no longer produce: symbol and
meaning in the dimension of art, brought into being through
the agency of language...

(Friedman 1981: 97–8)

If any one figure on the British literary scene was instrumental in this
upheaval, it was the American poet and critic Ezra Pound, who was
Yeats's secretary, Joyce's literary and financial supporter, and Eliot's
close friend (they met in 1915). As mentioned at the end of Chapter 1,
Pound argued that the first task of the new poetry was to break the
hold of the iambic pentameter. The fragmentation of metre that
resulted, as witnessed by Eliot's poem, can be seen as a sign of the
times: evidence of a world breaking free from the constraints of
Edwardian society. After the sentimental Romantic poetry of the late
Victorians and the Georgians, Pound advocated a return to Classicism,
to precise descriptions and dry, hard images. In this espousal of
concrete, objective verse Pound and Eliot were influenced by the writings of the philosopher and founding imagist T.E. Hulme, especially his
prewar manifesto 'Romanticism and Classicism' which contributed to
Eliot's attack on the emotionalism of the Romantics in his well-known
essay 'Tradition and the Individual Talent' (1972 [1919]). By 1912, the
founding principles of imagism had been established by Pound, H.D.
(Hilda Doolittle), and Richard Aldington: direct treatment of the
subject; no superfluity of words; musical not metronomic composition.[1]
Pound, using Hulme's vocabulary, wrote that 'An "Image" is that which
presents an intellectual and emotional complex in an instant of time.'
Many of these ideas were used by Eliot, who argued for a renewed
synthesis of intellectual and emotional sensibilities, in writing *The
Waste Land*. They were used again by Pound in editing the poem, when
substantial chunks were cut – 'Death by Water', for example, had been
of comparable length to the other sections. Despite his valorisation of
high culture, Eliot did not advocate intellectualism; instead he argued
for 'the nervous distrust of abstract ideas, the insistence on the poetic
transmutation of thought into sense-experience, the imagist emphasis
on the hard, precise image as "containing" its concept, yoked to the
symbolist preoccupation with poetry as music' (Eagleton 1976a: 147).
Symbolism, which is discussed in the next chapter, was a late
nineteenth century French style of poetry, indebted to Baudelaire,
realised by Mallarmé, and made widely known in Britain by A.J.
Symons's book *The Symbolist Movement in Literature* (1899). Symbolism
differs importantly from the anti-Romantic approach of imagism in the

poet's attempt to transcend materiality and reach spiritual planes through the symbol, a concentrated moment or (sometimes mystical) vision in which the experience of life is expressed.

In contrast to the social realist writers of the nineteenth century, modernist writers focused on psychology, introspection, and individual consciousness. Also, while realists depicted history using a similar set of tools to historiography, the modernists felt that authorial omniscience and third-person narration were misleadingly 'objective' techniques which did not allow for the position of the story-teller. Similarly, the present always surely stood in the way of any clear and direct explanation of the past. In *Ulysses*, Stephen Daedalus declares pessimistically and introvertedly that 'History is a nightmare from which I am trying to awake.' Writers such as Joyce turned against forms of historical understanding, seeing greater meaning in the individual than in society: 'we live as we dream, alone', as Joseph Conrad had written. In two ways, modernist criticism engages with this issue as forcefully as modernist writing: the New Critics similarly turned away from historicism, but other theorists were staging the debate in terms not of morality and the importance of 'the words on the page' but of ideology and society. This debate is frequently contextualised in terms of the opposed stances of the Marxist writers Georg Lukacs and Bertolt Brecht. Lukacs' position is best outlined in his late essay 'The Ideology of Modernism' from 1957, where he argues that modernism involves a 'negation of history' (Lukacs 1972). By this he means that modernist writers are interested in the personal, spiritual, or mystical transcendence of their surroundings, and so the social environment in their texts is little more than a backdrop. Lukacs argues that this concern for the human rather than the social condition manifests itself in two ways: first, the protagonist is delimited by personal experience, unmarked by historical specificity, and second, the individual is isolated, neither forming or formed by the world. Such a subjective representation of reality seemed to Lukacs profoundly reactionary and anti-Marxist, suggesting that culture could be separated from history, human beings from their actual material conditions. Lukacs championed what he saw as historical realism's dynamic presentation of dialectical change in preference to Joyce's historical stasis, which Lukacs thought reflected the individualism of bourgeois society.

Against this viewpoint, the dramatist Bertolt Brecht countered that the purpose of art was not to reflect social conditions but to attempt to change them – and this could only be done through the shock tactics of avant-garde modernist aesthetics. Real social conditions such as poverty and inequality should not be shown as either fixed or acceptable, as suggested by their naturalised depiction in most realist writing, but as abhorrent, outrageous, and unjust. Brecht's approach in his own plays, which intentionally alienated the audience from the characters and conditions they saw on stage, was in many ways the (formal but not ideological) incarnation of Ezra Pound's dictum that modernist artists should always 'make it new'. As social conditions changed, as capitalist forces adjusted to and assimilated revolutionary forms of art, those means of artistic representation had themselves constantly to change in order to force people to reappraise their lives. From such a perspective, the shock of a poem such as *The Waste Land*, which students actually did declaim through megaphones at Cambridge university in the 1920s, was its most important feature: challenging accepted notions of poetry and of modern life.

However, there are different views which take us beyond these polarised opinions and interpret modernist writing in other ways which are illuminating when applied to poetry such as Eliot's. Theodor Adorno, a major figure in the Frankfurt School of critical theorists, maintained that art and literature, and particularly modernist art, could function as a kind of negative or contradictory criticism of society, in thought-provoking experimental texts. With theories that parallel some of Eliot's ideas, Adorno argued that difficult texts provoked new, unfamiliar, estranged conceptions of life. Which is to say that the dissonances and fractures of modernist art expressed the individual's loss of control, centredness, and harmony in the contemporary world. For Walter Benjamin, a champion of Brecht's attempt to prise art from the confines of traditional bourgeois forms, such fragmented existence was reflected in the work of the Parisian poet Charles Baudelaire, whose graphic portrayal of urban life was to influence Eliot's London scenes in *The Waste Land*. However, the chief impetus for this depiction came, according to Bertrand Russell, from the war:

> After seeing troop trains departing from Waterloo, I used to have strange visions of London as a place of unreality. I used in imagination to see the bridges collapse and sink, and the whole great city vanish like a morning mist. Its inhabitants began to seem like hallucinations.... I spoke of this to T.S. Eliot, who put it into *The Waste Land*.
>
> (Fussell 1975: 326)

The last critic I want to discuss in this connection is Fredric Jameson. In his 1982 book, *The Political Unconscious*, Jameson again takes up the issue of modernism's relation to history. In particular, he is interested in the division between realism's transparent representation of history, based on a principle of verisimilitude, and modernism's insistence on the difference of each individual's experience and interpretation of life. Jameson argues that all interpretations are in fact transcendent and ideological, but that many deny this and repress historical forces through 'strategies of containment', such as symbolism. The purpose of interpretation is therefore to penetrate to the text's 'political unconscious', to the historical contradictions and the social conflicts it has repressed. In fact, it is only through this analysis of the ideological subtext that history can be approached – history is the absent cause of the text which must be read back into it. In this light, the formal experiments of the modernists appear as textual strategies to resolve the problems of contemporary society. We will see below how this might work as an approach to *The Waste Land*, but for now it is worth inquiring what it was that Eliot attempted in his texts.

To begin with, we can immediately record that he believed he was writing a poetry of the moment, a verse suited to the times. In 1921, Eliot wrote in his essay 'The Metaphysical Poets':

> We can only say that it appears likely that poets in our civilisation as it exists at present, must be *difficult*.... The poet must become more and more comprehensive, more allusive, more indirect, in order to force, to dislocate if necessary, language into his meaning.
>
> (Eliot 1932: 289)

For Eliot, because the modern world was complex and various, in terms of philosophy and society, poetry also had to be. As the above quotation suggests, one of the problems was the relationship between the world and language. On the one hand, modernist writers felt they could no longer express reality through language as the Victorians had. Eliot wrote in 1920 in 'Swinburne as Poet':

> Language in a healthy state presents the object, is so close to the object that the two are identified. They are identified in the verse of Swinburne solely because the object has ceased to exist, because the meaning is merely the hallucination of meaning, because language, uprooted, has adapted itself to an independent life of atmospheric nourishment.... But the language which is more important to us is that which is struggling to digest and express new objects, new feelings, new

71

aspects, as, for instance, in the prose of Mr. James Joyce or the earlier Conrad.

(Eliot 1932: 327)

On the other hand, as this quotation suggests, the modernists believed language and object *could* be made to fit together, to match each other. Modernist theory generally did not doubt, as postmodernist theory does, that there is a 'reality' of some kind to be expressed. For Eliot, the failure of language to an extent lay with poets: 'the bad poet dwells partly in a world of objects and partly in a world of words, and he never can get them to fit'. It also lay with the means of expression, with words which are only fragments of a reality that exists inside the mind. Eliot's idea in *Four Quartets* that words 'strain', or 'slip' and 'slide', has similarities to Derrida's poststructuralist notion of 'dissemination', of writing as a continual flickering, spilling, and diffusion of meaning (because the meaning of words never lies in themselves or in objects, only in other words, whose meanings lie in different words, and so on). But to Eliot, this was a barrier to expression, a failure of transparent signification in its attempt to be a window on truth – rather than a free play of meaning constituting relative 'truths' (Davies 1995).

For Eliot, the purpose of art, and therefore language in poetry, was to codify an emotion, to represent an 'internal reality'. Eliot famously wrote in his 1919 essay on *Hamlet* that:

The only way of expressing emotion in the form of art is by finding an 'objective correlative'; in other words, a set of objects, a situation, a chain of events which shall be the formula of that *particular* emotion.

(Eliot 1932: 145)

In *Hamlet*, Shakespeare attempted to express the 'inexpressibly horrible', and failed because Hamlet's feeling (his disgust for his mother) is greater than the situation Shakespeare represents. The expression of emotion through a chain of events is arguably what we have in *The Waste Land*: a sequence of objects and situations which attempts to express the sense of sterility in the postwar Western world. The association of thought and feeling provides an intellectual mapping of the individual's emotional experience. The poem's chain of images and events describes the modern, urban individual of the early twentieth century: someone who is marked by a personal more than a social meaning; who is inadequately represented in language; who is split between conscious and unconscious; who is divorced from history and alienated in the modern city.

Much of *The Waste Land*'s fragmentation and disorientation – the 'dislocated' language and the odd combination of objects and situations – can be discussed along these lines, but Eliot did also try to achieve a kind of design in his poem through the only force he felt capable of doing so: mythology. In 1923, Eliot referred in an article called '*Ulysses*, Order, and Myth' to 'the immense panorama of futility and anarchy which is contemporary history'. Having read the serialisation of Joyce's novel and understood the controlling power of *The Odyssey*, Eliot now saw myth as a way of giving contemporaneity shape and structure in literature. It was, he said, the only method of making 'the modern world possible for art'. From this perspective, we might best see *The Waste Land* as a bringing together of history and mythology, because the poet, for Eliot, needs to be alive to both. He writes:

> the historical sense compels a man to write not merely with his own generation in his bones, but with a feeling that the whole of the literature of Europe from Homer and within it the whole of the literature of his own country has a simultaneous existence and composes a simultaneous order.
>
> (Eliot 1972: 72)

Only through an oscillation between 'the temporal and the timeless' does the individual meet the 'traditional' for Eliot, and this is through a negation of neither the historical nor the contemporary.

The historical wasteland

> It was in 1915 the old world ended. In the winter 1915–16 the spirit of old London collapsed; the city, in some way, perished, perished from being the heart of the world, and became a vortex of broken passions, lusts, hopes, fears and horrors.
>
> (D.H. Lawrence, *Kangaroo*)

In his book *Criticism and Ideology*, Terry Eagleton claims that the postwar writings of D.H. Lawrence demonstrate an antithetical structure of 'female' and 'male' forces only brought together in the late *Lady Chatterley's Lover*, which contains in Mellors a character who fuses both principles. Eagleton sees Lawrence's contradictions, and their forced reconciliation, in terms of a fundamental ideological crisis in

1914–18 – years which feature the collapse of liberal humanism and the rise of corporate hierarchies, social atomism, and the mechanistic power of industrial capitalism (Eagleton 1976a: 157–61). In the wake of the war's destruction, Eliot similarly attempts a joining of opposites in *The Waste Land* as early as 1922. Male and female are mythologically united in Tiresias, the blind seer who has been both sexes (he was subsequently made blind by Juno, and given the power of prophecy by Jove, after supporting Jove's contention that women have more sexual pleasure than men). East and West are brought together by Eliot in the poem, as are past and present, asceticism and pleasure, mythology and naturalism, the poetic and the prosaic, the banal and the sublime, the city and the land. What is particularly important about the poem is that for the first time in Eliot's writing he concerned himself with a civilisation as much as an individual, with the world in addition to the self.

Contemporary reactions were diverse. Ezra Pound, who had edited the poem for Eliot, said it was 'the justification of the "movement" of our modern experiment since 1900'. I.A. Richards, though greatly influenced by the poem, thought it was over-intellectualised. Stephen Spender found it unnecessarily esoteric and elitist and thought that in the poem Eliot seems 'to describe the contemporary post-war situation of a certain very small class of intellectuals in Europe and America'. Later opinion is more in line with Samuel Hynes's view that

> the war book above all others in the 'twenties was *The Waste Land*...hence the two veterans who meet in the first part, and Lil's husband, who has just been demobbed, in the second, and the shouting and crying in part five, which Eliot's note identifies with the Russian Revolution. But beyond that, the world of the poem, with its heaps of broken images and its shocked and passive and neurasthenic persons, is a paradigm of war's effects, and of a world emptied of order and meaning, like a battlefield after the battle. And the *manner* of the poem – its ironic tone, its imagery, its lack of heroes and heroism, its anti-rhetorical style – is also a consequence of the war, an application of war-poet principles to the post-war scene.
>
> (Hynes 1976: 25)

Eliot says the poem is partly about a crisis in Europe – the train of events that shattered the European aristocracy from the collapse of the Tsarist regime in Russia in 1917, through the ousting of Kaiser Wilhelm II in the German revolution of 1918, to the demise of the

Habsburg empire in the aftermath of the war. However, the poem suggests that Western civilisation needs not just physical rebuilding but also spiritual renewal. The rebirth at the start of the poem, which can be seen in terms of class and the overturned social order, also seems to suggest this – that after the winter of war, the pain of rehabilitation and regrowth must take place. It paints a picture of a barren Western world of sexual and regenerative incapacity – and hence Eliot turns to Eastern religion, to the Hindu philosophy of the *Vedas*, for his final Sanskrit pronouncements of *Datta, Dayadhvam, Damyata*: give, sympathise, control.

In order that the poem's controlling mythological framework can be appreciated, I'll now begin a detailed discussion of *The Waste Land* by illustrating three straightforward ways to embark upon an analysis of the poem, all of which accentuate the theme of a desolated land in need of rebirth. It should be stressed, however, that the poem can be read from myriad perspectives, some more satisfying than others, but none wholly convincing because, as with any interpretation, coherence can only be achieved by foregrounding certain parts of the text and ignoring others.

First, there is the epigraph. This tells us that civilisations need to die in order to be reborn: 'For I with these my own eyes have seen the Sibyl of Cumae hanging in a jar; and when the boys said "What do you want Sibyl?" she answered, "I want to die."' The Sibyl was granted by Apollo as many years of life as there were grains of sand in a cupped hand, but she forgot also to ask for eternal youth. This story is used by Eliot to refer to Western civilisation, which has evolved but not stayed young. It would be a blessing to die – first, because death is a release and second, because only through death can there be rebirth. Tiresias, granted longevitiy and foresight by Jove, is in a similar position: jaded and weary, 'having foresuffered all'.

Second, there is the poem's opening sentence, with its meditation on natural, cyclical rebirth:

> April is the cruellest month, breeding
> Lilacs out of the dead land, mixing
> Memory and desire, stirring
> Dull roots with spring rain.

Each of the three starting lines finishes with a call for renewing activity: 'breeding', 'mixing', 'stirring'. April is cruel because it marks the beginning of spring, the time nature resumes its painful struggle for regeneration by spreading rain over the parched land. This is Eliot's image of the modern world – a land in need of spiritual reawakening. All the images of water and dryness in the poem return to this opening description. In this, they mimic the poem's theme of nature recycling itself, and of Western civilisation's need to do the same, to regrow. The third line mixes memory and desire, which respectively signal the past and the future, collapsing all time into the present of the poem. Moreover, all the figures in the poem are collected into Tiresias, Eliot says. The opening is additionally an allusion to the start of *The Canterbury Tales*, which also deals with an April journey, an annual pilgrimage for spiritual regeneration (to Becket's shrine at Canterbury), told in a diversity of styles.

Third, there are the section titles. Eliot based several of the poem's cardinal ideas on fertility rites and legends described in Jessie Weston's book *From Ritual to Romance*, the chief of which is that of the Fisher King. Weston refers to many vegetation ceremonies and cites numerous romances, including the legends of King Arthur, telling of a sexually wounded ruler whose impotence is reflected in the dead land of the kingdom. The titles of the first four sections of the poem revolve around ideas of death, sex, and sterility. 'The Burial of the Dead' alludes to the ceremony in the Christian prayer book which includes the throwing of a handful of dust onto the coffin. The section thus intimates a future rebirth, or rather resurrection, but this is far off. The second section's title, 'A Game of Chess', is initially a literary allusion to the playing out of the game of Bianca's seduction in Thomas Middleton's seventeenth-century play *Women Beware Women* (and, more literally, Middleton's *A Game at Chess*), but we should also remember that a game of chess is structured around the defence of a king who is also the weakest character on the board: if the king is lost, the game is over.[2] The Queen, the only woman, is the most powerful actor on the board, and most of the figures in *The Waste Land* are female, though what strength they have is a different matter. Many of the women are silent or powerless – figures such as Ophelia and Cordelia are abused, as is Philomel, who in Greek mythology had her tongue ripped out to prevent her telling of her rape by Tereus; in 'A Game of Chess' Lil and the society woman, who is often linked to the Belladonna of Madame Sosostris's Tarot cards, are treated dismissively; Madame Sosostris is a prophet, like the Sibyl, who is not listened to. Women who do talk in the poem speak of reproduction: sex and birth are major themes of the poem, and it is arguable that Eliot limits female agency to parturition. The third section, 'The Fire Sermon', named after a sermon by Buddha, could be called Death by Fire. This long section considers the modern world debased by meaningless couplings, by directionless passion devoid of spiritual values or even physical joy. It looks at examples from Eastern and Western theology of preaching against such dissipation, including Augustine's *Confessions*: 'I wandered, O my God, too much astray from Thee my stay, in these days of my youth, and I became to myself a waste land.' The section's theme is that fire, in its many forms, such as jealousy, passion, and anger, both destroys and consumes; but the hint of rebirth is also there in the possibility of purgation by fire. 'Death by Water' can be seen as a counterpart to 'The Fire Sermon'. Though it arguably alludes to baptism as well as ancient ceremonies about rebirth by water, the section implies that water both purifies – Phlebas forgets commerce – and drowns. (Despite its emphasis on death, the section uses cyclic images that again suggest that the sea gives rebirth: it refers to stages of age and youth; the whirlpool; the turn of the wheel.)

The fifth section is 'What the Thunder Said'. The thunder of course brings hope of rain to the arid land, but in the Bible God also often speaks with the voice of thunder. Finally, Eliot argues that spiritual guidance needs to be sought out – and it is heard in the commands: give, sympathise, control. This section, linking together ideas of rebirth and of Christ's resurrection, is formed around quests and questions as means of seeking rebirth. Consequently, it uses the knights' journey to the Chapel Perilous for the Holy Grail as a key device (the grail from the Last Supper held Christ's blood when he was wounded on the cross, and the poem here blends the various myths of wounded leaders – Christ, the Fisher King, King Arthur – as analogues for the modern world).

So, one of the poem's dominant modernist techniques is to contain the chaos of the present through mythology, a system of belief which is generally held to be antithetical to historical understanding. Eliot uses a mass of detail, including references to vegetation rites, to Egyptian theology, and to Wagner's Gods; and just as Joyce employs Greek mythology to force a structure onto the fast-paced rhythms of modern life in *Ulysses*, so Eliot incorporates references to the religious archetypes and common anthropological practices detailed in Frazer's massive cross-cultural study *The Golden Bough* (1890–1915). Eliot employs the contrast between modern life and the ancient (as well as the Elizabethan) world order as a way of criticising what he sees as the meaningless disorder of the contemporary world. He does this through the fragmentation of the poem, but also through its use of myth and allegory. Here we can return to the idea of modernist writing as a reaction to historical forces, even if unconsciously so. Fredric Jameson writes that 'Allegory is precisely the dominant mode or expression of a world in which things have for whatever reason been sundered from meanings, from spirit, from genuine human existence' (Jameson 1971: 71). Jameson takes his cue from Walter Benjamin, who argued in his 'Theses on the Philosophy of History' that allegory was characteristic of modern societies which had been stripped of intrinsic meaning. In capitalist society use-value has been totally superseded by exchange-value, and the modern world no longer places meaning in work or materials, emotions or friendship, only in commodities. The result is a turning to allegory for the delivery of meaning: for the morals and values which capitalism inadequately commodifies. So, Eliot writes *The Waste Land* in the way he does to symbolise a loss of spirituality, but Marxist critics argue this reflects the alienating moves of material capitalism.

Modernism is a literature of what Eliot calls the UNREAL CITY: a composite picture of urban life. In this image of London covered in a brown fog (like forgetful snow) Eliot takes much from Baudelaire's descriptions of Paris as fascinating and alienating: a claustrophobic, frenetic, over-populated world of machines that creates automatons. London is a place of 'crowds flowing' and 'hordes swarming'. Eliot's typist 'smooths her hair with automatic hand', his commuters go to work on the 'dead sound of the final stroke of nine', and all the while London Bridge is falling down. The people he describes are surrounded by death – one has a corpse in his garden, one asks, 'Are you alive or not?', and another says she is 'neither living nor dead'. The final section speaks of 'our obituaries' and says that 'He who was living is now dead / We who were living are now dying.' Alluding to contemporary eugenicist theory and to a declining birth rate (despite the increasingly large families of the working class), Eliot uses issues of sex and sexuality to create his divisions of class and gender which run through the poem but also suggest connections (Tate 1988). So, in 'A Game of Chess', scenes of seduction, beauty, and also rape preface the society woman's nervous sterility, which is distinguished from but related to the abortion of the woman in the pub, Lil ('What you get married for if you don't want children?'); similarly, the lack of communication between the sexes in the early part leads on to the threat to Lil of Albert's adultery or desertion later in the section. One social world is 'savagely still', the other marked by unwanted fertility and lust: 'She's had five already, and nearly died of young George…. if Albert won't leave you alone, there it is, I said.' According to David Trotter there is another dimension to the poem that needs mentioning in this regard: empire (Trotter 1988). At the turn of the century, urban degeneration was a common theme, and it was an often-voiced theory that empires decay from the centre unless rejuvenated from their outposts: from their contacts with new cultures (a similar view of English culture's need for regeneration from without was held by the Americans Pound and Eliot, who saw it as their task). From this perspective, Eliot's poem seems to begin from a picture of a decayed London and then move out in its later sections on journeys (Phlebas, the quest for the grail, the journey to Eumaeus) of regeneration. The list of fallen cities ('Jerusalem Athens Alexandria Vienna London') in part five links the modernist anxiety of decay with the imperial. It is therefore perhaps significant that Eliot turns to India – to Sanskrit, Buddhist sermons, and the Upanishads – for spiritual solutions to the West's materialist decadence (Trivedi 1995).

Throughout *The Waste Land* Eliot incorporates expressions of apocalypse and crisis that represent modernism's own condition as a radical break from the past, but there is also in the poem an attempt to put together the 'fragments', to rebuild the 'ruins' through aesthetic form. The poem or, to Eliot, the mind of the poet is the site on which this reconstruction can take place. E.M. Forster maintained that the purpose of art was to make order out of chaos and he used the motto 'only connect' for *Howards End* in 1910 because he felt the modern world was dividing between the privileged and the poor, between culture and materialism, men and women, city and country. Eliot instead used the common modernist device of classical imagery and symbolism for marshalling experience in writing. If, as Fredric Jameson suggests, this is a repression of politics and history, then it is worth noting that in Freud's analysis of dreams he observes that a symbol simultaneously expresses a desire to fulfil an impulse and the desire to suppress it ('coherence in contradiction expresses the force of a desire' as Derrida puts it), because it tries to represent something but does it by representing something else. This coincides with Eliot's attempt to contain social disorder and historical contradictions in the images and structure of *The Waste Land*. Nothing is explicit, everything is mediated through myth and symbol – and it is this 'art' that attempts to contain the detritus strewn before the bewildered reader. For Franco Moretti the poem denies (rather than represses) historical causation because it presents fragments, cycles, and repetitions forming a historical pattern – a 'natural' or extra-historical design that is basically static, unchanging and unchangeable (Moretti 1988: 222). But if we see Eliot's experiments with culture and time as allegorical rather than mythical they become not an organisation of contemporary chaos through literary patterning but representations of the kaleidoscopic experience of modern life. The poem's overall dissonance remains, but its piecing together of sounds and extracts draws the reader into a particular kind of incomplete (mis)understanding that itself becomes the poem's message.

Eliot, though he says the poem is not 'social criticism' but 'rhythmical grumbling', is also trashing modern life, an existence he calls in one biblical allusion 'stony rubbish'. While the Elizabethans wrote of courtly love or of Cleopatra's golden barge, modern living offers only the crowds streaming over London Bridge and the polluted Thames flowing underneath. Religion is reduced to the horoscopes and Tarot-card predictions of Madame Sosostris, love is reduced to caresses that are unreproved if undesired, and court poetry is reduced to music-hall innuendo. The poem berates popular culture throughout its five sections, as Eliot compares his observations of contemporary life with his knowledge of the past, viewed almost exclusively through poetry. The third section of the poem comprises a series of pictures of modern London juxtaposed with Elizabethan and Classical allusions (and also contrasts the sexual promiscuity of the typist, as well as Belladonna and Lil in the second section, with the restraint of lustful feelings by St Augustine and Buddha). Eliot is here part of a wider movement in English criticism that seems to want to reconstruct a lost Elizabethan utopia, where thought and feeling were one, where rhythms of speech expressed in poetry the intuitive consciousness of an organic community, and every individual recognised in the principle of order the necessity of submission to the proper authorities, social and divine.

However, interpretations of Eliot's poem that denigrate modern plurality in favour of a past order, and in so doing struggle for their own unity, can be read against the grain. For example, just as prose in the modernist period became more poetic, reflexive, and self-conscious, poetry such as *The Waste Land* moved towards the novelistic. Consequently, the Russian critic M.M. Bakhtin provides apposite terms in which to describe some of the features of Eliot's poem. The most relevant aspect of Bakhtin's overall argument is summarised by David Lodge:

> There is an indissoluble link in Bakhtin's theory between the linguistic variety of prose fiction, which he called heteroglossia, and its cultural function as the continuous critique of all repressive, authoritarian, one-eyed ideologies. As soon as you allow a variety of discourses into a textual space – vulgar discourses as well as polite ones, vernacular as well as literary, oral as well as written – you establish a resistance…to the dominance of any one discourse.
>
> (Lodge 1989: 22)

Unlike most previous poetry, which used one style or voice, and was therefore distinctly 'monologic', *The Waste Land* is characterised by what Bakhtin refers to as heteroglossia (multiple discourses), by polyphony (many voices), and by contested meaning. While poetry usually doesn't recognise other forms of language or discourse, *The Waste Land* steals genres and forms of speech: pub conversation and autobiographies of the aristocracy, Wagner and nursery rhymes, the Upanishads and the Bible, commerce and Dante; it almost revels in the social diversity of different speech types. Bakhtin says the novel is a 'struggle among socio-linguistic points of view' but the same could apply to Eliot's poem. Far from being a condemnation of social disorder this suggests that the poem is a mosaic of social discourses and ideological viewpoints.

Eliot's original title for the poem was 'He Do The Police In Different Voices' (from Dickens's *Our Mutual Friend*) and this is a clear comment on the way in which *The Waste Land* orchestrates and mimics a polyphony of speech. Bakhtin says that the diversity and importance of the novel is characterised by 'parodic stylization', by 'double-voicedness' and 'hybridity', features that abound in Eliot's cutting, suturing, splicing, and ironising of different snatches of other texts. The poem is also full of parody and double meaning. In a great deal of the text Eliot says one thing and implies another. Through the poem's proliferating associations, connections, and comparisons, meaning, in Bakhtin's terminology, is 'centrifugal' and not 'centripetal', which is to say that it is not centralised but dispersed. This is because, like much modernist writing, the text opens itself to multiple readings and even seems to encourage a plurality of interpretations.

Conclusion

A dialogic reading of *The Waste Land* seems to falter before the omniscient view of the narrator, whether it be Tiresias or Eliot. The dominant figure in the text arbitrates between the different voices and inserts a metacommentary above the poem's eclectic cultural fragments. Also, the implied reader is expected to sense Eliot's Classical allusions and to sympathise with a pejorative view of modern life. This is linked to Eliot's view of the poet's task. In his essay 'The Metaphysical Poets' he says that 'the ordinary man's experience is chaotic, irregular, fragmentary', but 'in the mind of the poet these experiences are always forming new wholes'. Eliot is here speaking of what the poet's experience should be like – it is the kind of fusion of intellect and emotion he finds in Donne but which has been missing in poets as well as in the common individual since the Metaphysical poets. *The Waste Land's* invocations of the need for fusion and regeneration apply as much to poetry as to life.

While a dialogic approach encourages the reader to see social diversity, hybridity, and irony in the poem, the dominant images and scenes of *The Waste Land* appear ugly, brutal, and unfeeling; they are moments of deterioration, danger, and mental decay portraying a desensitised, routine life surrounded by debris and pollution. As such the poem suggests a world-weary civilisation, shell-shocked, reeling, and numb from World War I; a society waiting to die in order to find, in Eliot's view, its rebirth and redemption. Yet ahead lay financial collapse, mass unemployment, fascism, and World War II. These were events for which a different kind of poetry, more urgent and politically engaged, would be written by poets who were both born in the twentieth century and too young to fight in World War I. But before we look at their work, we need to consider the importance of another poet for whom 1922 was a significant date: William Butler Yeats, who became a Senator in the Irish Free State established that year.

4

'DEMON AND BEAST'

The 1920s and W.B. Yeats

Introduction

In 1940, the year after Yeats's death, Eliot told an audience at the Abbey Theatre in Dublin: 'he was one of those few whose history is the history of their own time, who are part of the consciousness of an age which cannot be understood without them' (Eliot 1975: 257). The reverse is also certainly true and Yeats's writing should not be read outside of the context of Ireland's political and colonial experience. More than any other twentieth-century poet, his work parallels a public history which for him was also a personal one. His poetry evolves alongside social upheaval and debates over national identity, as Yeats 'the last Romantic' becomes Yeats the modernist, nationalist, and post-colonial poet.

Though his major work is written at the same time as Eliot's, Yeats is a very different poet of the modern world. As one of his biographers comments, Yeats seems to inhabit another time from his contemporaries:

> The bulk of the populations in developed countries live in conurbations with all the attendant stresses and opportunities. Yeats not only does not write out of this situation, he barely refers to it. Not only are there no factories or offices in the poems, there is scarcely a wheel.
>
> (Macrae 1995: 186–7)

In other words, though he is a nationalist poet, Yeats does not blend contemporary politics with its own society so much as with elements of the mythological, historical, personal, and spiritual. This can be interpreted in many ways: as a refusal of the modern industrial world; as a rebuttal to the impositions of English Imperialism; as an attempt to refashion Irish traditions and identity; and as a denial of the political democracy he hoped would soon be replaced by the hierarchies of an older aristocratic order.

In this chapter, I will look at two of Yeats's volumes of the 1920s: *Michael Robartes and the Dancer* (1921) and *The Tower* (1928). Yeats's output from 1889 to 1917 is primarily dramatic and lyric love poetry, but with his postwar writing, and in particular with these two volumes published in the 1920s, he addresses the political scene in Ireland and explores the attitudes he has to rebellion, independence, nationalism, and the civil war. However, as prologue, I want to consider the particular way in which Yeats adopted personas in some of his work, poetry that is concerned both with spiritualism and with politics, the mystical and the material.

Private and public

Yeats has been represented in many ways, but never in terms of a unified identity. Richard Ellmann's (1948) biography discusses him in terms of personas – most particularly those of the mystical, contemplative introvert and the campaigning, political activist. Alasdair Macrae, in a more recent biography, notes the same contrast between the images of a reclusive poet, looking out from his tower at Lady Gregory's Coole Park, and a passionate orator fighting for Irish nationalism: the individual who has the most-cited name in *The Oxford Illustrated History of Ireland*.

Yeats himself believed in the poet adopting a character or 'mask', a simplified antithetical self, with the clear aims and the lonely intensity of committed Irish national heroes, such as Edward Fitzgerald, Robert Emmet, and Wolfe Tone, who had led the 1798 Rising against the English. In general, Yeats admired strong leadership, and he supported Mussolini and Franco as well as the Irish Blueshirts' leader Eoin O'Duffy. Consequently, he has been accused of embracing fascism, and this is fair inasmuch as he believed in government by the few of the many, but he was firmly against violence, and in the six years he was a Senator in the Free State, Yeats opposed all censorship and any state discrimination against individuals.[1]

In addition to this public side, Yeats also valorised the role of the romantic dreamer or wild, mystical aesthete. He sometimes called the two personas Owen Aherne and Michael Robartes.[2] Robartes reflects Yeats's private self: his occult interests, his sexual desires, and his idealism. By contrast, Owen Aherne is the public man – less of a dreamer, but also less active and aggressive. As Robartes's opposite, he is a pious Catholic on the verge of becoming a monk – Yeats used Catholicism as a symbol of conventional and cautious belief – but he is also sometimes just 'the author'. Of most importance here, Yeats's two sides express less a split personality than an attempt to negotiate the divide between public and private life that had become enshrined in the course of the nineteenth century. Consequently, many critics position Yeats as mediating or caught between opposites, and his poetry arises in the tension between them. Therefore a famous piece such as 'Sailing to Byzantium' might best be seen as describing a half-wish, a desire that the poet knows is impossible, but which his imagination (fantasy) seizes hold of. George Orwell, who viewed Yeats as a feudalist, a snobbish aristocrat, and a hater of democracy, the modern world, and science, attempted to reconcile what he saw as the two fundamental sides to Yeats – his symbolic, mystical style of poetry and his right-wing political vision of society:

> [T]he very concept of occultism carries with it the idea that knowledge must be a secret thing, limited to a small circle of initiates. But the same idea is integral to Fascism. Those who dread the prospect of universal suffrage, popular education, freedom of thought, emancipation of women, will start off with a predilection to secret cults.
>
> (Orwell 1943: 84–5)

In his poetry, this predilection is most familiar in Yeats's theory of history, which I will come to when discussing *Michael Robartes and the Dancer*, and in his symbolism. In 1900, the year after Symons published *The Symbolist Movement in Literature*, which is dedicated to Yeats, Yeats wrote 'The Symbolism of Poetry', more under the influence of Blake than anyone else. In it he expresses his belief in inspiration, magic, transcendence, and to an extent irrationality: a very different aesthetic from Eliot's. Yeats claimed that 'All sounds, all colours, all forms...evoke indefinable and yet precise emotions.... Because an emotion does not exist...till it has found its expression...poets and painters and musicians...are continually making and unmaking mankind' (Yeats 1972: 30–1). Elsewhere, in an essay on 'The Philosophy of Shelley's Poetry', he wrote: 'It is only by ancient symbols, by symbols that have numberless meanings...that any highly subjective art can escape from the barrenness and shallowness of a too conscious arrangement, into the abundance and depth of Nature' (Yeats 1964: 72). Yeats believed there to be emotional and intellectual symbols which, though often personal, were always given by an external force (see Emig 1995). Mysterious and ultimately indefinable, these symbols evoke the shared human mind and memory, in similar ways to Jung's collective unconscious, which Yeats regarded as a scientific explanation of his ideas. Symbols for Yeats also have associations with history, and in 'The Tower' he speaks of past events 'in the Great Memory stored' (see this chapter's appendix).[3] Consequently, according to Yeats it is symbolism which has the power to move people in poetry. He wanted organic rhythms, an attention to form, an end to anecdotal description and brisk rhythms, and a return to imagination (he was 'certain that the imagination has some way of alighting on the truth that reason has not'; Yeats 1964: 53). In this, we can see why he disliked so much not just the poetry of Austin and Newbolt, but also of Wilfred Owen and Isaac Rosenberg. While Yeats's personal poetic usages are often specialised, symbolism itself draws upon the basic fact that all language is metaphorical: it is not the thing or concept it describes. Symons writes at the start of his book, 'Symbolism began with the first words uttered by the first man, as he named every living thing; or before then, in heaven when God named the world into being.' For Yeats, this also best expressed why the Word has great power, and why for him language was associated with magic, spirituality, and sacred truths.

In his pursuit of a traditional aristocratic order Yeats had little time for egalitarian socialism or progressive democracy. But he was also in many ways a radical national figure, the pioneer whose re-creation of a Celtic mythology was based upon a desire to build an Irish identity just as much as his political views were predicated upon a belief in elitism and the leadership of the many by the few. It is therefore important to remember that in his relation to the world, Yeats saw himself as both Owen Aherne and Michael Robartes.

Yeats and Ireland

Introducing his work, Yeats asserted as a first principle that 'A poet writes always of his private life' (Macrae 1995: 67). But he also believed that the autobiographical element was transmuted in art: by storytelling, fantasy, and symbol – but also by history. From his early years, Yeats's life is inseparable from contemporary events in Ireland and decisions taken in the British parliament. In repeated journeys that resemble the movements of ambassadors, the Yeats family migrated between the two foremost capitals of the British Empire while the English and Irish wrangled over Home Rule. Born into an Anglo-Irish Protestant minority in Dublin, Yeats was the son of a lawyer/painter father and a mother from a prosperous ship-owning family from Sligo on the West Coast, where Yeats spent many early holidays. Two years after his birth, Yeats's family moved to London in 1867, the same year that the Irish Republican Brotherhood – which Yeats later joined – staged a rising to seek independence from England by force. In 1880, soon after the Irish Land League was founded by Michael Davitt and Charles Stewart Parnell to rid Ireland of English landlords by burning them out, the Yeats family came back to Dublin. In 1883, Yeats refused to go to Trinity and took up art and poetry instead. Four years later, his family returned to England again and Yeats tried to publish his work in London. He met Oscar Wilde, William Morris, and John O'Leary, the Nationalist leader he revered. O'Leary introduced Yeats to Maud Gonne, an active Nationalist campaigner with whom he was to fall unreservedly but unrequitedly in love (she is the subject of nearly all his love poems). He also joined the Theosophical Society and the Order of the Golden Dawn. This was the year after the First Home Rule Bill was defeated in parliament, sparking riots on the streets of Belfast. In 1891, while many Irish Protestants were espousing Unionism and far more were treated with suspicion by the Nationalists, Yeats founded the Irish Literary Society.

Yeats's political awareness and activity increased in the 1890s. He campaigned against British action in the Boer War and opposed Queen Victoria's Jubilee as well as her visit to Dublin. He was involved in charity work and provided help for people threatened with eviction (Macrae 1995: 67). He supported the Nationalist struggle and attempts to organise trade unions in Ireland, while serving as an active member of the Irish Republican Brotherhood from 1896 to 1900. In his 1893 collection, *The Rose*, Yeats had already affirmed an Irish identity and heritage which he saw culturally and politically, placing himself as: 'True brother of a company / That sang, to sweeten Ireland's wrong' ('To Ireland in the Coming Times').

In many ways, the end of the century marked the decisive phase of Irish resistance to English rule, issuing from the Celtic and Gaelic revivals of the late nineteenth century. Douglas Hyde founded the Gaelic League in 1893, positioning the real, anti-colonial Ireland as essentially an agricultural community with a rural identity. Meanwhile, Yeats embarked on his forging of an Irish identity based on Celtic culture, publishing his collection of folk stories, *The Celtic Twilight*, in the same year. Over the next fifteen years, Yeats attempted to instigate a new Irish poetry, with himself at the helm, a National Theatre, and a unifying Celtic mythology, amounting to a National Literary Revival. Yeats also worked on a three-volume edition of Blake, published in

1893, through which he further developed his interest in symbolism. In 1896 he met Lady Gregory, who became a patron and invited Yeats to spend his summers at Coole Park. She encouraged his interest in the stage and this led to the founding of the Irish National Theatre Society in 1902 and, through the patronage of Florence Horniman, the Abbey Theatre in 1904. The production of Synge's *The Playboy of the Western World* at the Abbey in 1907 led to riots which Yeats volubly opposed but also perceived as marking a shift in Irish consciousness. After this setback, combined with the death of John O'Leary, Yeats lamented a change from a 'Celtic' to an 'Irish' movement, the work of 'a new class...without exceptional men' but comprising 'shopkeepers [and] clerks' (Cairns and Richards 1988: 97).

The next ten years saw significant alterations in Yeats's life that were poetical, political, and personal. Ezra Pound, who encouraged him to modernise his poetry, became Yeats's secretary briefly in 1912, the year of Marsh's first *Georgian Poetry* anthology and of the Third Home Rule Bill, later defeated in the House of Lords. In 1916, after the formation of military groups such as the Irish Citizens' Army and the Ulster Volunteer Force, the Easter Rising in Dublin revived and further stimulated Yeats's interest in Irish nationalism. In 1917, he proposed once more to Maud Gonne (her estranged husband was one of those executed by the English), and then to her daughter Iseult, and finally to Georgie Hyde-Lees, who accepted him. On their Sussex honeymoon, Yeats encouraged his wife to experiment with automatic writing, which proved such a success that he set out to encompass the resulting 'messages' in a comprehensive system.

In December 1918 the separatist Nationalist party, Sinn Fein, led by Eamon de Valera, won a convincing election victory. Its members refused to go to Westminster and established the Irish parliament (the Dail) instead, in Dublin. In 1919, they declared that Ireland had seceded from Britain, and, in the ensuing war, Michael Collins led the IRA against the British Black and Tans, composed of ex-World War I servicemen. Yeats returned to Dublin in 1920 to work for the nationalist cause, publishing anti-colonial poems that were to go into *Michael Robartes and the Dancer*: 'Easter 1916', 'Sixteen Dead Men', and 'The Rose Tree' (of Irish Nationalism). In July 1921 the war ended and a treaty was signed later in the year, splitting the Irish Free State from the north. In the Dail, the treaty was only narrowly accepted by sixty-four votes to fifty-seven, and soon civil war broke out in July 1922. When it ended the following year, Yeats, who was awarded the Nobel Prize in 1923, played an increased role in the Senate of the new Irish state, but was dismayed by de Valera's emphasis on Roman

Catholicism. It was important to Yeats, a member of 'the Ascendancy', or Anglo-Irish aristocracy, to establish alongside the Irish–Irish nationalist cause, an anti-British Protestant identity.

In some ways, Yeats's reasons for opposing colonial rule were out of the ordinary. To begin with, it was on the basis of incompatibility that he desired independence. For Yeats, while Ireland was essentially feudal, England was modern and democratic. Where Ireland was agrarian and spiritual, England was mechanised and materialistic, enslaved by 'progress' and science (a form of knowledge Yeats opposed to that of 'reverie'). He had written in 1903:

> England or any other country which takes its tunes from the great cities and gets its taste from schools and not from old custom may have a mob, but it cannot have a people.... The poet must always prefer the community where the perfected minds express the people.
>
> (Yeats 1964: 129)

Yeats wanted a nation in which an aristocracy ruled but fashioned a shared culture from the people, in an 'organic community'. These are the values and influences that shape his poetry in the years of World War I and after: the nationalist cause, the Protestant aristocracy, civil war, and traditional Irish identity, combined with his love for Maud and Iseult Gonne, his marriage to Georgie Hyde-Lees, the revelations of automatic writing and mysticism. In this time he composed many of the poems that make up *Michael Robartes and the Dancer* (from November 1914 to September 1919 – their composition overlaps considerably with that of the poems in *The Wild Swans at Coole*) and *The Tower* (September 1920 to March 1927, aside from 'The New Faces' and 'Owen Aherne and his Dancers' which were written earlier).[4]

Michael Robartes and the Dancer (1921)

In 1919, Yeats said of his poetry 'I had three interests: interest in a form of literature, in a form of philosophy, and a belief in nationality' (Parkinson 1970: 50). All of these are apparent in his 1921 volume. The book has an arrangement which can, for our purposes, be explained simply. The first poem, 'Michael Robartes and the Dancer' is about Yeats and Iseult Gonne (as is 'Owen Aherne and his Dancers' in *The Tower*). It opens the volume by posing arguments about education versus experience; the flesh versus the mind; men versus women. The following three personal poems, 'Solomon and the Witch', 'An Image from a Past Life', and 'Under Saturn', concern Yeats and his wife Georgie, although they are haunted by the presence of Maud Gonne. The next five, from 'Easter 1916' to 'The Leaders of the Crowd' are political poems dealing with the events of the previous half-decade. The penultimate five blend Yeats's two sides because they mix elements of his and Georgie's visions with his mystical and historical theories: 'Towards Break of Day' recalls the synchronicity of identical dreams that Yeats and Georgie had; 'Demon and Beast' relishes the moment when the demon hatred and the beast desire are both still, though with some regret because 'every natural victory / Belongs to beast or demon'; 'The Second Coming' anticipates the arrival of a terrible new age in history; 'A Prayer for my Daughter', which dwells on the women Yeats has loved, hopes that Anne Yeats will not inherit extremes of beauty or enmity, but will value the rituals of custom and ceremony while beginning all things in 'merriment'; and 'A Meditation in Time of War' again reflects on the quiet moment when warring parties, like those in Ireland, or the beast and the demon, are expunged from the mind. The final poem, 'To be Carved on a Stone at Thoor Ballylee', is a solemn tribute and future epitaph for himself and Georgie at the Tower.

This summary gives a flavour of the way in which Yeats oscillates between events that seem important at a national or local level, seguing between the personal and the historical. However, the complexity of the poems requires considerably more detailed analysis of at least some of them to build a reasonable overview of the issues with which Yeats deals.

As an opening salvo against theory over practice, 'Michael Robartes and the Dancer' contrasts knowledge learned at school (education) with that gained from a mirror (reflection). It is a poem of seduction in which neither side wins, though Robartes's arguments are consistently countered. Against the dancer's role as 'woman of ideas', Robartes tries to take the position of the 'tutor' – which is somewhat ironic as it is against such pedagogy that he is arguing in his affirmation that beauty should be its own teacher and should learn from the body. It is important that he is in dispute with a dancer: someone who 'embodies' a union of abstract knowledge (knowledge of the dance) with physical beauty (the performance of the dance). She appears open to his alternative form of physical knowledge but remains unconvinced: his denunciation of abstract knowledge uses theoretical reasoning. Her every comment outmanoeuvres his logic in one way or another and yet plays along in the game of flirtation. In terms of its historical context, as Elizabeth Cullingford has noted, the poem stages the debate between suffragists and anti-suffragists, touching on the feminist debate over the body as source of pleasure or danger (Cullingford 1993: 86–92). This, like the following three poems, concerns the sexual and spiritual side to Yeats's life, while the next five turn to Yeats's persona of 'Owen Aherne' and to public events, particularly those of the Irish Rebellion of 1916, which Yeats initially thought unwise but came to see in the light of previous Irish resistance to English Imperialism. The Rising was to prompt his most famous poems in support of the nationalist cause.

In an earlier volume, *Responsibilities* (1914), and in particular in poems such as 'September 1913', 'Paudeen' (a derogatory term for the Irish, from the Gaelic for 'Paddy'), and 'To a Shade', Yeats's disillusionment or, as he put it, discouragement, is clear:

> Where Celticism had allowed Yeats access to a species of sentimental connection with the people-nation through folklore and landscape, his new and profoundly anti-popular discourse furnished a critique of the leaders of the people-nation which saw their mediocrity defined by the very solidarity of outlook between them and the people-nation.
>
> (Cairns and Richards 1988: 100–1)

Yet, after the Easter Rising, Yeats decided that he had underestimated the Irish and their capacity for heroism. Before 1916 even most Catholics in Ireland opposed complete Home Rule. And it was not the Rising itself that changed their minds but the British reaction. Yeats was similarly affected, and particularly so by the brutal reprisals. While England was at war with Germany it seemed to the nationalists an ideal time to strike for independence. In the six days of the Rising, about 1,500 republicans were involved, mainly in the capital. The major focus of the fighting was the Dublin Post Office, held for several days, from which Patrick Pearse read out a declaration of the Irish Free State. Several nationalists were killed in the fighting but sixteen were condemned to execution and large numbers imprisoned when the British retook control (Freyer 1981: 62–6). Yeats's response was the poem 'Easter 1916' (the sense of a religious sacrifice is important), written in the months following the executions.[5] He was in England at the time and appeared at first somewhat annoyed not to have been informed of the Rising but soon realised that it expressed a kind of idealism he himself sought in the Irish. Edward Said positions Yeats alongside other poets resisting Imperialism, whom he resembles in

91

his anger at the schemes for partition...the celebration and commemoration of violence in bringing about a new order, and the sinuous interweaving of loyalty and betrayal in the nationalist setting.... Like all the poets of decolonization Yeats struggles to announce the contours of an 'imagined' or ideal community.

(Said 1990: 86–7)

Ambivalent to the new order, Yeats's poem plays off against each other the aversion to violence and the commitment to change that he found hard to reconcile in his mind. This is also present in his work after independence in such poems in *The Tower* as 'Meditations in Time of Civil War': 'We had fed our heart on fantasies, / The heart's grown brutal with the fare.' T.R. Henn attributes Yeats's change after the Rebellion to a recognition that the aristocratic culture that had been so important before World War I had lost its centrality in (a certain kind of ideal) Irish life. It was in some ways ironic that the independence movement Yeats had supported and campaigned for, was antagonistic towards the country-house tradition (e.g. Lady Gregory received death threats) that represented so much of his own hopes for the future (Henn 1984).

Subsequent poems in this short volume mix the mythological and the political in Yeats's understanding of historical cycles and personal drives: 'I had long perned in the gyre, / Between my hatred and desire' ('Demon and Beast'). His personal, mystical views blend with his historical ones as he seeks to identify the forces that are leading the world into such widespread violence: in World War I, the Western empires, and Eastern Europe. Yeats thus shared Eliot's view of the world as being in turmoil and decay, for example in his famous poem 'The Second Coming': 'Things fall apart; the centre cannot hold; / Mere anarchy is loosed upon the world.' Yeats thought events in the early part of the century were the herald of a major phase in history. In 'The Second Coming' he offers a view of the Western world spinning (in a perne or reel) through history towards a new aristocratic age, reversing the twenty centuries of democracy inaugurated by Christ's birth. In a system that drew upon Nietzschean philosophy, magic, lunar cycles, and aristocratic values, Yeats believed the world moved back and forth in 2,000 year periods, or 'gyres', and was coming to the end of what he called a 'scientific, fact-accumulating, heterogeneous civilization'.[6] Cairns and Richards explain:

While the Christian cycle had been preceded by an aristocratic, antithetical cycle, dominated by Greece, the annunciation of which had been Zeus' rape of Leda, the Christian cycle had been primary or democratic in its essentials. Hence, the coming cycle would be antithetical or aristocratic, and as the democratic developed to its apotheosis, the new cycle was simultaneously being prepared.

(Cairns and Richards 1988: 122)

Recent violent eruptions such as World War I, the Russian Revolution, and also, in Ireland, the Easter Rising (compare the refrain of 'Easter 1916', 'A terrible beauty is born', with the last two lines of 'The Second Coming') were interpreted by Yeats as announcements of the coming new age. In other words, his philosophy of history allowed him to understand the world, the future, and Ireland's economic backwardness in terms that suited him: contemporary events heralded the aristocratic revolution he desired and Ireland's technological position simply placed it closer to an ideal Grecian order (Deane 1985: 40).

When reading 'The Second Coming', it is helpful to remember its position in *Michael Robartes and the Dancer*. As Hugh Kenner has shown in a discussion of *The Tower*, Yeats's imagery in one poem is often made clearer, though never fully *explained*, by considering its place in the volume's overall sequence (Kenner 1956). So, the references in 'The Second Coming' to 'perne' and 'gyre' are taken up from the previous poem 'Demon and Beast', while the idea of a 'ceremony of innocence' is expanded upon in the following poem, 'A Prayer for my Daughter', which itself echoes the refrain of 'Easter 1916'. In 'The Second Coming' Yeats argues that the best 'lack all conviction' while the worst are 'full of passionate intensity'; but John Lucas asks:

who are the worst? Those who make revolutions? Very probably. Political radicals, then, even communists? Quite likely. For though in 'Easter 1916' Yeats acknowledges the worth of Pearse and Connolly, he knew that both were communists; and the 'blood-dimmed tide' of 'The Second Coming' may well catch up the events and aftermath of the Easter Rising as well as the Bolshevik rising and, then, assassination of the Czar and his family. Communists and their sympathizers and radical allies are 'Leaders of the Crowd', Helens of 'social-welfare dream,' or dreamers of 'some vague utopia.' As such, they let loose 'a roof-levelling wind,' which threatens to destroy everything that stands in its way, including, of course, 'monuments of unageing intellect'.... [T]he champions of mass democracy...was what history had let loose, and it was from *this* that civilization had to be saved, even if such salvation had to be accomplished in the pages of a book. There, if nowhere else, could be the celebration of 'beautiful lofty things'.

(Lucas 1996: 87)

As I said at the start of this chapter, Yeats presents several personas; it is also appropriate to regard him in several lights historically: as an Irish nationalist, an anti-communist, an anti-democratic aristocrat, and as a member of the British Empire, a resident of southern England as much as Ireland. In his belief in Ireland, Celtic mythology, and the Protestant Ascendancy there is at least continuity. As part of a mock-trial of Yeats after his death, W.H. Auden wrote in his defence:

From first to last [Yeats's poems] express a sustained protest against the social atomisation caused by industrialism, and both in their ideas and their language a constant struggle to overcome it. The fairies and heroes of the early work were an attempt to find through folk tradition a binding force to society; and the doctrine of Anima Mundi found in the later poems is the same thing...

(Auden 1939: 62)

Yeats can be read in many ways: Orwell sees him as crypto-fascist, Auden places him as a believer in community, and Edward Said understands Yeats's poetry as part of an attempt to mount a resistance to English colonialism through a unifying national identity. One of the reasons that there are so many views of Yeats is precisely that, while retaining certain fundamental beliefs, he changed with the times. The Yeats of *Michael Robartes and the Dancer* is a sceptic and a nationalist, a mystic and a politician writing at the time of the birth of the Irish Free State. His next volume was written from a very different perspective.

The Tower (1928)

The Tower includes poems written in the first years of Ireland's independence and in the years of Yeats's fullest public life. The collection suggests the changes in Yeats's life in the 1920s: moving between homes in Dublin and at the Tower in Galway, becoming a Senator, winning the Nobel Prize, starting a new family life, and seeing the publication of his mystical theories in *A Vision* (1925). The poems rage at, in personal terms, age and, in public terms, violence. The whole of the volume, published when Yeats was 63, dwells on decay and shows a concern with transience, destruction, and Ireland's warring.

A treaty between Ireland and Britain had been signed in December 1921, giving not Republic but Dominion status to the new Irish Free State. Six of the Ulster counties in the north which had a Protestant majority remained under British rule but with a devolved parliament in Belfast. As has happened almost everywhere else that the British divided territories at independence, such as India and Cyprus, civil war broke out in Ireland (between those who accepted the treaty, headed by Michael Collins, and those who rejected it, led by Eamon de Valera). In the midst of this, though he agreed to be a Senator in the new Dail in 1922, Yeats's disenchantment with politics was evident. For example, to record the impact of the war on the country, on his own life, and on Ireland's heritage he wrote 'Meditations in Time of Civil War', a poem of anger and contempt, ending with a section enti-tled 'I see phantoms of hatred and of the Heart's Fullness and of the Coming Emptiness'. To Yeats, approaching his sixties, politics appeared not less important but so much less satisfying than art; while he wished to see Ireland united by culture and tradition, it seemed that war was succeeding war. All of this dissatisfaction, despite his happiness with Georgie, is apparent in *The Tower*, from its opening celebration of the permanence of art in distinction from the transience of nature, through the long meditations on war's destruction, to the more abstract poems which again entwine world history with Yeats's mystical beliefs or compare his interest in education as a Senator with his theories on the acquisition of knowledge.

Yeats planned his volumes with care and their arrangement is important.[7] The first poem in *The Tower* is 'Sailing to Byzantium' and it announces Yeats's desire to escape from his own mortality and from Ireland's violence: to move out of nature and into 'the artifice of eter-nity'. On early Byzantium, which Yeats saw as the summit of European artistic achievement and spiritual philosophy, he wrote:

> maybe never before or since in recorded history, religious, aesthetic and practical life were one.... The painter, the mosaic worker, the worker in gold or silver, the illuminator of sacred books, were almost impersonal, almost perhaps without the consciousness of individual design, absorbed in their subject-matter and that the vision of a whole people.
>
> (Yeats 1925: 244)

Yeats wanted a similar unity for Ireland, and much of his work can be seen as a groping towards appropriate forms, in a national literature, mythology, and theatre. Edward Larrissy argues that 'Sailing to Byzantium' offers 'an extreme version of bitterness towards Ireland' because Yeats is growing old while all around him nature is celebrating its transient youth and regeneration (Larrissy 1994: 170). Above all, in its recommendation of artifice or insight over nature or life, despite their inseparability, it stands as an overture to the rest of the volume.

After 'The Tower', in which Yeats again rages at decrepitude and attempts to transcend physical and sexual loss through poetic and imaginative potency, the following seven-part poem, written during the civil war of 1922–3, concerns Yeats's questioning of the forces that shape and create civilisation. He asks whether violence is necessary for 'greatness' or progress, and then turns for reassurance to his own home, the Tower in Coole Park, a symbol of human effort and of the need to create even in the most discouraging times. The sections are indeed '*Meditations* in Times of Civil War' and they come to no definitive conclusions, but dwell on themes of decay, commitment, industry, and destruction.

The succeeding poem concerns the war four years earlier which had followed the declaration of Ireland's secession from England in January 1919. Edna Longley writes:

> Yeats's dramatic-lyrical sequence, 'Nineteen Hundred and Nineteen', was at least as epoch-making and epoch-defining as *The Waste Land*; and it may have proved more paradigmatic of poetry in this century. Written at roughly the same time…the poems have certain common factors: pessimism about contemporary conditions; a grand historical perspective on such pessimism; a sense that western civilisation, as an imaginative and spiritual construct, has been 'broken in bits'. In each case poetry confronts all its enemies, its own ruin. But Yeats's elegy for fallen civilisation is also a war-poem.
>
> (Longley 1986: 18)

The poem's original title had been 'Thoughts upon the Present State of the World' and it is an attempt to extrapolate a world-view from specific, local events, such as the 'horrors at Gort', which were atrocities committed by the British Black and Tans, particularly the shooting of Ellen Quinn with a baby in her arms in November 1920. For Yeats, the war signalled the depressing realisation that the modern world was failing and not yet working towards a preferable civilisation. The first stanza dwells on destruction – in Greece, not Ireland. It then moves on to consider Ireland's similar heritage and how it was mistakenly thought wars were at an end: 'all teeth were drawn...and a great army but a showy thing'. Now the times are apocalyptic and cruel, but perhaps this realisation can itself bring about change. Yeats in the next section imagines humanity whirling in history (the twenty centuries of the Platonic Year) like the body of a Chinese dancer spinning in cloth. Section three considers the soul moving through history, and section four envisions the terrible stage it has reached, particularly in the present Anglo-Irish conflict's rejection of the hopes of the Third Home Rule Bill in 1912. In section five, Yeats mocks the optimists and the progressives, and then mocks the mocker, while the final section accumulates dark, threatening visions of destruction. It is Yeats's most sombre and bleak poem of the period and needs to be considered alongside the preceding meditations and the short verse that follows: 'The Wheel', a simple parabolic eight-line poem about human discontent and restlessness, which Yeats allies to his old age (his fears are mixed with the hopes expressed in 'A Prayer for my Daughter', written soon after her birth in February 1919). Yeats wrote of the time:

> In my own neighbourhood the Black and Tans dragged young men tied alive to a lorry by their heels till their bodies were rent in pieces. 'There was nothing for the mother but the head' said a country man.... The one enlivening truth that starts out of it all is that we may learn charity after mutual contempt. There is no longer a virtuous nation and the best of us live by candle light.[8]

'Leda and the Swan' is another poem of male violence, but it has been read as an attack on censorship in an Ireland which defined its independence in terms of the ethical code of the Catholic authorities (Cullingford 1993: 142). The poem records an initial great shock or blow as history is transformed by the intervention of the divine, and at first appearance it might seem to have little to do with Ireland. However, Edward Said sees the poem in terms of the birth of colonial violence and the problematic co-ordination of anti-colonial resistance. He interprets the question 'did she put on his knowledge with his power / Before the indifferent beak could let her drop?' as an issue of the relation between reason and force in acts of opposition:

> More precisely, Yeats's greatest theme in the poetry that culminates in *The Tower* is, so far as decolonization is

97

concerned, how to reconcile the inevitable violence of the colonial conflict with the everyday politics of an on-going nationalist struggle, and also with the power of each of the various parties in the colonial conflict, with the discourse of reason, or persuasion, of organization, with the requirements of poetry. Yeats's prophetic perception that at some point violence cannot be enough and that the strategies of politics and reason must come into play is, to my knowledge, the first important announcement in the context of decolonization of the need to balance violent force with an exigent political and organizational process.

(Said 1990: 90–1)

Though this is fair comment, Yeats's ideas of reason are themselves of an understanding that is not abstract, but drawn from experience – and if Said is correct, then Ireland's knowledge, like Leda's, can only be born out of violence. Another key poem in the collection which comments on this issue is 'Among School Children'. Like 'Michael Robartes and the Dancer', it contrasts two forms of knowing: the abstract and the concrete. Yeats opposes the philosophers who, from Plato on, come to see through deduction that the real is only an embodiment of the ideal: 'Plato thought nature but a spume that plays / Upon a ghostly paradigm of things.' Against such abstract thinking Yeats places 'images' worshipped by nuns, children adored by mothers, and living 'knowledges' that are only comprehensible in their physicality: like the tree's beauty (a tree needs no philosophy, no knowledge of itself) or the dancer's embodiment of choreographed movements which have no meaning other than in their performance. That the real is an enactment of the ideal can be seen in life, argues Yeats, without the aid of philosophical reflection. The last lines of the poem, which again suggest the inseparability of art and nature or form and content, have provoked as many interpretations as any in Yeats's work, including political and social ones. Said, who is perhaps thinking of Yeats's comment that 'All men are dancers' in 'Nineteen Hundred and Nineteen', argues that 'The range of references in the closing strophes of "Among School Children," suggests that Yeats was reminding his audience that history and nation were not separable, any more than a dancer was separate from the dance' (Said 1990: 92). Yet, the poem also concerns Yeats's position as school inspector and Senator, and so hints at his support for better education – the poem was written soon after the School Attendance Bill of 1925 – and for divorce and contraception in Ireland (Yeats's first Senate speech in 1925 was in favour of divorce and while the sale of contraceptives was legal until 1935 their advertisement or promotion was outlawed). These were reforms which he believed would lead to greater happiness, unlike the prohibitions of the Catholic Church. In this light, for example, the final lines suggest that the 'theory' of marriage has to be an enactment of the 'practice' of love and sex (Cullingford 1993: 184–202). As Yeats had realised from Maud Gonne's failed marriage, to refuse divorce when love has broken down simply results in unhappiness. Similar conclusions drawn from experience, from action not abstraction, animate the rest of the volume which rests again in tensions: between sensuality and spirituality; the triumph of Irish liberation and the nadir of the destruction of ancestral houses; the weakness of age and the strength of wisdom; private desires and public duties.

Conclusion

In 1960, Yvor Winters caricatured the kind of Ireland that Yeats wanted:

> Such a society would be essentially agrarian, with as few politicians and tradesmen as possible. The dominant class would be the landed gentry; the peasants would also be important, but would stay in their place; a fair sprinkling of beggars (some of them mad), of drunkards, and of priests would make the countryside more picturesque.... What Yeats would have liked would have been an eighteenth-century Ireland of his own imagining...
>
> (Winters 1984: 124)

Though simplistic and distorted, Winters's view that Yeats was averse to the political turmoil of revolutionary Ireland is not entirely wide of the mark. Yeats wrote that his vision was of an 'aristocratic civilisation in its completed form, every detail of life hierarchical, great wealth everywhere in few men's hands' (Orwell 1943: 84). Politically, Yeats, with Eliot and Pound, was soon to find himself out of step with a new generation of poets who absorbed the style and aesthetics of the modernists but transmuted them under a social and psychological view of the world that was antithetical to their politics. The 1930s' poets would have agreed with the Irish struggle for independence from England, and yet they were generally silent on issues of Empire, turning instead to the European continent for their battlegrounds and ideologies. On the occasion of Yeats's death in 1939, W.H. Auden wrote a tribute, 'In Memory of W.B. Yeats', in which he famously speculated that 'Poetry makes nothing happen', being only 'A way of happening, a mouth'. The lines are often thought simply to express Auden's disillusionment at the end of the 1930s, but in the context of Yeats's work they suggest the parabolic movement from an attempt to forge a national consciousness through Celtic literature to a conviction that 'monuments of unageing intellect' are prized little alongside the achievements of the natural cycle, from the building of Thoor Ballylee to the Easter Rising: the realisation that historical events are propelled by the violent drives of hatred and desire, demon and beast.

Appendix: aspects to Yeats's symbolism

Swan   The form Zeus took when he raped Leda, conceiving Helen of Troy; also linked to the dove (holy spirit) that visited the Virgin Mary at the Annunciation (both signalling huge changes in the course of history – but opposite kinds). In 'Leda and the Swan' we can see the destruction of Troy (and death of Agamemnon, etc.) as revenge for Zeus's violent act against Leda. Her daughter has taken on some of the God's power, and it is a negative, destructive, violent, vengeful epoch.

White birds/swans   are generally images of the soul (e.g. see part III of 'Nineteen Hundred and Nineteen') and of poetic creation.

Rose   Beauty, spirit, love, Maud Gonne, or Ireland in 'To Ireland in the Coming Times'.

Stone   The fanatic heart that has lost its humanity but gained a power; the idea of Independence/Home Rule and the fight for it in 'Easter 1916'. The stone is a symbol of the constancy but hard-heartedness of those fighting a political cause.

Moon   The light of poetic imagination – opposed to the 'prosaic light of day' in 'The Tower'. Also linked with aloof beauty or with madness, though, if waxing/waning with ascent/decline.

Falcon   Violence and loss of control in 'The Second Coming'.

The Tower   particularly Yeats's Norman Tower, Thoor Ballylee at Coole Park in County Galway (1915 onwards). The tower is for Yeats (haunted by) history, itself a repository of 'the Great Memory' (a similar shared store of human symbols to Jung's collective unconscious).

Winding Stair (especially at The Tower)   Upward struggle for initiation and artistic development; also of the gyres of history.

Ancestral Houses   Symbolic of the Protestant Ascendancy in Ireland, which is ambivalent for Yeats as it brings to mind the violence of their making as well as the sense of continuity and the past's monuments.

Troy   The symbol of a great civilisation destroyed by barbarians.

Spiritus Mundi   (spirit of the world)   This is the great repository from which Yeats draws his images, especially in his mystical system worked out in A *Vision*.

The Rough Beast   In 'The Second Coming', this seems to be 1917 Russian Revolution bolshevism (Yeats thought this period in history equivalent to that which announced the 2,000-year upheavals that commenced with the Trojan wars and then with Christ's birth).

Mythologized figures   such as Helen (will to passion), Caesar (will to power/conquer) and Michaelangelo (will to create) are archetypes – expressing recurrent patterns in history and in human experience.

5

IN/BETWEEN THE WARS

Poetry in the 1930s

Think of what our Nation stands for,
  Books from Boots and country lanes,
Free speech, free passes, class distinction,
  Democracy and proper drains.
      (John Betjeman, 'In Westminster Abbey', 1940)

Introduction

As great a variety of poetry was produced in the 1930s as at any other time in the twentieth century, and yet the decade's heterogeneity has frequently been undervalued. Because the decade is often considered to belong to Auden and his circle, I want to begin by stressing the breadth of verse published in the 1930s. Yeats and Eliot composed some of their best poems and the second edition of the influential work of the Victorian-as-modernist Gerard Manley Hopkins appeared in 1930. Of the well-known war poets, Graves, Sassoon, Blunden, Jones, and Gurney were still writing, as were Kipling, Masefield, and Arthur Symons. Surrealist poetry, promoted by David Gascoyne in *A Short Survey of Surrealism* (1935) and practised by Gascoyne, Roger Roughton, Herbert Read, and Hugh Sykes Davies, was temporarily in vogue in the second half of the decade and influenced Dylan Thomas (see Connor 1995). New writers, such as Stevie Smith and John Betjeman, though outside the mainstream of the 'Auden generation', were writing original poetry that was both idiosyncratic and comic. The small but significant number of women poets published in the 1930s has until recently been ignored, though they range from exemplary figures such as Elizabeth Daryush and Anne Ridler to those better known as novelists such as Winifred Holtby and Sylvia Townsend Warner. This was also the decade in which the Irish successor – more than Louis MacNeice – to Yeats, Patrick Kavanagh, started to publish.

In his most famous piece, *The Great Hunger* (1942), he describes the impoverished life of Irish farmers in the 1930s by drawing on his own experience of working on the land from the age of 13. Lastly, the most successful Scottish poet since Burns, Hugh MacDiarmid, had been writing in Scots in the 1920s but ceased doing so in the mid-1930s (his 'A Drunk Man Looks at the Thistle' (1926), is one of the finest long poems of the century). A founder member of the National Party of Scotland (1928) and an outspoken Anglophobe, he had advocated Italian fascism in the 1920s only to become a fervent communist in the 1930s (Bell 1995). A modernist writer by style, MacDiarmid was one of the most polemical and forceful poetical voices on the political left in the 1930s. He considered himself a radical working-class socialist, alongside whom the likes of Auden and Spender were fellow-travellers.[1]

But it is these 'fellow-travellers' who have come to be most closely associated with the decade. They were brought to the fore by Michael Roberts's publication of *New Signatures* in 1932. With this collection, the expectation of a fresh *generation* of writers was introduced. The time was itself ripe for such a discovery, not least because the idea of succeeding generations was formed by the experience of World War I, since which the judgement that the old men had betrayed the young had been repeated in several memoirs. By June 1933, after the publication of Roberts's second anthology, called *New Country*, a critic in *The Listener* was already talking about a new school of poetry led by W.H. Auden (Poster 1993: 1). Another reason why the 1930s have become enshrined as a literary decade like no other this century is the publication of Auden's first collection, *Poems*, in 1930. Though some recent critics have sought to correct the imbalance created in previous surveys of the decade, the 1930s continue to be identified with Auden, and vice versa. In 1939, Auden left for America and on the outbreak of war wrote 'September 1, 1939' in which he famously summed up the previous ten years as 'a low dishonest decade'.

In numerous studies, the 1930s poets are sharply contrasted with those of the 1920s, but it is too simplistic to see the new generation, many of whom were clearly influenced by the imagists, Futurists, and surrealists, as uniformly anti-modernist. For example, a recent collection of essays sees them instead as forming a transitional phase between modernism and postmodernism (Williams and Matthews 1997). Yet it remains generally accepted that the most often cited poetry of the 1930s is different in several ways from that of the 1920s. The earlier decade's writing is seen as individualist, metropolitan, experimental, and dominated by metaphor, whereas the later decade's is collectivist, suburban, realist, metonymic, and self-mythologising. The motifs of 1930s poetry are the journey, the documentary, landscape, and images of war; it has keywords such as 'history', 'love', 'struggle', 'Europe', 'deluge', and even 'the', a word used repeatedly to evoke the collective through its invocation of the concrete (e.g. in Auden's 'Spain'). The decade foregrounded the approaches of travelogues, newsreels, diaries, and journalism. Also, with the growth in forms of transport and the first intimations of a media society, 'mass communication' arrived in Britain's cultural vocabulary. There is the emergence of domestic anthropology in the fashion for new 'documentary' techniques and the inception of the Mass Observation Movement, launched to study ordinary British life, by the critic Humphrey Jennings, the poet Charles Madge, and the sociologist Tom Harrisson.[2] Unprecedented interest in photography and cinema meant that terms such as lens, film, record, and focus were common metaphors in descriptions of the way people perceived the world. Writing of the 1930s also evinces a concern with testimony: words such as 'homage' and 'witness' recur frequently and the journal, account, and notebook are popular forms of recording experience. The survey approach of film, which can provide aerial shots, zooms, panning and cutting techniques is evident in poetry. Auden's 'Consider' is a famous example of the new perspective, citing the viewpoint of the hawk or 'the helmeted airman'. The shift to politics is also fundamental to most understandings of the decade. Auden wrote in 'The Poet and the City' that 'In our age, the mere making of a work of art is itself a political act.' For this reason, Stephen Spender calls the 1930s writers the 'Divided Generation', caught between their literary vocation and their need to oppose fascism. In his autobiography *World Within World*, he concludes that

> the qualities which distinguished us from the writers of the previous decade lay not in ourselves, but in the events to which we reacted. These were unemployment, economic crisis, nascent fascism, approaching war.... The older writers were reacting in the 'twenties to the exhaustion and hopelessness of a Europe in which the old regimes were falling to pieces. We were a 'new generation'.
>
> (Spender 1977: 139)

From Eliot's view that history is both 'now' and 'England' ('Little Gidding') to Auden's insistence on 'to-day the struggle' ('Spain'), the decade's poetry on the political right and left can be seen to be threaded with themes of conflict and history's importance not to the past but to the present. John Cornford, fighting in Spain, argued that 'Time present is a cataract': 'history forming in our hand's / Not plasticine but roaring sands' ('Full Moon at Tierz: Before the Storming of Huesca'). After the declaration of society's collapse in the 1920s, most forcibly expressed in the cultural dissonances of *The Waste Land*, came a series of affirmations and evocations directed at rebuilding unities and solidarities that were to be tested in new military conflicts, from the civil war in Spain to Mussolini's annexation of Abyssinia, and finally World War II itself.

The contested decade

Struggles other than military ones are located in the decade, and Auden at one point asks readers of *The Orators*, in 1930, what they think of England, a country in which everybody is unwell. The 1930s have been stereotyped as the depression years and as those which gave birth to the leisure society of the late twentieth century. Also, the literary complexion of the prewar years has been hotly debated. Adrian Caesar argues that several decades in this century have been mythologised, in the sense of the term used by Roland Barthes (Barthes 1972). That is to say, the association between the 1930s, as a decade of poetry, and four Oxford graduates, W.H. Auden, Stephen Spender, Cecil Day Lewis, and Louis MacNeice, has become axiomatic and naturalised. Such assumed connections are in need of de-mythologising but not ignoring. To begin with, it is helpful to note that this was a literary decade divided in its allegiances to the two strands of poetry we have considered so far. Caesar explains that

> Most poets of the 1930s sought, in their various ways, to build upon two distinct developments of nineteenth-century Romanticism: the modernism of Eliot, Pound, and Yeats with its reactionary political flavouring, and the more liberal, specifically English, Georgian tradition through poets like Wilfred Owen and Edward Thomas.
>
> (Caesar 1991: 1–5)

On the one hand, Thomas, and Owen in particular, were perceived as poets who had shown that in the chaos of the fast-paced, urban, alienating, strife-ridden twentieth century it was possible to write in a popular, accessible style and still produce genuinely affecting, accomplished, engaged and even politicised poetry. On the other hand, Auden, for one, felt that he moved from the sensibilities of Rupert

Brooke to those contained in *The Waste Land*. For many of the writers of the 1930s, Eliot's poem

> seemed to offer a vision of what civilisation had been brought to by the errors of former generations.... The idea that the subject matter of poetry could be ugly, or merely ordinary, was still a shocking and exciting one in 1930. Eliot's methods...set the poetic fashion for poetry that was compressed, strongly visual and, ultimately, obscure.
>
> (Tolley 1975: 36)

And as for Yeats, up to his death months before the war he consolidated his position as elder statesman and reactionary – while the 1930s poets admired his poetry, he disliked theirs greatly and wrote in 'A General Introduction for my Work' in 1937:

> The young English poets reject dream and personal emotion; they have thought out opinions that join them to this or that political party.... They are determined to express the factory, the metropolis, that they may be modern.... they express not what the Upanishads call 'that ancient self' but individual intellect.
>
> (Yeats 1964: 269)

For Yeats, these poets turned to intellect not emotion, and were attempting to lead, not draw their inspiration from, their culture.

In terms of social history, the decade is divided between accounts of its progress and its crises. However, the two need to be considered together in order to begin to encompass the heterogeneity of contemporary events. From one perspective, the interwar years can be characterised by the rise of entertainment: the dance palace, the cinema, spectator sport, the loudspeaker radio, rambling, annual holidays, dog racing, and so on – the unexceptional but important pleasures Louis MacNeice describes as 'the solace / Of films or football pools' (*Autumn Journal* III). Expansion also took place in the construction industry and there were massive housing programmes, bringing a wave of Tudor-style buildings, a vogue for art deco, and a proliferation in design styles. Technological advances were also now being mass marketed for domestic use, as gramophones, irons, vacuum cleaners, lights, and mains radios became common. After the forming of Ramsay MacDonald's National Government in 1931, state intervention spread to almost every social sphere and right across trade and industry (e.g.

tariffs and subsidies multiplied, and coal, air travel, and London's transport were nationalised). With over two million cars in Britain by 1939 the expansion of the road network created new patterns of work and leisure; the Electricity Board's grid network was established; and there was a massive extension of suburbs, the significance of which was battled over by such writers as Spender, Betjeman, and Smith (Dentith 1997).

Three important areas of change in leisure patterns were film, radio, and reading. The 1930s was the 'golden era' of the cinema, which became the great social meeting place in the latter half of the decade as up to twenty million tickets were sold each week. Hollywood dominated the screens in Britain but not the rest of Europe. French and German cinema prospered because the competition was always subtitled, but in Britain Hollywood's stars both monopolised the screen and set the fashions in clothes, hairstyles, and babies' names. Films were also popular with writers because they suggested different narrative techniques. In the face of such new media, the nature of art itself had seemed to change. A very useful essay with respect to cinema in the 1930s is Walter Benjamin's 'The Work of Art in the Age of Mechanical Reproduction' written in 1936, which analyses aesthetic works in terms of alienation and commodities (Benjamin 1973). Benjamin argues that in a world of printing, duplication, and photography, artistic works have lost the 'aura' that their uniqueness once gave them. The new technologies of artistic reproduction have dispensed with the idea of a work's authenticity – the idea of an authentic photographic or film print makes no sense. Benjamin thought this moved art's function from the realm of ritual into that of politics, with dire consequences for the 1930s (fascism renders politics aesthetic, he felt, whereas communism politicises art). The political significance of film was a matter on which the left was divided. The cinema was seen by many as enormously important because it could reach a huge audience and set its agenda. As an observational form, film seemed like the art of the left because it was a mass medium: it was communal, had popular appeal to a mass market, and could be a great educative force. Also, it was not surrounded by a rarefied aesthetic discourse and was not inherently bourgeois – anyone could take a picture. Importantly, film dealt with groups and not individuals, and was externally oriented, unlike the introverted prose of writers. Auden declared it the 'democratic art' because it required no technical skill. Alternatively, he condemned the movies themselves as little more than a capitalist sweetener for the poor and MacNeice wrote that 'the cinema gives the poor their Jacob's ladder / For Cinderellas to climb'

(*Autumn Journal* XVII). While many writers thought of educational and documentary film after sound was introduced in 1929, the 1930s were first and foremost the decade of stars such as Shirley Temple, Fred Astaire, and Ginger Rogers, characters such as Tarzan and Frankenstein, and big-budget films such as *Gone with the Wind*. There was social comment in some Hollywood films, for example Chaplin's *Modern Times* and Ford's *The Grapes of Wrath*. But, for the most part, the picture-palace was considered a distraction from daily life, at least for the 25 per cent of the population who were going twice a week. As Day Lewis's poem 'Newsreel' has it: 'Enter the dream-house, brothers and sisters, leaving / Your debts asleep, your history at the door.'

Radio, though another mass medium, was not properly exploited by writers as it was not by anyone else until the late 1930s. Millions of sets were sold but the programmes were conventional, establishment oriented, and middle class in focus. There were national and regional BBC stations, but they mainly offered light music. Although often considered also to have had its 'golden age' in the 1930s, before television, radio was politically and religiously orthodox: the BBC, under John Reith, saw one of its chief functions to be the maintenance of cultural stability and social reassurance in an age of political change (Giddings 1997).

Perhaps most important for the 1930s' poets, however, was the enormous increase in the level of literacy and the profitable markets which arose to cater for the new 'reading-public'. With the introduction over the previous decades of mass education, reading habits were changing rapidly. By 1939, 67 per cent of adults bought a daily paper. The *Daily Mail* and the *Daily Express* were the big sellers, running into several million copies per day, while the *News of the World* sold four million copies every Sunday. Most writers were scornful of the papers' reactionary stances which reinforced the status quo; for example, in *The Orators*, Auden simultaneously insults press barons Lord Beaverbrook and Lord Rothermere as 'Beethameer, Bully of Britain'. The *Express*, which proclaimed in 1939 that there would be no war, was famed for taking nothing seriously. Day Lewis makes these papers, and Beaverbrook in particular, the subject of his excoriating attack in *The Magnetic Mountain* 20: 'Scavenger barons and your jackal vassals, / Your pimping press-gang, your unclean vessels.' The other new aspect to come under scathing criticism, particularly from Orwell, were newspaper adverts and advertising hoardings. Cult favourites of the 1930s were: 'Keep that schoolgirl complexion with Palmolive' and 'Bovril beats that sinking feeling'. Shredded Wheat was sold under the slogan: 'Britons make it – it makes Britons'.

In general, the *New Statesman* and *Left Review* were the prescribed reading for the left and the *Spectator* for the right. In terms of radical papers, the *Daily Worker* (which later became *The Morning Star*) was financed by the Communist Party and sold about 100,000 copies from its foundation in 1930. There was also a moderately successful feminist-slanted weekly called *Time and Tide*, poems from which are included in Jane Dowson's anthology, *Women's Poetry of the 1930s* (1996). The more conservative women's magazines, focused on home and family, continued to be popular. New publications like *Womans Own* were extremely successful in the 1930s, and, for many families these magazines provided their only advice on diet, clothing, and childcare. 'Romance' magazines also sold well, with titles such as *True Romances*, founded in 1934. Middle-class children were encouraged to read the books their parents had grown up with: Beatrix Potter's tales, *The Wind in the Willows*, and *Peter Pan*; children probably more willingly read *The Hotspur* and *The Wizard* which were started in the 1930s, as was *Just William*. Most importantly, the paperback was invented. The first Penguin book came out in 1935 at a price of 6 pence when most hardbacks cost around 10 shillings, which is why the majority of books in the early 1930s were borrowed rather than bought. Paperbacks dealing with contemporary events were published for the first time too, and were often sold-out immediately. The first ever book clubs were founded in the mid-1930s. In particular, there was the Left Book Club, which published Orwell's *The Road to Wigan Pier* and was created to provide socialist-inclined literature to a mass market. Lastly, the Cambridge literary critics came to further prominence, especially after F.R. Leavis set up the journal, *Scrutiny*, and in 1932 Q.D. Leavis published *Fiction and the Reading-Public*, a virulent attack on middlebrow novels and criticism. An analysis of reading trends since the seventeenth century, Leavis's book charts the growing divergence between those seriously interested in 'the novel' and those who consume romances, detective novels, and sensationalist fiction.

Despite these significant increases in leisure pursuits and in entertainment, it is even more difficult to avoid the counter-image of the decade as the 'grim 'Thirties' as David Gascoyne could call it already in 1940 ('Farewell Chorus'). From another perspective, all of this activity, from rambling to reading, was simply seen as an escape from the realities of daily life: 'Cyclists and hikers in company, day excursionists, / Refugees from cursed towns and devastated areas,' wrote Day Lewis (*The Magnetic Mountain* 32). Jem Poster considers the poetry to be 'fundamentally reflective of a generation's sense of actual loss and imminent disaster' and it is certainly true that the 1930s literary mythology has become inseparable from the decade's social and economic mythology (Poster 1993: 52). There was the Wall Street Crash and the Great Slump of 1929; the conciliatory policies of successive National Governments right up to the war; the Means Test in 1934; the Jarrow Hunger Marches of 1933 and 1934 (when unemployment in the town was nearly 70 per cent, although across the decade there was never a national unemployment figure above 25 per cent); and the military and political events leading towards World War II. Far more than the 1920s, this decade was dominated by international events: Hitler's appointment as German Chancellor in 1933; German and Italian expansion; the Spanish civil war (which recruited 4,000 British volunteers); imperial unrest in India and elsewhere; the Sino-Japanese fighting; and the international rise of the far right (including the founding of the British Union of Fascists under Oswald Mosley). The differences between standards of living in the north and south were considerable, as were those between classes and between the waged and the unemployed ('Thy mother is crying, / Thy dad's on the dole', wrote Day Lewis in his 'Carol', published in 1935). Despite the massive boom in house building in the south-east, in the north instances of three families living in one house or families of five living in a room were not rare: 'Mrs Carmichael had her fifth, looked at the job with repulsion, / Said to the midwife, "Take it away; I'm through with over-production"' (MacNeice, 'Bagpipe Music').

Despite state expansion in education, only 20 per cent of the population stayed on at school when they could leave and only 6 per cent went on to university. Distinctions at school between children of different social classes were not only academic: for example, public school children were on average six inches taller than their council educated peers at 14, the official leaving age. The most famous 1930s poem on education is Stephen Spender's 'An Elementary School Class Room in a Slum'. Spender protests against the conditions he finds but offers no solution except to throw open the windows and take the children to the countryside – to make a connection between culture and nature: 'the white and green leaves open / The history theirs whose language is the sun.' In its idealism and abstract solutions, the poem exemplifies the good but somewhat rarefied intentions of the bourgeois writers, and the language differs greatly from the unsentimental lines of Hugh MacDiarmid: 'all these lives, these lovers, / Lapse into cannon-fodder, sub-humanity, the despised slum-crowd' ('In the Slums of Glasgow').

Spender's more striking and successful poems praise the rise and rhythm of industry, mass transport and mass communication, in 'The

Pylons', 'The Express', and 'The Landscape Near an Aerodrome'. The first resulted in the title 'pylon poets' being applied to those who wrote about machinery or, influenced by Futurism, used the rhythms of the new industries to structure their verse and reflect their politics: 'After the first powerful plain manifesto / The black statement of pistons' (Spender, 'The Express'). However, by the end of the 1930s, Spender was already renouncing his earlier creed as mechanised power was now almost synonymous with weaponry.

The rise of machinery accompanied the long process of rearmament in the interwar years and war is a key subject of 1930s poetry at the start of the decade as much as at the end. Spender's planes, for example, are considered with awe for their capability as much as their beauty, when their mass production prefigures so many deaths: in the future 'Poor panic-stricken hordes will hear that hum, / And Fear will be synonymous with Flight' ('Thoughts in 1932'). John Lehmann's 'This Excellent Machine', written in the same year, also considers the ease with which modern machinery will be able to kill at the press of a button: 'We stand and stare, expecting to be minced – / And very few are asking *Why not scrap it?*'. The prospect of World War II is ever present and the debates over rearmament, disarmament, pacifism, and the peace movement never really abated between 1919 and 1939. The international conflict which crystallised these feelings was the Spanish civil war, in which several poets died (Bell, Caudwell, Cornford) and to which almost every poet felt obliged to travel. In his 1937 'Sonnet' Rex Warner described his options as either war preparation or living 'as some kind of fungus'. Auden, who went to Spain to become an ambulance driver but never in fact did, only composed one poem about the war, the notorious 'Spain', with its 'conscious acceptance of guilt in the necessary murder' and its 'poets exploding like bombs'. The war, which actually began in Morocco in July 1936, seemed to bring to a head the conflicts of the decade: Franco's fascism against the International Brigade's communism, a democratically elected Popular Front government against a militia funded by Hitler and Mussolini, the armed resistance of peasants and anarchists fighting against professional soldiers. In his poem, Auden unravels a progression (Spender says it is a Marxist dialectic) in which economic decisions and scientific development structure history, from all our Yesterdays through To-day's struggle to To-morrow's return to ordinary domesticity, while 'History to the defeated / May say alas but cannot help or pardon.' The moment of the present becomes freighted with the enormity of freedom and immediacy: 'I am your choice, your decision. Yes, I am Spain.' Spain certainly was a turning point for Auden, who returned disillusioned with communism and unsure of his political role (Mendelson 1981: 304–32).

Similarly, looking back in *World Within World*, Spender decides

> The 1930's which seemed so revolutionary, were in reality the end of a Liberal phase of History. They offered Liberal individualists their last chance to attach Liberal democracy to a people's cause: specifically to the cause of Spanish democracy. The total armament of the civilised world drowned all individual efforts in a rising flood of mechanised power.

He thought people had become 'half-slaves of these machines' which he had himself so celebrated in the early 1930s (Spender 1977: 286–90). For Spender, there was now an end to the belief that the individual could change society or shape history, rather than merely protest against events in a 'public fate'.

Many women poets, few of whom appear much influenced by Auden, were also involved in the war. For example, Nancy Cunard was an indefatigable campaigner for the republican cause. Her poem 'To Eat To-day' works by comparing a German bomber-pilot with the Spanish people on the ground below (in terms of what they see, what they eat, what they think): the one concerned with conditions of life, the other with causing death. Cunard, an important petitioner, editor, and publisher (she published the first pamphlets of Auden's 'Spain') had also solicited and compiled the *Left Review* document, 'Authors Take Sides on the Spanish War'. Sylvia Townsend Warner and Valentine Ackland travelled as Red Cross aid workers to Spain. Warner's poems differ from the detached judgement of Auden's 'Spain' by foregrounding the involvement of the narrator: 'I am the stink in the nostrils / of the men of Spain' ('Port Bou') and 'We saw him rise up singing / Where the freshet leaps and fails' ('*El Heroe*').

Nearly all those who travelled to Spain fought or worked on the side of the republicans. Among the young poets, left-wing politics was the orthodoxy (Roy Campbell and Laura Riding would be notable exceptions) and the common cry was that found in Rex Warner's 'Hymn' of 1933: 'All power / to lovers of life, to workers, to the hammer, the sickle, the blood.' Edward Upward asserted that 'no book written at the present time can be "good" unless it is written from a Marxist or near-Marxist viewpoint'. One of the reasons why several prominent 1930s writers turned to the left was their early experience of Germany and the rise of fascism: Auden, Isherwood, Spender, and Upward were all in Germany around 1930 (primarily in search of sex and experience). Nearly all the prominent 1930s poets went to Oxford or Cambridge, and had previously been to public school. The poets for the most part were middle-class, highly educated, male southerners. Generally, they gave the impression of writing for the same kind of people; Orwell writes 'when you go to the industrial north, you are conscious...of entering another country'. This was true in at least the sense that Liverpool, for example, had twice as many people living below subsidence level in 1930 as London. Orwell's view was that writers had gone over to the left in order to have something to believe in; the feeling was so pervasive that it was considered eccentric in literary circles not to be more or less left wing. Julian Bell wrote in the *New Statesman* in 1933, 'Communism in England is at present largely a literary phenomenon – an attempt of a second post-war generation to escape from the Waste Land' (Caesar 1991: 24). However, Orwell's other valid criticism was that most writers were toying with communist politics without having the vaguest idea of what it was like to be poor or to be subject to a communist government. At the margins of left-wing thinkers, he observes that it is easy to play at being 'political' in a liberal society, and to an extent the red flag *was* intertwined with the old school tie. In terms of a shift from the 1920s, it seemed to many that modernist angst was now simply being channelled into a cause. Frank Kermode's conclusion is representative when he says that the proletarian body was 'fantasized by the bourgeois Communist sympathizer, transferring his sense of what it meant to be outcast, alienated, *maudit*, to the worker' (Kermode 1988: 47); Spender writes in his autobiography that his lover was 'almost another sex': 'I was in love, as it were, with his background, his soldiering, his working-class home' (Spender 1977 [1951]: 184). Yet, to balance the view that intellectuals in the 1930s suffered from political bad faith, we would have to say that to many people it genuinely seemed as though the capitalist system was coming to an end – the Wall Street Crash, followed by economic depression and mass British unemployment at 3 million, made it appear that each person *had* now to choose between fascism and communism. The dilemma was summed up in Orwell's essay title, 'My country, right or left?'.

Writers of the 1930s, especially Auden, were also very aware of the legacy of Freud, whose theories of the personal psyche were as important as Marx's theories of the social struggle. In poetry, self-analysis was both a common strategy and a common subject: MacNeice, for example, writes of his deepest desires for sex and murder, 'Which fantasies no doubt are due to my private history, / Matter for the analyst' (*Autumn Journal* III). It is therefore equally wrong to turn aside completely from biography and personal circumstances to the forces of history as it is to ignore a wider society when analysing texts – it was in the 1930s that writers made it their creed that poetry is produced at the intersection of the personal and the political. It is also at this point that the canonical view of 'thirties poetry' often inserts itself to reduce our understanding of the decade's diversity.

Poets of serious purpose

The term 'thirties writing' connotes a style as well as a period; not all literary texts written in the 1930s are talked about as 'thirties' literature, just as not all works written around 1800 are thought of as examples of Romanticism. In other words, a pattern has been mapped on to the decade's literature, just as it has on to its history. Robin Skelton's 1930s anthology demonstrates this well. His chosen poets are all male except for Anne Ridler and were all born between 1902 and 1916. The collection begins with four poems, one by each of Auden, Spender, MacNeice, and Day Lewis: the 'MacSpaunday' poets whose style and views have come to epitomise 1930s poetry.[3] Orwell sums up the change in literature in his essay 'Inside the Whale':

> quite suddenly, in the years 1930–35, something happens, the literary climate changes. A new group of writers, Auden and Spender and the rest of them, has made its appearance, and although technically these writers owe something to their predecessors, their 'tendency' is entirely different. Suddenly we have got out of the twilight of the gods into a sort of boy scout atmosphere of bare knees and community singing. The typical literary man ceases to be a cultured expatriate with a leaning towards the church and becomes instead an eager-minded schoolboy with a leaning towards communism. If the keynote of the writers of the twenties is 'tragic sense of life', the keynote of the new writers is 'serious purpose'.
>
> (Orwell 1962: 30)

Orwell's evocation of a boy scout or walking tour atmosphere is not unique and, discussing the Auden group, even Skelton acknowledges that there is an 'adolescent' quality to their writings. The communal atmosphere of various kinds of club and the general emphasis on group activity were increasingly common: though the scouts and guides had been around for two decades, the Youth Hostel Association was founded in 1930, and hiking in numbers became a cult in the decade.

114

Nearly all reviews of the 1930s emphasise the importance of W.H. Auden. One argument for this singling out centres on Auden's poetic ability; another considers him primarily as a social poet. Arnold Kettle argues that

> What Auden did supremely well in his early poetry was to explore and speculate on the condition of Britain in the period between the wars.... His almost constant use of a 'persona' is a device which allows him to dramatize situations without depersonalizing them or adopting the rather heavy, hectoring tone which poetry concerned with public issues can easily fall into.
>
> (Kettle 1979: 94)

Some of the ways in which Auden might be said to do this are: his concern with psychological theories of repression from Freud ('Miss Gee') to Homer Lane ('Sir, no man's enemy'); his direct questioning of political labelling and convictions ('A Communist to Others'); his interest in heroism and leadership ('Easily, my dear, you move');[4] his observant, often satirical analyses of social life ('The Unknown Citizen'); his belief in the transformative and regenerative power of love ('May with its Light Behaving'); his ability to turn sentiments and ideas into characters and narratives ('Song for the New Year'); his use of plain, rhythmic poetry to accompany film ('Night Mail'); his anatomies of contemporary Britain ('Letter to Lord Byron'); and his ability to create or summarise the mood of an event ('Spain') or time ('September 1, 1939'). Alongside his internationalism and his Englishness, his easy use of light verse and complex syntax, it is above all the way that, in terms of sentiment and reference, Auden blends the personal with the public, and the everyday with the esoteric, that makes him seem both indebted to Eliot and markedly different from him; such that in his autobiographical 'Letter to Lord Byron' Auden can mention Disney, the Great North Road, Baden-Powell, Sunlight Soap, Kodak cameras, and even quantum theory, without making the reader feel that the images jar or are being used to suggest the degeneration of culture.

The 'Auden generation' grew up in the heyday of Georgian poetry to see it overthrown by the revolution of modernism: in Gavin Ewart's lines from 'Audenesque for an Initiation', 'We've given up the Georgian poets, teaching dance bands how to croon'; or, as Auden himself phrased it in his autobiographical verses, 'For gasworks and dried tubers I forsook / The clock at Grantchester, the English rook'

('Letter to Lord Byron'). Yet, the inward-looking focus of modernism was unsatisfactory. Many young writers had hopes of creating a new non-bourgeois aesthetic. T.S. Eliot had famously said that great poetry must be difficult. Most 1930s writers responded that for a poem to be affecting and effective it must first be comprehensible. Additionally, they believed that one's private life was also political and that intellectuals had a responsibility towards society more than themselves. Too often writers had considered their own class and not the poor or disenfranchised: 'How many times smelling the smell of poverty / Have you tried and turned for good to your cornfield and garden' (Bernard Spencer, 'Evasions').

The dominant tendency towards documentary and reportage created a paradox that writers were aware of: they made formal use of detachment and objectivity, but they also had definite views. Louis MacNeice put it like this: writers 'have desires and hatreds of their own and further, they think some things ought to be desired and others hated'. Therefore, authors had to write as individuals but they were committed to international causes and often wished to write representatively. Their views were socio-historical ones, not personal ones, as the modernists would have known them. MacNeice's great work of the 1930s is *Autumn Journal*, a long meditation on social life written in the last months of 1938, in the shadow of the war. By interlocking his own life with that of Europe he creates a pervasive sense of loss and disappointment combined with expectation and commitment. The tone is melancholy and regretful, but there is a quiet determination before the inevitable war, to which the previous years seem inexorably to have led. All local happenings, such as the cutting down of trees and the loss of a neighbour's dog, have wide symbolic resonances, while European events, such as the Munich conference and the Spanish war, have a deep personal significance for the 'I', 'we', and 'you' who populate the poem.[5] MacNeice was brought up in Northern Ireland but lived most of his life in England. After attending Marlborough and Oxford, he taught Classics for six years at Birmingham University ('And to hear the prison-like lecture room resound / To Homer in a Dudley accent', *Autumn Journal* VIII), but greatly preferred the surrounding countryside to the city itself. The poem 'Birmingham' uses a seemingly chaotic and jumbled form to imitate the clutter of metropolitan living. Indebted to Eliot's London, 'Birmingham' presents a picture of trains, cars, shops, and 'trams like vast sarcophagi'. The poem seems to argue that ideals (Platonic forms) are incompatible with the 'jerry-built beauty and sweated labour' of the mundane urban sprawl. Here and elsewhere MacNeice's diction and use of dialogue are

116

representative of the decade's shifts. Like Auden, he uses ordinary and colloquial speech in an unpretentious way which, as in 'Bagpipe Music', turns around Eliot's slightly contemptuous use of the vernacular. His poems are also explicitly dialogic, from the formal argument over the merits of country and city, tradition and progress in 'An Eclogue for Christmas' to the meditative debate on 'logic and lust' in 'London Rain'.

While MacNeice is perhaps the most observant poetic reporter of 1930s social scenes, the vogue for instructive political art crossed with documentary forms is best illustrated not by MacNeice but by Auden. In 'Psychology and Art Today' (1935), Auden made the distinction between escape-art and parable-art. He argued that pre-1930s writers had been too introverted and highbrow, indulging in escapism. Parable-art was more accessible, illustrative, and committed. He said it was not didactic, like propaganda, but revealing: it rejected current society only to project a better one. Auden's essay thus echoed with the common critical vocabulary of the time in which the words 'parable', 'fable', and 'allegory' were common. His ballad of failed quests and of human limitations, 'The Witnesses', is a good example of the kind of parable-art he recommended, warning against the hero-worship and unrealistic expectations of an idealised communism. In conjunction with this allegorical approach, Auden in his poetry created a distinctive rugged landscape of moors, hills, and mountains, and this approach was much imitated, for example in Day Lewis's *The Magnetic Mountain* (1933). However, Samuel Hynes considers Day Lewis's magnum opus an example of propagandist escape-art because of its inability to imagine the revolution that the poem's ascent towards communism requires (Hynes 1976: 117–30). The poem pictures cutting out the cancer of corruption and greed in capitalist society, but in language which typifies the excess of 1930s rhetoric: 'It is now or never, the hour of the knife, / The break with the past, the major operation' (*The Magnetic Mountain* 25).

Auden's parable-art landscapes are usually in northern settings, for their symbolic significance in contrast to those of the south and for their associations with Scandinavian mythology.[6] The settings are also allegorical, from the very opening of his *Poems* (1930) in the poetic drama *Paid on Both Sides*. The result is to politicise landscape and thus to strip it of a meaning outside of the social. In Tom Paulin's reading of Auden and MacNeice's *Letters from Iceland* the two poets achieved a radical break from tradition such that it would afterwards be impossible to write (or read) nature poetry innocently of allegorical import: 'Without human or political content nature means very little, and to

describe it in isolation from that content is to abdicate the responsibility to be relevant which Auden and MacNeice impose on
themselves and us' (Paulin 1976: 78). After 1930, the north itself
became a privileged area over the south for intellectuals, though many
of them only visited, toured, or journeyed above the Midlands (as
though the north bore the same relation to them as somewhere like
Iceland). Despite MacNeice's assertion of the 'powerful ethics of Going
North' ('Letter to Graham and Anne Shepherd'), hardly any prominent writers actually lived there.

A related mapping of women's bodies has been outlined by Janet
Montefiore, who sees the male poets identifying body with landscape,
as in the image of the fertile field in *The Magnetic Mountain* or
Spender's 'feminine land indulging easy limbs' in 'The Landscape Near
an Aerodrome' (Montefiore 1996: 104–12). In the mythological world
of the Auden generation, women also achieved a comparable level of
symbolic significance to the working class, but instead of representing
the future and the cause, they continued to personify possession and
dispossession, suppression and repression in the usual fixed stereotypes
of virgin territory, Lady Bountiful, betraying body, and passive nature.
But there were other poets – women – who wrote differently of female
experience and history. For instance, Anne Ridler discusses menstruation in 'The Crab Is In', while Ruth Pitter expatiates on motherhood
in 'Maternal Love Triumphant' and spinsterhood in 'Old, Childless,
Husbandless'. To take a particular example, Elizabeth Daryush's poems
demonstrate an awareness of exclusion and loneliness beside privilege
and (self-)deception. 'It is pleasant to hang out' berates false offers of
comfort while 'Off Duty' describes the difficulty for the true carer to
leave off caring. 'Children of wealth' and 'Still-life' both record the
way in which money is cocooned from poverty, in terms of emotion as
much as possessions, as does 'You should at times go out': 'visit the
slums of doubt / and feel what the lost feel'. Overall the poems suggest
a world of privilege which is itself 'unloved, alone, afraid', and Daryush
emerges as a poet of considerable abilities as well as social relevance,
despite her absence from the well-known anthologies.

In *Feminism and Poetry*, Montefiore offers a cautionary tale in which
she chronicles the almost complete lack of discussion of women poets
in literary analyses of the 1930s (Montefiore 1994: 20–5). Adrian
Caesar, for example, explains that he deals with few women poets in
his study because they were infrequently published or discussed at the
time, and the literary world of the 1930s was male-dominated (Caesar
1991: 8). This is true, but as an argument for discussing few women
writers, it seems only to compound the exclusion. The recent publica-

tion of Jane Dowson's volume, *Women's Poetry of the 1930s* (1996), means that a selection of women's poetry is now widely available and Montefiore has contributed a discussion of women poets in her *Men and Women Writers of the 1930s* (1996). While their range of subjects is in fact greater, it is immediately noticeable that the poems in Dowson's anthology share the same characteristic themes of the decade as men's poetry. For example, the emphasis on leftist politics is obvious from the titles of Valentine Ackland's 'Communist Poem 1935' and Naomi Mitchison's 'To Some Young Communists from an Older Socialist' (Ackland and her lover Sylvia Townsend both worked extensively in conjunction with the British Communist Party). The preoccupation with war is there in Naomi Mitchison's 'Thinking of War', and the preoccupation with technology can be found in Daryush's 'Invalid Dawn' or Holtby's 'The Man Who Hated the Spring'. The decade was also analysed and appraised at its end: in 'September 1939' Vita Sackville-West compares the hopes of the decade with the failure represented by the war: 'Nothing remains but active faith / And courage of a high despair.'

Kathleen Raine, who is discussed in some critical works, and Anne Ridler, included in Skelton's anthology, are the two exceptions to the general exclusion of women poets from reviews of the 1930s. Another writer who should appear in far more volumes and studies is Laura Riding, who continued the experiments of modernism and was very much apart from the dominant literary circles of the 1930s, although she saw herself in terms of the poetic tradition (Montefiore 1991). An opposer of anthologies, much feminism, and women-only collections in particular, Riding has been underdiscussed in literary reviews although many have seen her as an important influence on Auden. An innovative and obscure writer, her themes of subjectivity and language make her now a more theoretically productive writer than most of the heavily anthologised 1930s poets, even if she is less engaged with political and historical issues.

Conclusion: the 1940s

I have been dealing in this chapter with two overlapping bodies of work: poetry produced in the fourth decade of the century and 'thirties poetry'. For Jane Dowson, the first group can be characterised by a need to (re-)evaluate the significance of the present within history: 'What most unites all the poets, regardless of age or gender, is a preoccupation with finding a language with which to marry the sense of the moment with the sense of tradition' (Dowson 1996: 13). To a degree, the second group is one result of the dynamics of literary history, of the drive to identify a successor, whether an individual or a movement, to the modernist poetry of the previous decade. The idea of 'thirties poetry' is also partly sustained by its putative demise: at the end of the decade there was the disruption caused by the war, the departure of Auden from Europe, and the cessation of the major periodicals, *New Verse*, *Twentieth-Century Verse*, *Criterion*, and even *New Writing* (temporarily). On the one hand, Auden by the end of the 1930s, writing from America, seemed now to believe poetry to be separate from social influence: 'For poetry makes nothing happen' and 'Art is not life and cannot be / A midwife of society'. On the other hand, the new world war changed sensibilites and complacencies just as the earlier one had. To counter the picture of fragmentation offered in *The Waste Land*, T.S. Eliot wrote *Four Quartets*, published together in Britain in 1944, to present a vision of a nation's cultural and agricultural continuity at threat, such that 'the whole poem holds up the idea of an England worth defending' (Corcoran 1993: 4).

The poetry of World War II has not had the same press as that of World War I, even though fine work was produced by Keith Douglas, Roy Fuller, and Alun Lewis among others. Henry Reed's three-part 'The Lessons of War' is a famous and excellent illustration of the differences between World War I and World War II verse. It is not a bitter satire or protest poem, but a short parody – its first part, 'Naming of Parts', compares military drill with the rhythms of nature, while the second considers the restricted logic and language of army training. Exemplifying the shift away from committed political poetry, the poem also begins with a stanza parodying Auden's 'Spain', pointing out the boredom of military life, rather than its historical import: 'Today we have naming of parts. Yesterday, / We had daily cleaning. And tomorrow morning, / We shall have what to do after firing. But today, / Today we have naming of parts.' For poetry, the war and its aftermath has often been seen as a hiatus between the established corpus of 'thirties' writing and the emergence of the Movement poets in the 1950s. The canonisation of Auden has been said by Adrian Caesar to have been because of his appeal to a 'liberal middle-class conscience' which has constructed the decade's value and significance. Many of the most well-known writers of the 1940s, several of whom began publishing in the 1930s, were socially and politically different from the previous 'generation': two of the leading poets, Dylan Thomas and George Barker, were from lower middle-class backgrounds and entered neither public school or Oxbridge (Barker went to a London polytechnic while Thomas did not go on to higher education at all). In the work of *The New Apocalypse* writers (including Henry Treece, J.F. Hendry, Dorian

Cooke, and Norman MacCaig) Romantic poetry had a resurgence, as did the visionary poetry of Yeats and the experimental poetry of the surrealists. The Apocalypse poets rejected social realism and believed that society should adapt to the individual, who was determined by myth (which amounted to the individual's 'aspirations and inspirations'). There is not space to dwell on their poetry here except to say that it aimed to be organic rather than mechanistic, personal rather than public, abstract rather than social; and it came to seem anxiously obscure. Rejecting the communal social perspective of the 1930s, Hendry declared in modernist style in his 1943 essay 'The Art of History' that 'There *is* no history – except the history of self-realisation' (Tolley 1985: 104). This contrasts sharply with Auden's personification of a portentous communal history 'that never sleeps or dies, / And, held one moment, burns the hand' ('To a Writer on His Birthday'). The new London poets, such as David Wright, Michael Hamburger, and John Heath-Stubbs, had not grown up haunted by World War I, and led a bohemian lifestyle more concerned with pleasure than politics. Others, such as Vernon Watkins and Kathleen Raine, concentrated on metaphysics, like the older Edwin Muir, and gained inspiration from mystical writers such as Swedenborg and Yeats. But it was the intervention of the war in literary history which put a stamp on 'thirties poetry', leaving it monolithically isolated and simplistically defined. The poetry of the decade had been engaged and committed, aware and prophetic, in complete contrast to the complacent conservative verse which preceded World War I. It was also a decade in which the British had forgotten their Empire: the poetry of the 1930s makes almost no mention of Africa, India, or the colonies. On the left, this was partly because the Empire was an embarrassing hangover from an inglorious national past and partly because Europe had become obsessed with its own wars and divisions. On the right, it was partly because there were few poets writing and partly because, with increased travel and with concerted opposition such as Gandhi's, the Empire had ceased to have the aura of or to play the role in 'Englishness' that it once had. With the advent of World War II, however, and the need for a new assertion of national and international loyalties, the Empire's continued significance was again apparent and the subject for Churchillian sentiment, as in the poem with which this chapter began, John Betjeman's sardonic 'In Westminster Abbey':

Keep our Empire undismembered
   Guide our Forces by Thy Hand,
Gallant blacks from far Jamaica,

Honduras and Togoland;
Protect them Lord in all their fights,
And, even more, protect the Whites.

The war was the culmination of the divisions and conflicts of the 1930s but it was a watershed for poetry. While art responded to the war with such a shocking evocation of suffering and pain as Francis Bacon's 'Three Studies for Figures at the Base of a Crucifixion' (1945), poetry lacked anything so immediately forceful. Literature seemed to respond instead with the muted irony and sadness of Evelyn Waugh's *Sword of Honour* trilogy and the hieratic symbolism of the Apocalypse poets. Also, when the 1940s was over, the poetry that came to the fore rejected the modernism of the 1920s and the commitment of the 1930s. The Movement writers of the 1950s, whom I shall consider in the next chapter, reminded contemporaries of Edward Thomas and of the war poets, but it is perhaps not an abstract 'literary history' that pushed Larkin and his contemporaries to centre stage so much as social commentators who sought a quiet, non-metropolitan, ironic and commonsensical poetry after the perceived social and poetical excesses of the previous forty years.

6

'PHILOSOPHICAL SUNDIALS OF HISTORY'

Poetry after the war

Now answer History with a marvellous golden yes
As she steps up asking all possible questions
(George Barker, 'Elegy I', 1943)

In this old country, we are falling asleep, under clouds
That are like wide-brimmed hats. This is just right.
(Douglas Dunn, 'A Poem in Praise of the British', 1969)

Introduction

This chapter spans the range of responses to history and society delimited by Barker and Dunn above, from enthusiastic engagement to
ironic comment on national decline. My intention is to place postwar
poetry and history alongside each other in an attempt to suggest how
one is a measure of the other. Adorno writes that in poetry

> various levels of society's inner contradictory relationships
> manifest themselves in the poet's speaking. I should repeat
> that neither the private person of the poet, his psychology,
> nor his so-called social viewpoint are to come into question
> here; what matters is the poem itself as a philosophical sundial
> of history.
>
> (Adorno 1989: 164)

The poem is a guide to history but society also throws its shadow on
poetry – this is what I intend to show in this chapter and a range of
poets will be cited; however, to give some focus to the discussion,
Philip Larkin, the voice of postwar England for many critics, will be
referred to often.

Like those in the 1930s, postwar poets continued to offer varied responses to contemporary events and beliefs, such as: the decline of organised religion (as in Ted Hughes's pagan Crow poems); imperial dismantling (Larkin's many laments up to 'Homage to a Government' in 1969), and colonial leftovers (D.J. Enright in Singapore); American cultural hegemony and the rise of youth culture (Thom Gunn); Auschwitz (from Plath to Dannie Abse's 'A Night Out'); and science and the legacy of Hiroshima (Donald Davie's 'Eight Years After'). But since the 1930s, both the issues and the poets had changed. During and after the war, as David Lodge puts it, 'the leading writers of the 1930s became disillusioned with politics, lost faith in Soviet Russia, took up religion, emigrated to America or fell silent' (Lodge 1977: 212). Most clearly, the work of the postwar poets responded to changes in British society and culture: the levelling of classes, the appearance of consensus politics, new forms of mass entertainment, the rise of service industries and consumerism. While Auden had written tributes to Yeats and Freud, Thom Gunn wrote poems about motorcycle gangs, 'Black Jackets' and 'Elvis Presley': 'He turns revolt into a style, prolongs / The impulse to a habit of the time.'[1] In poetry, the social revolution spawned a plain, direct, colloquial style which engaged with the new consumer culture and addressed the ordinary 'man': as Larkin put it, the 'sullen fleshy inarticulate men...fathers of cold-eyed lascivious daughters on the pill, to whom Ramsay MacDonald is coeval with Rameses II, and cannabis-smoking jeans-and-bearded Stuart-haired sons' (Larkin 1983: 298). Several 1950s poets looked back to the war, and some, such as Kingsley Amis, Donald Davie, Charles Causley, and Robert Conquest, had been in the forces. However, most chose to consider the contemporary postwar scene and their own or the country's future.

There were few poets who responded to the new social conditions in the way that Eliot had to the aftermath of World War I, even though Patricia Waugh characterises Larkin's representation of society as a kind of 'welfare-world Waste Land' (Waugh 1995: 10). Undoubtedly, there was a general sense of disillusion at Britain's diminished role in the world, but more importantly there was a determination by government not to make the socio-economic mistakes of the interwar period. The Beveridge Report of 1942 had outlined the kind of social provision a postwar state ought to provide. It advocated a general policy of universal welfare but also identified key areas for improvement, such as housing and education, and specific innovations, such as a National Health Service and National Assistance. In 1945, the general election brought a Labour government to power with almost half of all votes and there was a period of social consensus lasting at least up to 1957 and the Suez disaster, which put an end to any continued imperial pretensions: 'soon if the government didn't act there'd be all kinds of nasties / gushing up out of the drains, Britain would be [is] engulfed' (Peter Reading, *Stet* – on his childhood misunderstanding of the 'Suez' crisis).

Inside the UK, spatial relations were changing as travel became more economical and people could move between places in less time with less expense. On his *English Journey* of 1933, J.B. Priestley had found three Englands: old England, industrial England, and suburbia. People rarely moved between these three Englands before the war. In the years 1938 to 1950 however, road travel by bus and coach, in terms of passenger miles, had increased by 150 per cent. Of all travel, 75 per cent was now by road though Britain's first motorway was not opened until 1959. By 1970 there were nearly 12 million cars and vans in Britain, and domestic air travel had doubled over the previous ten years. Train travel was also still increasing and featured prominently in the work of Betjeman and Larkin.

Class was a different issue postwar, if still a considerable one. In 1948, people assigned themselves to the following classes: upper (2 per cent), upper middle (6 per cent), middle (28 per cent), lower middle (13 per cent), working (46 per cent), 'no reply' (5 per cent).[2] High taxation was reducing the economic power of the upper middle class while collective bargaining and the threat of strikes had raised the standard of living of the working class. There was little intention or possibility of allowing a return to the mass unemployment and poverty of the 1930s. With regard to literature, small shifts in class power were reflected in the number of newly published poets from lower middle-class backgrounds and in the intention of academics such as Richard Hoggart, Raymond Williams, and E.P. Thompson to study working-class and popular culture.

Increasingly, that culture became characterised by consumption: not just in terms of shopping, but sex, drugs, pop music, television, and advertising. Not surprisingly, as their purchasing power rose and the pace of technological change increased, the majority of people also enjoyed more leisure time. In 1946, one-third of the population was going to the cinema once a week and the popularity of film was soon to be matched by that of broadcast television. In 1953, the coronation of Elizabeth II was watched by over 20 million people and commercial television was made legal in 1954. By 1961, over 70 per cent of families had a television set, and by 1971 the figure topped 90 per cent at a time when fewer than 50 per cent had telephones. As Cecil Day Lewis

125

had discussed 'Newsreel' in the 1930s, Ian Hamilton composed 'Newscast' in the 1960s, observing that the Vietnam war for most people took place on television. Many postwar poets themselves have had roles in the media, from George MacBeth (a BBC producer) to James Fenton (a foreign correspondent). Famously, one of the reactionary voices against the new social order was T.S. Eliot, who, in his 1948 *Notes Towards the Definition of Culture*, opposed state intervention and welfare engineering which he thought eroded religious, educational, and personal values by subverting traditional institutions. For others, it was precisely the 'decadence of the upper-middle-class social and artistic hegemony' which had now led to a stagnant period in literature in the 1940s and early 1950s.[3]

The later 1950s and the 1960s in Britain have a revolutionary cultural climate which, Christopher Booker argues in his book *The Neophiliacs*, parallels that of the 1920s in the US. Change was noticeable in

> the prominence of youth, the frenzied dance crazes, the short skirts and exhibitionistic dress, the self-assertive towers in architecture, the rigidly conformist rebellion against 'convention' and 'Victorian' morality or just the all-pervasive sense that society was somehow moving rapidly into an unprecedented age.
>
> (Booker 1992: 51)

The emblems of the time are from popular culture and tabloid headlines: the Beatles and the Stones, freely available drugs and sex, the pill, the mini and the mini-skirt, pop art, the scandal of the Profumo Affair, the lifting of the *Lady Chatterley* ban, and the *Oz* trial. Legislation seemed to sanction the permissive society as liberal reforms were passed on obscene publications (1959), capital punishment (1965), abortion (1967), and homosexuality (1967) – but these need to be set against, for example, Mary Whitehouse's pro-censorship campaigning in 1964 and Enoch Powell's 'rivers of blood' speech in 1967.

Seeming to reinforce Macmillan's late-1950s pronouncement that Britons had never had it so good (e.g. average male earnings almost doubled between 1951 and 1961, and did double over the next decade), the 1960s saw a boom in commerce and advertising, which for the first time became a substantial industry in itself (poets responded with ambivalence at best: think, for example, of the melancholy of Larkin's parody of a marketing paradise, 'Sunny Prestatyn'). In the title of Michael Hamburger's satirical poem, the postwar years contested 'The Soul of Man Under Capitalism'. Consumer goods, which were comparatively if not actually declining in price, sold well and many thought in the 1960s that J.K. Galbraith's 'affluent society' had arrived in Britain as on the one hand it seemed an 'Establishment' was forming to constrict political power and on the other hand it appeared individuality was losing out to large industrial organisations (Lloyd 1986: 361). The commercial character of modern living was nicely parodied in 1961 by Peter Porter in his poem 'A Consumer's Report' where one disgruntled customer offers feedback on a rather uneconomical, messy, purposeless, and awkward invention: 'The name of the product I tested is *Life*'. Porter's customer ends by asserting 'We are the consumers and the last / law makers.'

Massive social alterations also took place in terms of gender and race – these will be discussed in later chapters – but the final defining agenda of the time was set by the antiwar and anti-nuclear movements. CND was founded in 1958 and it soon had the support of between a third and a quarter of the population. Its campaigning influenced the Labour Party's decision to recommend unilateral nuclear disarmament at its 1960 conference. The following year, Porter published a satirical poem, 'Your Attention Please', about a government announcement instructing citizens how to behave after an enemy country has launched a nuclear attack, to which 'our president' 'Has already given orders for / Massive retaliation.' A year later in 1962, the face-off between Russia and the US over the Cuban Missile Crisis brought the West closer to nuclear war than at any other time since 1945.

Retreating to 'England'

In his poem, 'Hawkshead and Dachau in a Christmas Glass' Donald Davie argues that Yeats and Rilke 'died' at one of the concentration camps. It is certainly true that poetry after 1945 appeared in some ways to turn back into itself as a reaction to the war. According to one critic there was a 'celebration of specifically English themes: the countryside, domesticity, all the familiar landmarks of English life now no longer under threat of violent eradication' (Williams 1987: 71). Postwar poetry has thus been seen, for example by Stephen Spender in *The Struggle for the Modern* (1963), as a partial return to the style, nostalgia, and introspection of Georgianism: Larkin and Hughes treat similar themes, if in more intellectual terms, to Edward Thomas or Walter de la Mare, and they have also eclipsed the Georgians' level of popularity since some of their volumes have sold over 50,000 copies.[4] Renewed

127

visions of national identity manifested themselves in an increased interest in the poetry of (displacement and) place: Geoffrey Hill's Roman Britain, John Betjeman's suburbia and metropolis, Ted Hughes's feral primeval landscapes, Donald Davie's piecemeal reworking of English counties through memory in the *The Shires*, and Larkin's 'deflated urban pastoral' of rundown churches, commuter trains, and bedsits.[5] To an extent these preoccupations suggest an insular attitude, one that is overly concerned with the condition of 'English' identity after an international war.

Ted Hughes sympathetically but also a little disparagingly remarked that the male poets of the 1950s wanted to 'get back into civvies and get home to the wife and kids and for the rest of their lives not a thing was going to interfere with a nice cigarette and a nice view of the park' (Perkins 1987: 418). In line with this, Seamus Heaney argues that

> Larkin's England of the mind is in many ways continuous with the England of Rupert Brooke's 'Grantchester' and Edward Thomas's 'Adlestrop', an England of customs and institutions, industrial and domestic, but also an England whose pastoral hinterland is threatened by the very success of those institutions.
>
> (Heaney 1980: 168)

Yet the spectrum of postwar poetry is much broader than this summary, focused on the 1950s, suggests. The 1940s, both during and after the war, are characterised by an outward, international tendency, and the subsequent return to Englishness has to be seen as a reaction to the war poets' international perspectives, the decline of Britain's Imperial profile, and the loss of an obvious poetic mainstream with the eclipse of the Auden coterie and a new generation's determination to move poetry's centre away from London.

In and immediately after the war, the experimental, hieratic poetry of the 1940s returned to many of the modernist practices eschewed by the 1930s poets, and so was not widely popular. While literary publishing in general thrived postwar, the market for poetry contracted: fewer volumes were produced, journals (such as Cyril Connolly's *Horizon* and John Lehmann's *Penguin New Writing*) were closed down, and the 1951 Festival of Britain Poetry Competition flopped disastrously. The most highly rated of the 1940s writers was Dylan Thomas, whose work influenced the romantic personalism of the Apocalypse poets mentioned in the last chapter, such as J.F. Hendry, Henry Treece, Vernon Watkins, Norman MacCaig, and

128

Nicholas Moore. These New Romantic poets met with a bad press in the 1950s and 1960s as the literary pendulum returned towards a vogue for anti-modernism.[6] For example, Philip Hobsbaum wrote in 1965: 'In English poetry of the forties, obscurity grew so fast and rhythms broke down to such an extent that the whole attempt at modernism collapsed in the nerveless verse and chaotic imagery of the New Apocalypse' (Hobsbaum 1970: 384). Even Robin Skelton's anthology of the poetry of the 1940s begins by saying that 'many of the poets found notable by those years now appear to be dismal failures'. He characterises their difference from the 1930s writers in this way:

> many poets of the forties rejected the view that the poet should be a social commentator, school master, mass observer or lay psychiatrist, and wished him to take on, if not a prophetic mantle, at least a sprig of the divine laurel.
>
> (Skelton 1968: 15, 29)

However, the reputations of Dylan Thomas, David Gascoyne, and George Barker, Skelton's three figureheads, plus those of Bernard Spencer, Lawrence Durrell, Roy Fuller, and Kathleen Raine, are still high, if somewhat eclipsed by the *New Lines* poets who followed them.

Make it New

In 1983, the critic and poet Andrew Crozier could still write that 'our sense of the situation of poetry today is conditioned by the arguments of 1956–66' (Crozier 1983: 220–1). By this, he means primarily the controversy between Robert Conquest's 1956 *New Lines* anthology and A. Alvarez's *The New Poetry*, first published in 1962 and revised in 1966. In his introduction to *New Lines*, Conquest argues for the idea that each decade has its own poetry. Consequently, he attempts to define that of the 1950s and includes only poets born since 1920. The volume is not concerned with poets whose writing was interrupted by the war, but with ones who established careers after it, amounting to a rebuttal of the 1940s poets whom Conquest saw as too emotional, metaphorical, theoretical, and subjective. For Conquest, the *New Lines* poets returned to the 'cardinal traditions of English verse', but their qualities, other than empiricism and writing for the 'whole man', are defined by him through negatives: they submit 'to no great systems of theoretical constructs nor agglomerations of unconscious commands', are 'free from both mystical and logical compulsions', and so have 'a negative determination to avoid bad principles'. Conquest argued that the 'stage needed sweeping' in poetry, and his new writers, from a *Spectator* article of 1954, were known as being 'In the Movement'. This article identified a group of writers who were 'sceptical, robust, and ironic', seeing themselves as commonsensical and middlebrow: Kingsley Amis, Donald Davie, D.J. Enright, John Holloway, John Wain, Larkin, and Conquest (also, less helpfully, Thom Gunn and Elizabeth Jennings).

Conquest's introduction to *New Lines* is therefore often seen as a kind of manifesto for the Movement, stressing the poets' return to earlier literary forms and concerns, bypassing modernism and its 'grander themes' (as Kingsley Amis put it), and yet even here Conquest argues that the anthology's atmosphere is 'concentratedly contemporary' and that 'To be of one's own time is not an important virtue, but it is a necessary one.' The *Spectator* article speaks of a 'modern Britain' of the 1950s which was substantially changed from the country it had been prewar. It went on to observe a parallel metamorphosis in literature, declaring that Auden, Thomas, and modernists from Henry James to Kafka and Proust, are 'all gone, utterly gone, and vanished'.

The Movement poets differ in their views and practices – not all of them were happy about being rounded up into a group – but certain standpoints and features are representative of the majority. Their aesthetic attitudes are expressed by Larkin's well-known objections to tradition, allusion, and myth, to the ideas behind poems like *The Waste Land* and 'The Tower'. Their provincial, male, social and ideological characteristics have been said to 'bespeak a high degree of social root-lessness, and a complementary degree of personal isolation and self-dependence': 'the Low Church and middle-class origins; the concern with classlessness and upward social mobility; the hostility to the 'posh' and the 'phoney', and the nostalgia for traditional order; the connection with provincial universities' (Crozier 1983: 208). However, this belated shift in poetry is partly analogous to the reorientation in politics and society initiated by the Labour election of 1945. The new poets' rejection of modernism, which was never likely to appeal to a mass audience, seems entirely consonant with the socialism of the time as does their belief in popularity, plain-speaking, and emotion over intellectualism; but the writers were hardly champions of the new meritocracy or even highly politicised. For example, Thom Gunn asserted in 1957 that 'The unions are as powerful as they could wish to be.... National health has been around for ten years, and the village squires are all dead' (Perkins 1987: 424).

While, as Donald Davie argues, there is a case to be made for saying that the prominent poets from each decade from the 1920s to the 1960s came from Oxford, and to a lesser extent Cambridge, the Movement poets were not associated with the upper class, Bloomsbury, bohemia, the south, or, after their undergraduate days, Oxbridge (Holloway 1956/7). With these lower middle-class, suburban poets, the equivalents in poetry to the 'angry young men' of drama and fiction, we again find a change in diction, such that Kingsley Amis can even interrupt his own poem to ask 'Going well so far, eh?' ('Here is Where'). The familiarity with the reader is also entirely typical and shows how the Movement writers not only rejected the dominant style of the 1940s, but also, in looking back to the 1930s, found a role model in Orwell far more than Auden. Yet it is to the poetic hegemony of the 'Auden generation' that the influence of the Movement writers is often compared (see Morrison 1980a: 9).

More helpfully, the *New Lines* poets' preoccupations can be located in their time, just as they can be set against those of other poets who surfaced in the twenty-five years following the war, such as the Group writers' use of violent imagery to oppose the Movement's gentility, Sylvia Plath's transatlantic dislocations of gender, the Mersey poets' *pop vox*, and the anti-establishment values associated with Michael Horovitz's anthology *Children of Albion: Poetry of the 'Underground' in Britain* (1969). The conscious 'Little Englander' approach in some of the Movement poets also has to be seen as a response to England's crisis of postwar, post-Imperial decline and has to be set alongside other voices from the British archipelago: poets from Wales (R.S. Thomas, Dylan Thomas, Vernon Watkins, David Jones, Alun Lewis), Ireland (Patrick Kavanagh, Louis MacNeice, John Hewitt, and John Montague), and Scotland (starting with the rejuvenation occasioned by Hugh MacDiarmid's 'Scottish Renaissance' of the 1920s and on to W.S. Graham and Norman MacCaig).

One atypical writer from *New Lines* whose work deserves more study than it currently receives is Elizabeth Jennings. A poem such as 'Identity' explores a familiar theme in her writing by comparing the self's perception of (it)self with that assembled by the other. 'The Island', echoing John Donne, also concerns the search for identity in others, the quest of 'Seekers who are their own discovery', while 'In the Night' and 'A Way of Looking' meditate in their different ways on the relationship between the mind and its attempted apprehension of objects. Jennings, whose later poems, following a nervous breakdown, focus more explicitly on mental instability, is interested even here in the mind's inability to grasp reality and yet, in Movement style, contains the potentially threatening content of her poems in highly ordered, rational forms. As she wrote in 1955: 'Big questions bruised my mind but still I let / Small answers be a bulwark to my fear' ('Answers'). She is also greatly concerned, in poems like 'Piazza San Marco' and 'Not in the Guide-Books', with the relationship between thought and word, sound and meaning, signifier and signified. Her attempt in language to connect identity with a world of objects and others outside the self is an important precursor to the struggles of Sylvia Plath and later more theoretical poets concerned with the culturally constructed matrix of the subject and society.

New Lines was itself soon challenged by the publication of the provocatively titled The New Poetry in 1962, with its forthright intro-duction by A. Alvarez. Alvarez thought that in the 1940s English poetry had been at its 'nadir'. In this he had an ally in Conquest, but Alvarez also thought the Movement poets were too orderly, controlled, and 'genteel'. By launching a general attack on the 'academic-administrative verse' of the New Lines writers, but still including half a dozen of them, he inaugurated a struggle over poetry in the present rather than in relation to the past. Alvarez began his anthology with the innovations of American poets such as John Berryman and Robert Lowell, then turned towards English followers, like Ted Hughes and Thom Gunn, who were accompanied by such diverse poets as Charles Tomlinson, John Fuller, Geoffrey Hill, and Norman MacCaig, who was too old by ten years to have been included in Conquest's collection. In the 1966 edition, he introduced the work of Sylvia Plath, who had died three years earlier. Where the Movement poets wrote as 'ordinary, decent people' of what they saw, Alvarez's preferred poets intimated that the dislocations of the war and the political struggles of the last twenty years had revealed depths to both society and the individual which had to be confronted and explored. If poetry had responded to history by retreating from it in New Lines, the war's psychological and moral repercussions were to be brought out by The New Poetry.

The clearest difference between the two anthologies lay in the opin-ions and temperaments of their editors. Advocating a traditional, plain-speaking, genial poetry, Robert Conquest's view was the antithesis of Adorno's famous declaration that there could be no poetry after the horrors of the Nazi concentration camps. By contrast, in his influential preface to The New Poetry, Alvarez asked for poets to engage with the modern 'forces of disintegration', with the horrors 'of two world wars, of the concentration camps, and the threat of nuclear war'. One poem Alvarez included, Peter Porter's 'Annotations of Auschwitz', is an obvious example, with its seven parts each detailing in a mixture of humour and horror different kinds of torture that implicate in the psychopathology of the holocaust every aspect of postwar life, from tube-travelling to meat-eating. Yet, Alvarez did not hail his poets so much as their potential. In direct contrast to Conquest's faith in a return to English poetic tradition, his belief was (not that English poetry had been rejuvenated but) that the *New Poetry* might 'come to' something if it followed the lead of the Americans, as it had in the days of Pound and Eliot. Social issues seemed to be resurfacing less in the subject matter of these emerging poets than in their tone, which is not whimsical and colloquial but impassioned and earnest, seeming to Alvarez to reach back 'into a nexus of fear and sensation'. Even Ted Hughes's poems are, according to Stan Smith, repressions of history which, in their deep anxieties about loss and recovery, mimic the mood of their time and contain history in displaced forms (Smith 1982: 150–69). No doubt seeing this same reaction to history reflected in the 'sharp details which bring [his poetry] so threateningly to life', Alvarez preferred Hughes over Larkin for his seriousness, for his poetry's display of a 'powerful complex of emotions and sensations', and for his direct portrayal of a brute world which is 'part physical, part state of mind'.

Two examples: Larkin and Plath

And the intricate, well-worked hills undeceived by the dream
That life could be utterly different, somewhere else.
(Carol Rumens, 'The Lisburn Road List' [variations on a theme of
Philip Larkin])

Where Hughes delivers a rural England that reminds him more of Ireland, and Betjeman is unremittingly nostalgic, Donald Davie says of Larkin 'the England in his poems is the England we have inhabited' (Davie 1973: 64). Which is to say that Larkin's England is no longer one of the country, or even of the city, like Eliot's, but of the suburb and the province. With a self-deprecating irony and a paradoxically sentimental detachment, Larkin confronts his society and its particularity. Patricia Waugh argues that Larkin 'presents the promise of 1945, the optimistic projection of national unity into a peacetime world of justice and abundance, as simply a temporary refuge from something which is actually "nearly at an end"' (Waugh 1995: 29). Larkin expresses England's social changes since the 1930s, but there is a pervasive sadness which makes every change appear unsatisfactory if not regrettable. In his poetry there is a nostalgic longing for familial unity alongside his almost misanthropic protestations of independence, a mourning for Empire beside his evident distaste for the social miscegenation necessitated by post-Imperial immigration. The demise of the English countryside, mourned by other writers over the previous century, is greeted by Larkin with resignation even if with slight surprise at its speed: 'And that will be England gone, / The shadows, the meadows, the lanes' ('Going, Going'). This poem, in an earlier form, first appeared above the picture of a chemical works as a prologue to a government report on the environment entitled *How Do You Want To Live* (Lindrop 1980: 46–7).

Larkin's world is one in which, famously, your parents 'fuck you up' and sexual intercourse started too late, in 1963 ('This Be the Verse' and 'Annus Mirabilis'). Oddly, the reader gets the sense that in the recent past things were bad but now they are worse: sexual repression has been replaced by a desensitising sexual promiscuity. To be less deceived is also to be less happy, as faith in religion, belief in love, hope in the future dissolve into sceptical detachment. One kind of unhappiness is replaced by a worse, amounting to a creed that asserts 'Life is first boredom, then fear'. On the other hand, Larkin does not believe in tapping into tradition, whether literary or historical. He does not draw from a storehouse of images like Yeats or allude to Renaissance poetry and Classical mythology like Eliot. More as an assertion against the poetry that has gone before than as a declaration of his own convictions, he has said: 'Form holds little interest for me. Content is everything' (Lodge 1977: 214). The content of Larkin's poems is decidedly contemporary: fags and gravy, pills and diaphragms, televisions and toasters, perms and prescriptions, bri-nylon and cotton wool. It is, however, a poetry of observation that is tinged throughout with nostalgia and melancholy. Its 'Englishness' is stereotypical: the poems are unassuming and understated, often self-denigratory and class-conscious.

A librarian at Hull University for most of his adult life, Larkin believed strongly in the work ethic: 'Why should I let the toad *work* / Squat on my life?...For something sufficiently toad-like / Squats in me, too' ('Toads'). Larkin described his daily routine as 'Work all day, then cook, then eat, wash up, telephone, hack writing, drink and television in the evenings. I almost never go out' (Larkin 1983: 57). A stereotypically British anti-intellectualism appears in his comments. He declared himself to read little other than light fiction, to have no interest in foreign languages or writers, and to dislike 'studying' poems. Born in the year of *The Waste Land*'s publication, Larkin disliked the modernist revolution of Pound and Eliot, as well as that of Picasso and Charlie Parker. He characterises it briefly:

It seems to me undeniable that up to this century literature used language in the way we all use it, painting represented what anyone with normal vision sees, and music was an affair of nice noises rather than nasty ones. The innovation of 'modernism' in the arts consisted of doing the opposite.

Modernism, Larkin felt, by undervaluing the importance of communi- cation, emotion, pleasure and ordinary speech, had reduced literature's audience and made poetry the preserve of academics and intellectuals. By contrast he felt that he had, in his anthology *The Oxford Book of Twentieth-Century English Verse*, 'made twentieth-century poetry sound nice' (Larkin 1983: 72–3). His early work, published in *The North Ship* is greatly influenced by the premodernist elements in Yeats, but it is the three subsequent volumes, *The Less Deceived* (1955), *The Whitsun Weddings* (1964), and *High Windows* (1974) that have won him high praise.

At the time of the publication of *The Less Deceived* in 1955 Larkin was considered a member of the Movement. Like them, he had a dislike for the artistic experimentalism of the 1920s, for the committed poetry of the 1930s, and for the neo-romantic surrealism of the 1940s; plus a liking for writing that expressed rationality, intellect, and morality in poetry that was often conversational and ironic but usually in traditional forms. Larkin's poems of this time are colloquial, obser- vant and gently quizzical, familiar but detached, sincere but unsentimental. The themes and tones vary, although the subjects are nearly always scenes from contemporary life, and in particular those that illustrate the gap between expectations and experience. The poems attempt not to eradicate but to lessen a little our illusions and (self-)deceptions, whether they be about settling down ('Places, Loved Ones'), or travelling ('Arrivals, Departures'), or getting away from it all ('Poetry of Departures'). At the same time, being 'less deceived', Larkin concludes, affords no pleasure or comfort.

One of Larkin's most pervasive themes is ageing and dying (e.g. 'Triple Time' and 'Next, Please'), a subject which appears to apply as much to the British Empire or the English countryside as to Larkin. He once said he didn't think happiness was really possible 'if only because you know that you are going to die, and the people you love are going to die' (Larkin 1983: 66). Growing older worried him 'dreadfully' (see 'The Old Fools') and the pervasive melancholy of his work is in no small part due to his 'dread' of 'endless extinction' (Larkin 1983: 66, 55). Larkin's poetry seems both to note the unsatisfactoriness of life and to mourn deeply the passing of it, when 'Simply to choose stopped all ways up but one' ('To My Wife'). Any choice marks the end of other possibilities, adulthood is a pale shadow of childhood hopes, time an enemy, and life a prelude to death. Stability is little more than stasis but change is always both a possible wrong decision and a step closer to death. Larkin sees having children ('Why did he think adding meant increase? / To me it was dilution', 'Dockery and Son') and getting married ('Where's the sense / In saying love, but meaning interference? / You'll only *change* her', 'He Hears that his Beloved has become Engaged') as unsatisfactory, depreciatory, and almost arrogant acts. To an extent, they are examples of the ways in which people try to improve their lives but, for Larkin, merely alter them; the larger forces in life, such as time, drives, needs, and decay, determine our experience. Though his last volume of poetry was published in 1974, Larkin's sentiments continued to suggest the mood of the 1950s: a sense of anti-climax after the war. The flip side of Jimmy Porter in Osborne's *Look Back in Anger* (1956), Larkin comes across as not an angry, young man but a disappointed, middle-aged one who would still agree that there are no good, brave causes left. As Tom Paulin concludes, 'the England he addresses is a cold country inhabited by hard-working Anglo-Saxon Protestants who wear cheap, ugly clothes and drink beer' (Paulin 1992: 249).

Broadly speaking, Larkin's poems deal with the customs of English life, but the rituals and gatherings he describes are usually very traditional and often in decline, as with the holiday on the coast ('To the Sea') and the agricultural show ('Show Saturday'). Other, seemingly perennial, rituals (often semi-religious) are sad, a little painful, and routine but suffused with solemnity and a necessary seriousness. In 'Church Going', Larkin contemplates the significance of religion and religious buildings in a post-Christian age. Assuming religion's decline to be inevitable, the poem meditates on the purposes churches will be put to in the future. Will some be made into show pieces, while others are left abandoned or claimed by the superstitious? Typically, Larkin's musings move from idle speculation to serious meditation and he ends by noting the church's function as a solemn place in which birth, marriage, and death are 'robed as destinies', thus fulfilling an ever-present social or personal desire for meaning, explanation, and formality in the face of mortality. It has been said of Larkin that 'Death-in-life is as much his preoccupation as it was Eliot's' (Kirkham 1983: 298). Whereas Auden argued that suffering takes place amid normality and indifference, Larkin notes that 'Nothing, like something, happens anywhere' ('I Remember, I Remember'). The melancholy in Larkin's poems appears in many ways to reflect the mood of the times. While the years from World War II to the oil crisis in the early 1970s can be seen as three decades of rising prosperity, the feeling in Britain is also that of slow recovery, imperial decline, and postwar disillusionment. The United States, which poured millions of dollars of aid into Europe, and more into Britain than any other country, was now undeniably the major world power, followed by Russia. Larkin's feelings about America, or at least about academics from the US, are quite clear in two poems about cynical, selfish careerists: 'Naturally the Foundation Will Bear Your Expenses' and 'Posterity'. English tradition and ceremony, particularised in an Armistice Day parade, are dismissed as 'solemn-sinister wreath-rubbish' and the poet himself is seen as just 'One of those old-type *natural* fouled-up guys'. Britain, bombed, rationed and with debts of 3,000 million pounds, had an aura of fallen 'Great'-ness in the world context: the government began its imperial dismantling with the secession of India in 1947, and introduced the welfare state as a sign that no citizen should have to return to the shortages of the war or the poverty of the interwar years.

Yet, for Larkin there also appears to be some consolation in ritual and ceremony. At the end of 'Show Saturday' he seems both to celebrate and to bless the traditional communal event: 'Let it always be there.' As a kind of 'strength' resisting mortality and decline, social customs provide rhythms, continuities, and reassurances, even if they often seem, to Larkin, pale reflections or comical parodies of their ideal selves. There is additionally a sense of union, however uneasy, in the way that many of Larkin's poems move from the personal to the social, and this is often signalled by a shift from first person to second or third (such as in 'Church Going' or 'The Whitsun Weddings'). Aiming for this anxious, ambivalent sense of communion with society or the reader, Larkin's poems also sometimes end in an idiosyncratic uncertainty or self-doubt, such as 'Mr. Bleaney' ('I don't know') or 'He Hears that his Beloved has become Engaged' ('Still, I'm sure you're right.') or 'Self's the Man' ('Or I suppose I can'). Other critics have pointed out that many of his best lines operate through negatives, which create an overall impression of mediocrity and never more than cautious, insecure optimism.

The reason why Larkin seemed to speak for what his biographer calls 'the disillusion of the post-war years and for the value of conserving traditions' is clear from his most famous poems which start from concrete examples (often associated with solemnity and ceremony: a church, funerals, a tomb, weddings) and move through central verses of unsentimental meditation on their contemporary worth or meaning, to a final summing up, such as: 'What will survive of us is love' ('An Arundel Tomb'). As Larkin said of 'The Whitsun Weddings' in a letter to Anthony Thwaite, 'success or failure depends on whether it gets off the ground on the last two lines' (Larkin 1992: 301). And the movement of that poem, a reversed bathos, imitates the movement of the train as Larkin surveys England in his journey from the country to the capital city. 'The Whitsun Weddings' belongs to the genre of 'England from a train' poems that runs from Edward Thomas's 'Adlestrop' to Peter Reading's *Stet* (1986) through Betjeman's 'Pershore Station', 'From the Great Western', and 'Great Central Railway' or Larkin's own 'I Remember, I Remember' (Paulin 1992: 286–7). Auden's great force for national unity, the night train delivering mail, is replaced by passing trains that just occasionally move in and out of stations with which the detached, contemplative travellers have few connections and can muster only awkward passing thoughts.

If Tom Paulin thinks Larkin's 'real theme' is national decline, Larkin says that the dominant emotion of his poetry is 'sadness' – both are perhaps true (Paulin 1992: 233). In an interview, Larkin has said that 'Deprivation is for me what daffodils were for Wordsworth', such that he thinks of himself as quite funny but that 'writing about unhappiness is probably the source of my popularity, if I have any – after all most people *are* unhappy, don't you think' (Larkin 1983: 47). This 'sadness' has become his trademark, just as Larkin thought Sylvia Plath's principal subject was suicide.[7] The significant difference between them, for Larkin in an essay entitled 'Horror Poet', was that his theme was universal whereas Plath's was unusual and extreme (Larkin 1983: 278–81). Yet, this appears a superficial judgement on Plath, whose direct experience of suffering is inextricably tied up in her poetry with fundamental postwar issues of anonymity, torture and pain, the relationship between the individual and the mass-produced, the ownership of bodies and the production of identities. Just as Larkin exemplifies the cool, dry emotional stance of the *New Lines* poets, Plath can be considered a cardinal example of the engaged, committed poets of *The New Poetry*: Larkin's somewhat languid self-indulgent 'sadness' is more deeply felt, experienced, and acted upon, to the point of Plath's theme of 'suicide'.

If we use Plath, a writer rarely associated with history, to illustrate briefly this middle postwar period of the 1960s, it is salutary to remember that the poet Christopher Middleton complained in 1964 that

English poetry right now is suffering from this very dangerous cleavage of poetry from history. There are very few English poets who seem to have any sense of history as something happening in me and you and all around us all the time.

(Smith 1982: 16)

Plath does not write of history happening all around her, as Auden or Yeats might, but she does represent the manner in which it impinged upon her own life, in a way that is totally alien to Larkin. An atypical example of her oblique engagement with history is 'Cut', a gruesome narrative ostensibly concerned with Plath slicing the top off her thumb while chopping an onion. The poem uses a series of images for the thumb-stump which appear random until the reader realises that American history from the scalped pilgrims through to trepanned Vietnam soldiers is being recounted episode by episode. All of the pain and self-mutilation of the country's past is compressed into the image of Plath's self-inflicted wound.

Plath differs so greatly from Larkin that it is striking simply to consider the fact of their contemporaneity. If one subscribes to the view of isolated, individual, inspired poetic talent, then the fact of their shared historical moment means almost nothing. However, if the differences between them as poets are contrasted, each is placed in a light that illuminates the other. For example, their attitudes to marriage are dissimilar, especially in terms of gender roles, but revealing in their distrust both of the institution and of the motives of those who seek through matrimony to fill a vacancy in separate lives; and in this they anticipate a distinctly postwar disillusionment with marriage and, implicitly, the most recent crises of the family: 'It works, there is nothing wrong with it. / You have a hole, it's a poultice. / You have an eye, it's an image. / My boy, it's your last resort. / Will you marry it, marry it, marry it' (Plath, 'The Applicant'); 'He married a woman to stop her getting away / Now she's there all day, // And the money he gets for wasting his life on work / She takes as her perk' (Larkin, 'Self's the Man').

Patricia Waugh rightly speaks of Plath's linguistic extremism in terms of 'gender anger with no available politically formulated vehicle for its expression', but even here many of Plath's shocking images are drawn from history, and she herself maintained that 'personal' poetry should be 'generally relevant, to such things as Hiroshima and Dachau'.[8] These are not the concern of Larkin's poetry, and neither are Plath's other principal subjects, but they are the concern of their shared society. As can be easily seen from the realist films of the period, by Tony Richardson, John Schlesinger, and others, many of Plath's key themes, such as marriage ('Purdah'), childbirth ('Winter Trees'), family relationships ('Daddy'), illness and recovery ('Tulips'), are the sites of contested social issues in Britain, wrapped up with the NHS, the welfare state and family benefit, divorce laws, contraception, women's liberation, and the rise of the 'teenager'. Postwar divorce figures in 1947 (60,000) were ten times those prewar, but the number fell to a steady rate of about 25,000 per year in the 1950s. Marriage, however, had increased over the century, from including about half of women aged between 20 and 40 in 1911 to nearly three-quarters in 1951. The first postwar baby boom peaked in 1947 when there was an average birth rate of nearly twenty-one per thousand of population (five greater than in the interwar years). Families, because of urban living and social security, were contracting from extended to nuclear. Plath engages in the kind of identity politics that are more commonly found in feminism in the 1970s and debates over new ethnicities in the 1980s. Her dwelling on death, mutilation, (re)birth, and physical violence suggests a desire for regeneration and reshaping, as her poetry uses body imagery (sometimes women's but sometimes not, as in 'The Rabbit Catcher' or even 'Winter Trees') to express a psychic desire to change cultural constructions of gender and to posit and critique an 'emergent female selfhood', just as the women's movement was to confront gender oppression through representations of the body and femininity in the 1970s.[9] Similarly, her invocations of the Holocaust, for example in 'Daddy' and 'Lady Lazarus', and the attacks and defences over her position that have followed from critics, show the sense in which the personal and the political have become still more interlocked in a world where mass communication has heightened ideas of shared responsibility and where the rise of individual liberties has accompanied the slow demise of beliefs in human nature, liberal humanism, and universalism.[10]

Conclusion

The Movement's frequent preoccupations with loss and regret, retirement, contemplation, conservatism, the past and the countryside, are not ahistorical self-expression but part of a national attempt to come to terms with war, Empire, and the socio-economic transition to what we would now call postmodernity. The war had in many ways broadened English poetry, as writers in service or exile produced work with a refreshed vocabulary in numerous anthologies from, for example, Africa and the Middle East, while individuals wrote from Alexandria

(Lawrence Durrell among others), America (Auden), and India (Alun Lewis). Robin Skelton speaks of an 'internationalism' of the 1940s also partly caused by the influx of other nationals into Britain and the enthusiasm of magazine editors for poetry in translation.

The 'genteel' formalism of the Movement was seen by Conquest as part of a tradition running through English poetry which had been diverted by the modernists and then the influence of Dylan Thomas. In retrospect, it is Conquest's intervention which appears more of a diversion. In the year after *The New Poetry* was published, another collection of poets (with whom Ted Hughes was also associated) who opposed Conquest's principles appeared together in Philip Hobsbaum's and Edward Lucie-Smith's *A Group Anthology*; it included Peter Porter, George MacBeth, Margaret Owen, Zulfikar Ghose, and Peter Redgrove.[11] The volume took its title from the name that a fluctuating constituency of poets had given themselves since 1955 when they were meeting weekly in London. These workshops were based on Hobsbaum's experiences of Cambridge English tutorials, and their direct purpose was to share views on a previously circulated poem written by one of the members of the 'group'. Other than a belief in this process of discussion, they had no common agenda or shared convictions about poetry, and so cannot be said to have constituted a 'movement'. Among these poets, Peter Porter has consistently responded with perception and humour to contemporary beliefs. The poems in his first collection *Once Bitten, Twice Bitten* (1961) range over such issues as loss of faith ('We have our loneliness / And our regret with which to build an eschatology', 'The Historians Call Up Pain'), sexual promiscuity ('All the boys are howling to take the girls to bed. / Our betters say it's a seedy world', 'John Marston Advises Anger'), contraception ('The labour-saving kitchen to match the labour-saving thing / She'd fitted before marriage', 'Made in Heaven'), fashion ('Oyster-coloured buttons, single vent, tapered / Trousers, no waistcoat, hairy tweed – my own', 'Metamorphosis'), and the desire to escape conventional bourgeois life ('So give up thinking, work hard, buy a car, / Get married, keep a garden, bring up kids', 'Conventions of Death'). Porter's poems of sex and consumerism throughout the 1960s, up to *The Last of England* in 1970, offer an observant London-Australian's view of British life, and their heavy use of irony and parody betray his profession as an advertising copy-writer.

This chapter has left a lot out in order to include a little. Many other poets writing in the 1950s and 1960s are less well known but often more widely influential among practitioners. One example is the Cambridge School – a network of writers, including Peter Riley,

Wendy Mulford and J.H. Prynne, who, from the late 1960s, stood against the mainstream of British poetry, drawing on more innovatory American and European influences, and articulating a more complex idea of ethical subjectivity. A conservative in terms of form but in every other respect unique, up to his death in 1959 Edwin Muir wrote haunting poems which imply and convey far more than they state; though pitched at a high level of abstraction, some seem like Kafkaesque parables of modern life, particularly in relation to the war and the holocaust (e.g. 'The Horses' and 'The Shortage'). Additionally, Roy Fisher attacked misguided high-rise urban-planning policies of the 1960s in his poetic sequence *City*, while David Jones wrote late modernist poetry which in its use of Welsh culture, layers of language, mythology, and landscapes, aimed to present and re-present a non-metropolitan and non-standard British identity. Jones has this in common with two other important postwar figures who compile their own Wordsworthian memories of 'home': Basil Bunting in his complex meditations on Northumbrian history, religion, and dialect in *Briggflatts* (1966) and Charles Tomlinson in his evocations of Gloucestershire and Staffordshire.[12] Postwar poetry runs the gamut from John Betjeman's comforting images of a prewar world of tennis, tea, and railway compartments to the constant formal refashioning of Edwin Morgan's work.

In the 1960s and early 1970s, a proliferation of magazine and small press publications led to a 'Poetry Revival' which was in opposition to the literary orthodoxies of the 1950s and reassessed the work of the 1940s (Mottram 1993). It is also important to note the many experiments with visual and aural presentation such as Christopher Logue's fusing of poetry and jazz in the 1950s, the sound poetry of Bob Cobbing, and the few British experiments with concrete poetry by Ian Hamilton Finlay and John Furnival in the 1960s. The period in poetry is above all one of developing variety which parallels the shift in the socio-political sphere moving from a postwar consensus in the 1950s to an increasing multiplication of attitudes and styles throughout the 1960s.

In 1969, Larkin wrote his 'Homage to a Government' attacking Harold Wilson's decision to remove troops from 'East of Suez' – an act which at least symbolically marked the final stage of the British imperial reorientation begun by the Suez crisis of 1956. For Larkin, the withdrawal meant that 'Next year we shall be living in a country / That brought its soldiers home for lack of money.' Also in 1969, a somewhat younger librarian from Hull University, Douglas Dunn, published his first volume of poetry, *Terry Street*, a portrait of working-class life in the city. Much of it reads like Larkin because the poems are detached, lightly ironic, and use metonyms rather than metaphors. However, the collection marks a sharp move away from the values of Larkin's era. There is still an air of class voyeurism (quite explicitly, in a line such as 'Old women are seen wiping in doorless toilets', 'Ins and Outs'), but the poems are marked by both a warmth towards their subject and a deep indignation at the continuation of social inequalities, not at the existence of the welfare state but at its failure. Individual poems also suggest alternative visions to the 1960s stereotypes: the young women 'don't get high on pot, but get sick on cheap / Spanish burgundy, or beer in rampant pubs' ('The Clothes Pit'), while the old men 'are the individualists of our time. / They know no fashions, copy nothing but their minds' ('The Patricians'). To a degree, the shift from Larkin to Dunn can be explained in terms of class, from Larkin's lower middle-class Midlands alienation to Dunn's Scottish working-class rootedness in the traditions of community. Yet, with respect to alienation and class, Dunn has had problems of a new kind. In terms of the postwar social revolution, he represents the fulfilment of the 1944 Butler Education Act – instead of upper-middle-class poets such as Auden 'going over' to the working class, in the late 1960s the inner-city schoolchildren, like Dunn, Tony Harrison, and later Craig Raine, were breaking out of their parents' 'slums' to become poets. This was a move which threw up different considerations of class distinction as children were exposed to a culture which was foreign if not antagonistic to that of their parents. It also gave a different language and voice to a disenfranchised section of British society and by the end of the next decade, Dunn's sentiments about *Terry Street* had hardened into the angry class politics of his important fourth collection, *Barbarians*, published in the year Margaret Thatcher came to power. Dunn, noting that to the Greeks barbarians were those who did not speak their language, uses his poetry to range over several exclusions and separations (Scotland from England, the working class from the middle class, Conservative from Labour, children from parents) which seemed to be exacerbated in the late 1970s, but which were in fact to be marked by wider gulfs in the 1980s.[13]

7

'TED HUGHES IS ELVIS PRESLEY'

Recent anthologies by men

> So right, yer buggers then! We'll occupy your lousy leasehold
> Poetry.
>
> (Tony Harrison, 'Them and [uz]')

Introduction

In this chapter there are three subjects that I want to discuss. First, the collection published in 1982 as *The Penguin Book of Contemporary British Poetry* edited by Blake Morrison and Andrew Motion. Second, a number of narrative poems and social studies in poetry that have been published in the last thirty years. Third, the latest contentious anthology to have split critical opinions: *The New Poetry*, edited by Michael Hulse, David Kennedy, and David Morley, and published in 1993 by Bloodaxe.

As prelude, I want to say something in terms of a preliminary review of the period. The arts during the 1950s and early 1960s had been characterised by themes of class mobility, sexual adventure, and realist aesthetics. This was broadly true of drama, fiction, poetry, and also film. Women were still under-represented in publishers' prestigious lists but influential texts appeared from authors with varied backgrounds in terms of class and culture. Writers were less concerned with pushing at the boundaries of art and the medium of language than with exploring the material relations of contemporary social experience. This emphasis is consonant with a social and formal shift in the concerns of not just poetry but also the theatre (the kitchen-sink drama of John Osborne or Shelagh Delaney), fiction (George Lamming, Colin MacInnes, Alan Sillitoe, John Braine, and David Storey), and cinema (the 'gritty northern realism' of English working-class life filmed in *Billy Liar*, *Room at the Top*, and *A Kind of Loving*, all based on recent

144

novels). Central preoccupations were the 'promiscuous generation' and the 'national malaise'. In 1968, Nathaniel Tarn could write that 'We know about Britain's diminution of power. This, among other things, has turned the poet away from politics.... And yet, in the world we inhabit, a poetry divorced from politics is as unthinkable as a man divorced from society' (Tarn 1968: 396). This trend was to change in the next two decades, however, as the polarisation of the political field, more pronounced than at any time since the 1930s, was accompanied by more engaged poetry, from Seamus Heaney's treatment of the 'Troubles' in *North* to Linton Kwesi Johnson's condemnation of 'Babylon' in *Inglan Is a Bitch*. Pop music became more political when Margaret Thatcher came to power in 1979, producing a range of anti-government, often personal attacks, from the Beat's 'Stand Down Margaret' to Elvis Costello's vituperative 'Tramp the Dirt Down', about dancing on Thatcher's grave. Across poetry, there has also been an increase in direct socio-political statements, from Blake Morrison's attack on Thatcher in 'The Inquisitor' in *Dark Glasses* (1984), through the many poems on the Gulf War by writers as varied as Tony Harrison and Jo Shapcott, to Jackie Kay's 'Death to Poll Tax', in *The Adoption Papers* (1991). Sometimes seen as developments of and reactions to the social upheavals of the previous two decades, the political and economic changes of the 1970s and 1980s hovered around four domestic issues: inflation, the 'Troubles', industrial action, and unemployment. For example, inflation rose to 23 per cent in 1973, the year IRA bombing on the mainland commenced and the Three Day Week was introduced as a result of the miners' overtime ban, while unemployment peaked in 1985, the year of the Anglo-Irish agreement and of Tony Harrison's controversial poem about the previous year's miners strike, 'V', discussed below.

A different group of writers emerged in the 1970s – many of whom now constitute the established names of the 1990s. These were poets and novelists who had not experienced the war, the eclipse of the British Empire, or life before the invention of mass consumerism, rock and roll, and the 'teenager' in the 1950s, but had grown up instead with the welfare state and the Cold War, appreciating both high and popular culture, the literary tradition and television. The dominant themes of 1970s writing reflected in myriad ways the maturation of the postwar shift in social attitudes, sexual mores, religious consciousness, and youth movements, together with the growing Americanisation of British culture. TV and then video became central products of the mainstream mass-consumer culture which was widely and wrongly anticipated to bring about the commercial failure of both the novel and poetry.

145

In art, a shift has also taken place from the concerns of modernism to the buzzwords of postmodernism: simulacra, hyperreality, metanarrative, the sublime, legitimation, cultural logic, language games, ecstasy, and so on. Postmodernism's concern with history and its narrative construction has suggested that analysts of historiography need to pay attention to the same linguistic effects as literary critics: discourse, metaphor, fantasy, narration. A dissection of history, identity, and language is typical of postmodernist writing. In poetry, such concerns are evident in the narrative reflections of James Fenton, which show an awareness of the storyteller's artifice but also of history's construct-edness. The artificiality of 'character' is toyed with in Peter Reading's postmodernist satire of postmodernism, the short poem 'Fiction', with its Russian-doll set of created identities and its repeated line 'Even one's self is wholly fictitious.' In the 1980s, the concern with a social postmodernist verse evident in Reading's work gained greater currency in the poetry of Michael Hofmann, Ian McMillan, and Peter Didsbury.[1]

From the momentum gained by an increasingly militant movement in the 1970s, gay writing broke into the mainstream in the 1980s with such novelists as Jeanette Winterson and Alan Hollinghurst. Gender theory, body politics, queer theory, and media interest in (usually food-related) 'hysterical illnesses' all led to increased emphasis on sexuality and identity. In poetry, lesbian sexuality was celebrated by such writers as Maureen Duffy and Jackie Kay (e.g. in 'And I still cannot believe it' and 'Tulips'). Also, a number of new women's presses were founded in the 1970s and 1980s after the success of Virago. In terms of racial politics, as we shall see in the final chapter, there have been recent shifts to a concern with reclaimed histories, colonialism, the 'black Atlantic', and ethnic and religious differences. Since the 1970s, both literature and popular culture have witnessed a portmanteau of trends that have explored sexuality and politics, glam and punk rock, suburban and metropolitan attitudes, decolonisation and diaspora, eco-politics and drug culture. Alongside these movements has been a traditionalist reactionary force which the government dubbed 'Victorian values' in the 1980s and 'Family values' in the early 1990s. In the period overall, the backlash was spearheaded by Margaret Thatcher, who said 'We are reaping what was sown in the 1960s.... The fashionable theories and permissive claptrap set the scene for a society in which the old virtues of discipline and self-restraint were denigrated' (Weeks 1985: 18).

One of the poets mentioned above, Peter Reading, is an opposi-tional voice whose views have always been at variance with Tory values and, in particular, with Thatcher's: 'But your many wise policies / were saving your islet, / your filthy isle, and / made all equal with nil' (from *Evagatory*, 1992). His works amount to detailed records of social behaviour and prejudice, often centring on some of the most difficult subjects: *Tom O'Bedlam's Beauties* (1981) concerns mental illness and *C* (1984) is a hundred-part study of cancer. In the tradition of Eliot's *The Waste Land*, Reading's long poems are usually concerned with the worst aspects of the violence and decay of Britain's inner cities, in which filthy streets are stalked by 'pongoid subspecies', alienated masses pursuing a 'pastoral picnic under an ozone hole'. Tom Paulin has christened Reading's vision 'Junk Britain', saying that, in *Ukulele Music* (1985), he 'blasts the national consciousness into tacky fragments and exposes the insane ugliness of British life' (Paulin 1992: 291). A poem which variously focuses on mass unemployment, urban crime, sexual abuse, tabloid culture, future apocalypse, hollow jingoism, naval history, and imperial decline, *Ukulele Music* is an inventive, playful, heteroglossic, multi-voiced analysis of the condition of Britain in the mid-1980s. Its subject is a country that has forgotten 'the Actual' of daily life in its celebration of post-Falklands pride and free-market economics. To his detractors, who feel his work is excessively bleak, Reading replies in *Ukulele Music* that 'Too black and over the top, though, is what the Actual often / happens to be, I'm afraid. He don't *invent* it, you know.' In works like *Stet* (1986), Reading's subsequent poetry, which is often now visually and typographically experimental, has become more extreme and austere: 'You could see, in the estates and the new slum high-rises, Morlocks / sullenly honing rank fangs; telly-taught, butcherous, brute.' Full of scorn for platitudes and cant, Reading's literary-documentary works skilfully transform the underbelly of British life into poetry, and so force readers of poetry to engage with social realities.

Others have tried to transform poetry from within the publishing business. While new feminist imprints such as Virago and the Women's Press have made a huge impact on the gender imbalance in the book industry, new presses have also reoriented the publishing of poetry away from London in the last thirty years – especially Carcanet, now in Manchester, and Bloodaxe, in Newcastle, together with Anvil, Peterloo Poets, Enitharmon, and Seren (Poetry Wales). In the 1970s and 1980s, black presses such as New Beacon Books, Peepal Tree, Dangaroo Press, and Bogle-L'Ouverture also started to make significant inroads into the poetry market. This geographical and cultural shift has been accompanied by changes in the aesthetic production and reception of poetry. Poetry, in the view of one of the editors of Bloodaxe's recent *The New Poetry*, has changed from being an authentic utterance that is difficult, sacred, subversive, moral, national and personal but not political, to an open space in which anything can be written about; though what tends to be written is democratic, left-wing, socially relevant, internationalist but colloquial, humorous but serious, and above all recent (Kennedy 1996: 247–8). Poetry is culturally important again and is, for the moment, about and from the here-and-now.

This shift into the popular poetry, sometimes populist and commercial, of the present is discussed below. However, the reason why this chapter is not the last, but followed by two more, is that in this and the preceding chapter I have generally discussed white, male poets from the British mainland. It is largely they who still dominate the 'poetry business' in the UK and the five editors of the two anthologies I will principally be discussing are all 'English' men. After the war, the Movement poets forged a new poetry on the grounds of regionalism and class, not gender, and the same is largely true of the middle generation that followed with Tony Harrison, Douglas Dunn, and Seamus Heaney. The strong challenges to this hegemony have only come recently and will be discussed in the following two chapters.

Extending the 'imaginative franchise'

The Penguin Book of Contemporary British Poetry was (self-)consciously compiled in the light of Alvarez's *The New Poetry*, with the editors placing their effort as the first 'serious' anthology in the intervening twenty years. Morrison and Motion felt the significant differences between 1962 and 1982 were: an appreciation that Alvarez's belief in a correlation between heavyweight seriousness and high quality was 'simplistic'; the rise of the new Northern Irish poets spearheaded by Heaney; the resurgence of narrative poetry; a concern for metaphor, conceit, and defamiliarisation; and a belief in the imagination less as a well-spring of dark Freudian forces than 'a potential source of tenderness and renewal'. According to their introduction, Morrison and Motion's twenty poets were not confessional insiders, like Larkin or Plath, but storytelling outsiders who had grown up since the war, not with it. To many commentators at the time, the selection of poets by Morrison (a literary editor at the *Observer*) and Motion (Poetry Editor at Chatto and Windus, and then Faber) seemed narrow and the emphasis metropolitan – these were in general white males published by the big presses of the south-east. For the most part the poets were conservative and concerned with private matters – to suit the mood of the me-society after 1979, it appeared that poets since 1966 had been reacting against Alvarez's injunctions, creating instead what Eric

Homberger called a 'severe privatization of meaningful experience' (Spencer 1994: 4). Society, history, and politics (except in Northern Ireland) were overwhelmed by anecdotes of personal experience, even in discussions of class.

Several of the poets will be discussed in the next two chapters but I want here to review the volume as a whole, beginning with its gender bias. Elsewhere, Morrison has said he detects in many of these authors a concern with family and domesticity (in Craig Raine, James Fenton, Seamus Heaney, Tony Harrison, Paul Muldoon, Hugo Williams, and Michael Hofmann). Yet, more specifically, this is exhibited as a fascination with fathers and with masculinity: 'the metrical muscularity of Harrison, the metaphor-hunter gathering of Raine, the hard sophistication of Muldoon, the impersonality of Fenton' (Morrison 1987: 211). The poets, all men, exhibit a common tendency that seems if anything a crisis of masculinity, as embourgeoised sons of farmers (Heaney), mushroom-gatherers (Muldoon), boxers (Raine), and bakers (Harrison) come to terms with their estrangement from their working-class fathers. At no point does Morrison suggest that this preoccupation might have anything to do with the rise of feminism in the 1970s or with challenges to accepted notions of masculinity. As Luke Spencer writes of Harrison, his 'compulsion to find common ground on which he can meet and make peace with the memory of his father speaks of a powerful need for male acceptance and approval' (Spencer 1994: 3). This is less the 'filial art' than men coming to terms with alienation from their fathers, in terms of class and education, in a way that parallels the post-1960s exploration of reconstructed identity in contemporary women's poetry, as discussed in the next chapter.

The Penguin Book of Contemporary British Poetry inevitably caused much controversy on publication because it attempted to sum up the twenty years since Alvarez's collection using only twenty poets. Aside from poets I will discuss in the following two chapters, the volume appeared to be championing only two kinds of writing: narrative and 'Martian' poetry. Narrative poetry I shall discuss in more depth below; the 'Martian School' of Craig Raine and Christopher Reid (also David Sweetman) I will touch on here.

Craig Raine was poetry editor at Faber from 1981 to 1991 but his style of bizarre, if often unconnected metaphors was developed before he became an 'Establishment' figure, in his first two volumes *The Onion, Memory* (1978) and *A Martian Sends A Postcard Home* (1979). The latter volume led James Fenton to discuss Raine and others as a 'Martian School': a group of poets who specialised in imaginative similes, describing everyday objects in original ways that seemed extremely 'alien'. Raine constructed a world in which light switches stare like 'flat-faced barn-owls', light bulbs are 'electric pears', and 'Clothes queue up in the wardrobe' ('An Enquiry into Two Inches of Ivory'). His concentration on metaphor and domestic observation has earned him a reputation as a poet who avoids public and political themes, yet it has been argued that he personalises larger moral issues, as in 'Flying to Belfast, 1977', which compares the apprehensions of a new bride to an outsider's fears about travelling towards possible violence in Ulster (Robinson 1988: 18).

Dubbed another 'Martian' poet, Christopher Reid has rather suffered in the shadow of Raine, by whom he was taught at Oxford and for whom he deputised for a year at Faber. However, Reid is a more controlled, wry, affectionate poet than Raine. His poems show a humorous concern with form also, as the two line stanzas of 'A Whole School of Bourgeois Primitives' imitate the 'lawn in stripes, the cat's pyjamas' of the first line. Taking its theme from the paintings of Henri Rousseau, the poem satirises civilisation's domestication of nature which becomes tame and neat, comical rather than frightening. Reid's poems are also often more connected, as in the ironically named 'Big Ideas with Loose Connections' which uses the lens of the observers' love to turn park activity into a sexual endeavour, ending: 'A wriggling, long-tailed kite leaps like a sperm / at the sun, its blurry ovum.' Though more whimsical, Reid, like Raine, asserts that the essence of poetry is renewed perception: imaginative defamiliarisation.

Drawing on Berkeley's formula that 'to be is to be perceived', Raine constantly emphasises how naturalised and familiar the world is to us. In contrast, the alien in his most famous poem sees people who hide in couples at night 'when all the colours die' and then read about their lives 'with their eyelids shut' ('A Martian Sends A Postcard Home'). Raine is concerned with 'Daily things', including human beings, but strives to make them seem extraordinary by placing them in strange comparisons. 'An Enquiry into Two Inches of Ivory', the small surface Jane Austen said she worked upon, is an exceptional piece because nearly all the comparisons with 'the great indoors' are drawn from wildlife. Raine repeatedly inquires into what he terms 'the museum of ordinary art', and requires the reader also to look upon everyday objects as though they were on special display. However, critics have objected that, especially since Raine's editorship at Faber, unusual metaphor has too often become the definition of poetry, reducing valued writing to issues of perception and alienation – and this is another indication of the accusations levelled at the confining influence of Morrison and Motion. However, in his later work, in *Rich* (1984), and especially the mammoth verse 'novel' *History: The Home Movie* (1994), Raine has moved towards the kind of narrative poetry that Morrison and Motion themselves practise – although it might be countered that the thrust of *History* is to domesticate public events by wrapping the century around Raine's own family tree.

At the time of its publication, *The Penguin Book of Contemporary British Poetry* was objected to by Larkin because the editors, unlike Alvarez, had no position to advocate, no message to propound. More recently, Peter Barry and Robert Hampson write that 'the narrowness of poetic taste evidenced in the anthology's selection of poets and poems clashes with the representative claims implicit in the title' (Barry and Hampson 1993: 4). Morrison and Motion maintain in their introduction that little new happened in poetry in the 1960s and much of the 1970s, but Barry and Hampson point out that this is contradicted by the output of the presses publishing in the 1970s and 1980s, and the contents of two other anthologies: Andrew Crozier and Tim Longville's *A Various Art* and *The New British Poetry* edited by Gillian Allnutt, Fred D'Aguiar, Eric Mottram, and Ken Edwards. Which is to say that much of the invention of the twenty years prior to 1982 was occurring where Morrison and Motion were not looking: in women's poetry, black British writing, and the small presses. However, the Penguin anthology did also emphasise a new vogue for narrative poetry, which was often postmodernist and fantastical, but sometimes political and satirical.

From 1979 onwards, Britain moved decisively away from consensus politics. No longer were nationalisation and the welfare state considered to have been positive changes by both parties. In an *Observer* interview of 1979, Larkin said:

> Oh, I adore Mrs Thatcher. At last politics makes sense to me, which is hasn't done since Stafford Cripps....But I'm afraid I don't think she will succeed in changing people's attitudes. I think it's all gone too far. What will happen to this country I can't imagine.
>
> (Larkin 1983: 52)

Apart from Peter Reading, the poet who has perhaps spoken out most volubly against Thatcher and the spirit of the 1980s is Tony Harrison. Harrison features strongly in the Morrison and Motion collection, and I want to begin by saying something about both him and his short poems, most of which are in any case part of his evolving, tripartite sequence 'The School of Eloquence', before moving on to a discussion of his long narrative poem 'V'.[2]

To begin with, Harrison is acutely aware of class in two respects: first, with regard to his parents – underprivileged working-class northerners who had no voice, no power, almost no representation; second, with regard to himself – an educated poet internationally fêted by a bourgeois intelligentsia and distanced from the culture of his childhood (e.g. see 'Book Ends' and 'Long Distance'). He strives to speak for (not to) a disenfranchised class but is also acutely aware that his education has taken him out of it. Like a similar writer, Richard Hoggart, he is careful to guard 'against two romantic idealizations of the working class: as the earnest Jude the Obscure seeking after knowledge, or as the class-conscious political activist.'[3] By foregrounding education or politics, neither stereotype seemed to Harrison to approach the daily preoccupations of most working people. Yet, he is aware that he is in danger of falling into either category, having been educated at Leeds Grammar School, followed by Leeds University where he studied Classics, and having been deeply concerned with politics throughout his life. However, his work centres more obviously on the working-class culture he feels both to have grown up in and to have moved away from.

Harrison's parents are constant figures in his poetry as he scrutinises the relationship between his upbringing and his present position as a poet. With respect to Harrison's portraits in his ongoing sixteen-line sonnet sequence 'The School of Eloquence', Rosemary Burton writes:

> His parents are well-known to readers of the poems: Harry, the bakery worker, 'worn out on poor pay', saving to buy a ukulele he could not play, standing in the theatre in his one good suit and finding that something about his appearance made theatregoers assume he was there to check their tickets, helpless and pitiable after the loss of his wife; and Florrie, loving, ambitious for her son, unable to understand why he didn't become a teacher, heartbroken when his first poetry book, *The Loiners*, was published, because 'You weren't brought up to write such mucky books.'[4]

Harrison says in 'Book Ends' that what lies between himself and his father is not thirty years, but books and more books. He therefore also takes the language of his working-class background seriously, not least because he was encouraged to feel inferior for it at school: 'Poetry's the speech of Kings. You're one of those / Shakespeare gives the comic bits to: prose!' He elsewhere says of one of his best-known poems:

I'd always thought that my life couldn't be written about. I remember the day I began to change. It's in the poem I called 'Rhubarbarians'. I used to go walking with my father near East Ardsley where the rhubarb fields were; *tusky*, as we called it. He told me that 98% of British rhubarb came from Leeds. And my Dad said, 'Oh I was in a play once, I was; I held a spear in *Julius Caesar* at school.' He said they taught him, as they do in the theatre, to make indescribable crowd noises by saying *'rhubarb, rhubarb, rhubarb'*. So I always had that sense that saying *'rhubarb'* was what my life was about, whereas the central literary life was somewhere else.

(Hoggart 1991: 39)

This ambivalence towards literature and language is evident throughout his writing. For example, 'On Not Being Milton' considers Harrison's relation to poetry and to working-class history. He likens his meditation on his social inheritance to the West Indian Aimé Césaire's pioneering black consciousness essay-poem about negritude, *Notebook of a Return to the Native Land*, which champions an essentialist black identity shared by all those who have been displaced by the African diaspora.[5] Harrison considers his own displaced position as articulate, educated writer alongside the silent, stuttering, or tongue-tied expression of traditional working-class resistance. Its odd opening suggests that the poem has already been written. Self-consciously literary, it compares the Luddites' smashing of knitting frames to the Leeds accent's violence on received English. Harrison's point is that he is not a southern canonical poet like Milton, but representative of all that that culture rejects. The poem's underlying message is that if language, and therefore poetry, is 'owned' then all 'deviant' usages are political; hence the pun on writing/righting. The poem is dedicated to two prominent poet-politicians in FRELIMO, the Marxist ruling party in Mozambique, where Harrison wrote the poem in 1971. Harrison therefore draws parallels between his class's educational empowerment since 1945 (the culmination of Raymond Williams's 'Long Revolution') and the rise of anti- and post-colonial movements over the same period.

Most of Harrison's poems are about division, in terms of class, gender, race, and politics. As he says in 'V', 'These Vs are all the versuses of life / from LEEDS v. DERBY, Black/White / and (as I've known to my cost) man v. wife, / Communist v. Fascist, Left v. Right'. 'V', written during the antipathies and clashes of the 1984 miners' strike, plays and puns on the meanings of its title letter and on the word 'United'. Their common appearance in the fixture 'Leeds United v...' is Harrison's starting-point for analysing rivalries, hostilities and divisions. Consequently, the versus of the title also represents the verses of the poem. As a hand gesture, V stands for 'Up Yours' but also, when reversed, for 'Victory'. While 'United' is the desecrating graffito Harrison finds sprayed on his parents' tombstone, as a single word it can also be read as an expression of loyalty and devotion – of the union Harrison wishes to associate with his parents. The transformation of the word from expressing hate to meaning love suggests the forlorn hope for transformations in personal and public life that Harrison dwells on throughout the poem. As Terry Eagleton says, 'No modern English poet has shown more finely how the sign is a terrain of struggle where opposing accents intersect, how in a class-divided society language is cultural warfare and every nuance a political valuation.'[6] 'V' consciously echoes Gray's 'Elegy in a Country Churchyard' in its discussion of Beeston's cemetery, undercut by coal seams which provide Harrison with a link to the controversies of the miners' strike. Broadcast on Channel 4 in 1987, the poem created a furore in the right-wing press – indeed, because of its use of swear words, 'V' received more tabloid coverage than any other postwar poem.

Other poets associated with the Penguin anthology who work in the narrative mode are James Fenton, and Morrison and Motion themselves (less well-known examples of the long narrative poem, which is rarely favoured by anthologists, are W.S. Graham's 'The Nightfishing' and John Heath-Stubbs's 'Artorius'). Motion, who is also Larkin's biographer (1993), turns Larkin's post-Imperial lament into a personal narrative of loss in his long work *Independence* (1981). Like Larkin's poetry, Motion's considers the public in terms of the personal and, while bringing history closer to the individual through careful examinations of private response, seems to bypass the political implications of events. Blake Morrison's most socio-politically engaged poem is the long vernacular piece, *The Ballad of the Yorkshire Ripper* (1987), about Peter Sutcliffe's murder of thirteen women prior to 1980. The anonymous narrator ranges over issues of masculinity, effeminacy, male violence, identification and influence, bringing to the reader's attention the complicity of a prurient and masculinist society in 'Pete's' atrocities.[7] Overall, the concern with lost empire, observation, nostalgia, and male behaviour in Morrison's and Motion's own narrative work provides the best clue to the kind of poetry they support in the Penguin anthology.

Perhaps the most highly respected poet who works in the narrative mode, and who has written his own serial-killer long poem about the violence underlying rural peace, 'A Staffordshire Murderer', is James

Fenton. Fenton is employed as a foreign correspondent, and has worked in Germany and South-East Asia, but has also been the *Sunday Times* theatre critic, has published his journalism and travel writing as *All the Wrong Places*, has translated opera libretti, and written a considerable body of poetry. Much of his work has been narrative verse and Fenton's choice of this form is partly because of the lyric's comparative inability to deal in any detail with history and society. A proportion of his poems deal with international events and what he calls the 'memory of war', drawing on his own experience as a witness/journalist: 'A German Requiem', 'Tiananmen', or 'Wind'. Fenton's narrative poems often have unreliable narrators, who are frequently children, use irony and intertextuality, and move towards uncertain conclusions which eschew closure. Such poems leave the reader with interpretative problems of time, event, and meaning, as with 'Nest of Vampires'. This is a piece which, in its description of a young boy's alienation from the collapsing monied world of his aristocratic family, appears to allude to Marx's description of capitalists as vampires feeding off the blood of the people.[8] The indirect allusion, heightened by the play on 'nest of vipers', is typical of Fenton,[9] a well-read *bricoleur* who became politicised in the late 1960s, and has since used both his journalism and his poetry to protest at local and world events. His privately produced package from the Philippines, 'The Manila Envelope' (1989), contained a polemical manifesto as well as a series of new poems which dealt directly with the events he had witnessed as a reporter, as in 'The Ballad of the Imam and the Shah'. Fenton's often obscure narratives resemble the modern world in their concentration on confusion, displacement and violence, in their heavy use of surreal game-playing while 'subverting our familiar empirical confidence in reality' (Robinson 1988: 15). This last comment by Alan Robinson seems to sum up the effects we have been looking at in the Penguin anthology which is a collection of poems that 'make strange' not just everyday notions of reality, but class, domesticity, and society. It is for the most part a detached poetry and stands in contrast to the poetry of the later 1980s and 1990s, which leans heavily towards the subjective and the personal, the performance and the confessional.

'Plurality has flourished': *The New Poetry*

In the early 1990s, the latest resurgence of poetry, like that of stand-up comedy in the 1980s, led to its acquisition of the label 'the new rock and roll'. This voguish 'sexy' image is satirised in Ian McMillan's 'Ted Hughes Is Elvis Presley', a poem included in the book which capitalised on poetry's latest rejuvenation, Bloodaxe's *The New Poetry*. Published in 1993, this anthology positioned itself as a review of poetry both alongside and since the Morrison and Motion collection. Consequently, it included no poet from the 1982 anthology and no poet born before 1940, just as Morrison and Motion had eschewed Alvarez's poets and all others of their generation. Organised by age (unlike the Penguin anthology which seems to be ordered in terms of an idiosyncratic mix of 'importance', complementarity, and seniority), its aim is clearly to reflect what the editors see as poetry's current variety. Although, like the Penguin book, less than a third are women, its fifty-five poets range in age (over-50 to 30), present location (Stephen Romer in Tours to John Hartley Williams in Berlin), language (Gaelic to Jamaican Creole), nationality/place of birth (Sujata Bhatt was born in India, educated in the US, and now lives in Germany; George Szirtes comes from Hungary), and publishing career (e.g. Peter Reading's fifteen volumes to Ian Duhig's one). Above all, it is a volume which veers away from the Oxbridge–London axis, arguably completing a shift begun postwar by the provincial Movement poets. It also seems to complete the trajectory of Alvarez's new poetry by illustrating the translated or foreign influences, particularly American, on contemporary British poetry.[10] Yet, the volume cannot cope with the abundance of poetry published at the moment – for example, dozens of important women writers are omitted – and the book overall seems to signal the need to dispense with overarching anthologies that attempt to 'represent' contemporary poetry.

The editors open their introduction by asserting that 'plurality has flourished' and 'every age gets the literature it deserves', which in this case means a new cohesive internationalist poetry of 'accessibility, democracy and responsiveness, humour and seriousness...[and] the beginning of the end of British poetry's tribal divisions and isolation' (Hulse *et al.* 1993: 15–16). The suggestion is that under Thatcherism, poets rallied to mount a defence of class politics, language, feminism, regional identities, and social difference as well as diversity. The editors therefore discuss their poets in terms of the periphery answering back and moving in on the south-east Conservative 'centre' from the margins of class, country, or colour of skin.

According to one of the editors, the shift represented by *The New Poetry* – particularly its youngest poets Glyn Maxwell and Simon Armitage – can be described in terms of rhetoric, scepticism, eclectic intertextuality, popular culture and cliché, drama and self-referentiality, slang, jargon, and vernacular. 'England' itself is contained in the collo-quial, as the local 'bloke' starts to replace the national 'citizen' in

Armitage's and Maxwell's pictures of a dehistoricised and fragmented country (Kennedy 1996: 55–78). Consequently, the range of contemporary poetry seems principally to parallel the diversity and difference of contemporary British society. Anthony Thwaite laments that the editors of *The New Poetry* have no discernible thesis beyond 'plurality has replaced monocentric totemism' (Thwaite 1996: 4); but, according to Logan Spiers, two subjects and two genres have been favoured. Spiers detects, on the one hand, ideological confusion and angst, and on the other hand, post-Imperial, post-industrial fragmentation. The poetic genres promoted are those of flashy verbal arrangements and depressed urban imagery (Spiers 1996: 155). The objection here is that the poetry axis has only shifted from the upper-middle-class, male south-east to the middle-class, male Midlands, and that the poetry favoured is that which resembles the poetry of the three editors. The suburban dissections of Sean O'Brien are seen as examples of 'sour discontent' crowding out 'the really new poetry'. The verbal playfulness of Glyn Maxwell, John Ash, Selima Hill, and Peter Didsbury is seen as little more than whimsy without subject matter – the poetry of an age which is so self-aware, so self-conscious that it archly remarks upon its lack of anything to say, or any language to say it in: 'Language, fat and prone beneath her fountain, / idly dispenses curling parchment notes' (Peter Didsbury, 'Back of the House'). Spiers's preference is for the poetry of Eavan Boland (an Irish poet 'whose work is most likely to define the past decade in poetry'), Tom Leonard, Sujata Bhatt, and the British Caribbean poets who offer a 'more genuine' sense of place and displacement. Interestingly, Spiers's argument amounts to a reaffirmation of several of the qualities rejected by the Morrison and Motion collection: insider's reflections and firsthand experience, conclusions and positions, engagement and commitment. His disliking is for the alien outsiders (as in Michael Hofman's 'Nighthawks', Glyn Maxwell's 'Helen and Heloise', and Geoff Hattersley's 'Slaughterhouse') who observe and observe themselves observing. A celebrated example would be Simon Armitage, whose 'Poem' about an 'average' man, for example, ends with the non-judgemental lines: 'Here's how they rated him when they looked back / sometimes he did this, sometimes he did that.' A still better example of this uncommitted observation is Armitage's signature poem, the cinematic 'Zoom!', which tracks back from an end-terrace house to take in the whole planet. The poem creates a giddying sensation of rapid movement combined with loss of control: 'city, nation, / hemisphere, universe, hammering out in all directions'. Armitage argues that it is 'just words' that can accomplish this feat normally associated with camera tricks. He is reclaiming for the verbal that which over the century has been increasingly claimed by the visual. However, if cinema has taken its main element, narrative, from literature, it has fed back a range of techniques which would not be found in the same way, if at all, in previous centuries: the jump-cut and cross-cut, the tracking shot, focus, and flash forward.

Instead of this penchant for seemingly passive, disengaged 'observation', other anthology editors have placed more emphasis on writers who themselves have investments in the issues they discuss. Yet, the overall effect of many recent interventions is to centre discussion on diversity rather than quality. Poetry is bound up with the realm of aesthetics, even if it is also inseparable from politics, and it is vital to acknowledge the finest writing, according to different kinds of criteria, just as it is important to widen the 'imaginative franchise' beyond the limits suggested by the biases of recent anthologies. It is perhaps canon-defining collections of the kind I have discussed that will either fade away in the face of such variety or proliferate to the point that no particular one assumes, let alone achieves, a hegemonic status.

Conclusion

There are many poets that I have not mentioned from the two anthologies. There are also a considerable number of significant voices left out of the pair, such as, to consider men only, Lee Harwood (one of the closest British writers to the influential American poet, his friend John Ashberry), John Fuller (in many ways a forerunner of Raine and Reid), and John Whitworth (a poet in the comic mode, like Kit Wright or Gavin Ewart). Also, while I have singled out Northern Irish poets in the final chapter, many of the authors considered in other chapters are Welsh or Scottish, such as Dylan Thomas, Douglas Dunn, and Carol Ann Duffy. Scottish poetry in particular is thriving and distinctive at present. Hugh MacDiarmid's renaissance of the 1920s (though not always its 'synthetic Scots' language, Lallans) has had many inheritors: the poetry of George Mackay Brown, Sorley Maclean, Iain Crichton Smith, Robert Garioch, Norman MacCaig, Gael Turnbull, Edwin Morgan, who has influenced Robert Crawford and W.N. Herbert, and, more recently, alongside Jackie Kay, Frank Kuppner, and Kathleen Jamie, the demotic Scots of Tom Leonard and Liz Lochhead. With no Conservative candidates elected to represent Scottish seats at Westminster, Lochhead's apposite 'Bagpipe Muzak, Glasgow, 1990' superbly parodies Glasgow's marketing as European City of Culture and also echoes MacNeice's earlier similarly named poem in its rhythm and in the refrain 'It's all go', but concludes by denouncing a Tory government that Scotland did not elect: 'So – watch out Margaret Thatcher, and tak' tent Neil Kinnock / Or we'll tak' the United Kingdom and brekk it like a bannock.' A threat that seemed partially to come true when Scotland enthusiastically voted for parliamentary devolution in September 1997.

Though without a similar voice to proclaim 'It's all go the Nationalists', Wales has produced many poets who have variously been positioned as Anglophiles or republicans, from Dylan Thomas through David Jones, Vernon Watkins, Alun Lewis, and R.S. Thomas to Tony Curtis, Duncan Bush, and Dannie Abse.[11] Welsh is far more of a living language than the other Celtic languages and there is still a vigorous strain of poets writing in it. Which brings us to the question of 'British' anthologies. In an age where hybridity, plurality, and diaspora are taking over from 'home', 'purity', and 'unity', it is increasingly difficult to talk about 'British' poetry. Steven Connor has noted that amid these cultural cross-currents, transnational tensions, and international writings 'it is now hard to be sure of what "the British novel" may be said to consist' (Connor 1996: 27). The same is true of 'English poetry'. As national allegiances are rivalled by more local or international ones, the coherence of a national poetry has to be questioned: many poets hold two passports, have homes or family connections in more than one country, were born or now live 'elsewhere', travel extensively, and are acutely aware of the globalisation of culture. Language is also important here: to speak of 'English' poetry is increasingly problematic as it elastically stretches to include (or exclude) Creole, Scots, translated Gaelic, transatlantic English, and other kinds of hybridised dialects and languages. It is partly with a view to other possible groupings of literature that the last two chapters of this book consider women's and post-colonial poetry: to signal the fracturing of a national poetry which has been narrowly defined for so long that only with great difficulty can it now encompass that which it names.

8

'MY HISTORY IS NOT YOURS'

Recent anthologies by women

My history is not yours.
Long ago, I set up my pieces
against my father, as you did,
but it was only fun.

(Carol Rumens, 'A Poem for Chessmen')

Introduction

In Chapter 1, I briefly noted that in 1938 Virginia Woolf argued in *Three Guineas* that women were positioned outside a masculine patriotism that had appropriated English identity. More recently, in his broad survey of twentieth-century poetry from Hardy to Hughes, John Lucas concludes that ' "Englishness" turns out to be a largely, or even exclusively, male affair' (Lucas 1986: 8). Jane Dowson also makes the point that unified concepts of nation, as of gender, exclude women (Dowson 1997: 245). That nationality is an issue of gender becomes a common theme in contemporary women's poetry, explored, to take examples from the anthologies considered below, by Carol Rumens in 'A Lawn for the English Family', Eva Salzman in 'The English Earthquake', Maura Dooley in 'Apple Pie in Pizzaland', and Carol Ann Duffy in 'Translating the English, 1989'. The querying of what it means to be English or British is underlaid by the extent to which national identity has always been localised and gendered. Women are explicitly included but implicitly excluded, like 'foreigners' as Anne Rouse puts it in 'England Nil', her sonnet about macho football supporters 'representing their country' on the Continent: 'You've been Englished, but you won't forget it, never.' The over-association between country and male violence is also emphasised in Jo Shapcott's ironically titled 'Motherland', in which the speaker decides a none-too-distant history of nationalism, patriarchy, and colonialism has made national identity a matter of 'rotting pride': 'England. It hurts my lips to shape / the word.'

Similarly, women figure highly in recent literary history but do not appear greatly in men's reviews of poetry – even in Edward Lucie-Smith's 1984 edition of *British Poetry Since 1945* there are only half a dozen women out of a hundred poets. Traditionally, women in poetry have been required to adopt the confining roles of inspirer (comically reversed in Jo Shapcott's 'Muse') and helpmate (satirised in U.A. Fanthorpe's 'The Poet's Companion'), and this stereotyping persists in the biases of some reviews and anthologies of contemporary poetry, despite the changes discussed below. In previous chapters, I have looked at some poets who have achieved recognition despite such stereotyping, like Charlotte Mew, Elizabeth Jennings, and Sylvia Plath, as well as a range of poems by women in World War I and in the 1930s. However, since the 1960s, two particularly significant changes have occurred: first, more women have been published than ever before, and second, more women poets from the past have been recuperated and republished. The reasons for a separate chapter here are manifold and worth enumerating: many women-only anthologies have appeared in the last fifteen years, raising though not resolving the question of a separate tradition or an alternative mode of poetry; the introductions to these anthologies have necessarily engaged with the aims and varieties of 'women's poetry' and can be helpfully compared; and an attention to women's poetry foregrounds a version of contemporary history which is obscured by the preoccupations of the male poets and critics who have until recently dominated the postwar scene.

The debt owed by recent writers to earlier twentieth-century women poets is clear but the importance of addressing issues of literature and gender, though generally agreed upon, has not led to a consensus of opinion. Below, in discussing each of them, I will look at Medbh McGuckian's idea of 'always sexed' poetry alongside Anne Stevenson's belief in an unsexed tradition, and also Wendy Cope's undercutting of the male canon and its self-regard beside Carol Rumens's plea for a 'post-feminist' poetry. Initially, much of these debates can be seen as developing from Sylvia Plath's attempts to write a poetry beyond the male literary tradition. U.A. Fanthorpe's 'The Passing of Alfred', the first poem in Carol Rumens's anthology *Making for the Open: Post-feminist Poetry*, opens with the line 'Our fathers were good at dying. / They did it lingeringly'. The poem implicitly compares the 'worthy' and dignified death in his eighties of Tennyson, his hand on a copy of Shakespeare, with the death of Sylvia Plath, a young mother who, meditating on her own suicide attempts, and shortly before she took her life by gas-poisoning, wrote that dying 'Is an art, like everything else. / I do it exceptionally well' ('Lady Lazarus'). Plath, alongside Elizabeth Bishop and Marianne Moore, is a pervasive influence on women poets since the 1960s, and though she had no established political voice to use in her poetry, she engendered one for others. Stevie Smith is also an important forerunner (for example, the opening to Medbh McGuckian's 'The Weaver-Girl' owes not a little to Smith's famous 'Not Waving but Drowning': 'I was weaving all year, I was closer than you thought'), to the extent that Linda France's anthology, *Sixty Women Poets*, uses Smith's death as its starting point, as though all poetry published after 1971 is indebted to her. Patricia Beer's 'In Memory of Stevie Smith' therefore serves as a similar eulogy of a unique poet alongside Auden's 'In Memory of W.B. Yeats'. Reading them in the light of work by subsequent poets, Neil Corcoran identifies a feminist slant in several of Smith's poems:

> Their notoriously wayward procedures have come to seem almost prototypical of some subsequent feminist deconstructions of mythical archetype and fairytale. Such poems as 'The Frog Prince', 'Voices about the Princess Anemone', 'Die Lorelei', 'Persephone', 'Phedre', 'The Last Turn of the Screw' and 'At School' play their classic narratives into revisionist fables of anti-bourgeois hostility, of the sceptical mistrust of marriage, of painful familial feeling (particularly connected with mother/daughter relationships), of frustrated and transgressive libidinous desire.
>
> (Corcoran 1993: 72)

The influence of Elizabeth Jennings can in many ways be seen in the continuing predominance of the theme of identity, although Sylvia Plath is more often cited as a forerunner. According to Helen Kidd, it is the use of ambiguities and language-experimentation in women's poetry that has led to an important recognition of the way female subject identity is formulated (Kidd 1993: 159). This takes many forms: identity is negotiated through the shifting appellations of a life in Wendy Cope's 'Names', multiplied by deception in Elizabeth Garrett's 'Double', negated in the desire for brutishness in Selima Hill's diseased 'Cow', and simply accepted in Moniza Alvi's 'I Would Like to be a Dot in a Painting by Miró' echoing the 1930s surrealism of David Gascoyne's 'Morning Dissertation' which saw each of us as 'but one dot on the complex diagram'. Such experimentations with subject positions in language to explore the contours of the self have evolved over a number of decades. The first intimations of the women's movement have been said to have arisen in France in the 1950s, when Simone de Beauvoir's *The Second Sex* argued that formations of gender and sexuality have less to do with the realm of nature than that of social construction. Her emphasis on role-playing or, as Judith Butler reformulates it in her book *Gender Trouble* (1990), the performance of gender, has continued to be a striking political preoccupation of women's poetry (for example, Denise Riley, from her first book *Marxism for Infants*, 1977, has consistently taken apart the conventions of poetic identification as well as the subject positions allotted by representations and discourses). This connects well with Jan Montefiore's theory that women's poetry has moved through three stages: traditionalist poetry, ecriture feminine, and representations of self. Basing her argument on Julia Kristeva's essay on 'Women's Time', Montefiore argues that as feminism has shifted from equality politics, through assertions of radical essential difference, to a transcendence of essentialisms within identity politics, women's poetry has similarly moved to a third generation interested in a 'post-feminist synthesis' of the roles of victim and victimiser apparent in each person's identity.[1] In part, this is to say that in its challenge to accepted ideas of femininity/masculinity, much of the best contemporary women's poetry eschews didacticism for a playful exploration of roles and subjectivities performed by both women and men.

Anthologies

The literary world's a drinking club for men
And females aren't invited to that den.
(Fiona Pitt-Kethley, 'The Drinking Club')

The appearance in the 1980s of women-only poetry collections has to be seen partly as a reaction to the exclusions of the male literary scene but mostly as an affirmation of the shifts effected by the women's movement in the 1960s and 1970s, which had already had a significant impact on the publication of women's fiction. Four of the best-known anthologies are *The Bloodaxe Book of Contemporary Women Poets* (1985), *Making for the Open: Post-feminist Poetry* (Chatto, 1985), *The Faber Book of Twentieth-Century Women's Poetry* (1987), and *Sixty Women Poets* (Bloodaxe, 1993). Though the editors of the first three collections have an ambivalent relationship to feminism and consider the best poetry to be gender neutral, they have in their own poetry, as in their anthologies, published poems that demonstrate the changes wrought by the women's movement, and they also owe 'a great deal to the celebratory re-evaluation of women's domestic work offered by some versions of feminism' (Pykett 1997: 263).

Jeni Couzyn's *Bloodaxe Book of Contemporary Women Poets* showcases eleven established British poets. All were born this century and all were over 40 when the collection was published. In her introduction, Couzyn notes the small space devoted to women in the standard poetry anthologies she grew up with, such as John Hayward's *Faber Book of English Verse*, which gives over eleven pages out of nearly 500 to women poets. Couzyn also notes that such token inclusions of women have rarely agreed with each other: the selections are idiosyncratic and appear to depend on the editors' whims. She then characterises the three main stereotypes of the woman poet: 'Mrs Dedication' (e.g. Elizabeth Barrett Browning), 'Miss Eccentric Spinster' (Stevie Smith), and 'Mad Girl' (Sylvia Plath). The first is defined by her relation to a man, the second stigmatised by a lack of relations with men, and the third marginalised by her supposed hysterical perversity. Couzyn then sketches a brief history of the most familiar poets from Aphra Behn through to Emily Dickinson whom she credits with having opened the way for subsequent women. She ends by citing two other pioneering anthologies, Louise Bernikow's *The World Split Open* and Cora Kaplan's *Salt and Bitter and Good*, collections which she evidently feels have blazed a trail for her own anthology and for potential others (Diana Scott's *Bread and Roses: Women's Poetry of the 19th and 20th Centuries*, Virago, 1982, should also be mentioned).

Couzyn's book, with its small number of poets, its introductions to each, its photographs and personal touches, is an attempt to gain a higher profile for women poets and to 'encourage editors to celebrate and circulate the work of many other contemporary women poets I admire'. Its aim appears to be both to set up a canon and to heighten appreciation of women's poetry by devoting a volume to the work of a small group that the dust-jacket labels 'the leading British women poets'. In this it appears quite different from Carol Rumens's international selection of fifty-eight poets in *Making for the Open*, first published in the same year, which includes only two, Anne Stevenson and Fleur Adcock, of Couzyn's eleven choices. Rumens's subtitle, 'Post-feminist Poetry', has continued to receive adverse criticism for its implication that poetry moved further than feminism, or that feminism was in some sense over by 1985. In the preface to her revised edition of 1987, Rumens tried to counter the criticisms and explain that her intention was to include poems which she valued for their 'verbal intensity', irrespective of their political position: 'the greater part of explicitly feminist poetry has foundered on its own political imperatives: it is self-centred, uninterested in language and form, stereotyped in imagery'. Rumens, who has been poetry editor of both *Quarto* and *The Literary Review*, wanted to present an anthology of women poets in terms of the literary tradition and she describes a 'post-feminist aesthetic' which concerns itself with imaginative explorations outside the self (she quotes Charlotte Mew's 'The Farmer's Bride', discussed in Chapter 1, as an example). She sets this against inward contemplation and, for Rumens, the volume's subtitle represents 'a tiny gesture towards the day when gender-tags become obsolescent'. The anthology features only work published since 1964 but Rumens does not feel that post-feminist poetry started then – she uses the term in an ahistorical sense to denote poets who have thought outside the limits of their gender, to 're-imagine one another'. She argues that there is a tradition of poetry open to both sexes, and that poetry can operate as a species of moral corrective to politics: the well-observed anatomising of personal life is a way into commentary on wider society. Rumens's affirmation of a poetry of the imagination outside of politics seems somewhat naive and idealistic, reminiscent of Woolf's championing in the 1920s of Shelley as an androgynous poet in *A Room of One's Own*, but the compilation of an excellent anthology of women's poetry was itself a valuable political gesture in 1985, and it forcefully demonstrated the omissions of the recently published Morrison and Motion collection.

Like *Making for the Open*, Fleur Adcock's *Faber Book of Twentieth-Century Women's Poetry* is compiled in the knowledge of women's exclusion from mainstream anthologies. Adcock considers her grounds for selection not to be reputation or politics but merit (in terms of aesthetics and poetics), and claims to have no particular axe to grind or 'view' to 'propound'. Faber bill the collection as 'destined to establish a canon by which other, more partial anthologies will eventually be judged'. Adcock has little time for tradition, and considers women's poetry only to be different from men's by virtue of the fact that it has been in several ways neglected and undervalued. As a later anthologist, her fear for women's poetry is no longer that it won't be published, read, and studied, but that it may be 'shunted into a ghetto', shelved not under 'poetry' but 'women's studies'. Adcock comments on the quantity of wit in the poems she has included, and this is in fact quite a striking feature. Where Larkin, for example, has an acerbic, somewhat deprecating comment to make on most of life's activities, there is here even a celebration of excretion in the American Maxine Kumin's 'The Excrement Poem'. The choice of poets, from Charlotte Mew to Wendy Cope, inevitably raises further questions about exclusion (few black women poets) and criteria. Adcock chooses poets for their wit and detachment, which opens the same debate as Alvarez did with *The New Poetry* and has to place a question mark over the volume's desire to be canon-forming. ·

Adcock's sixty-four chosen poets were all also over 40 at the time of publication, and this makes a sharp distinction between her volume and Linda France's 1993 *Sixty Women Poets*, in which almost half the poets were born since 1945, Adcock's cut-off date. France uses 1971 as her starting point for selecting poems rather than poets. She begins by mentioning the 'non-exclusive tradition' established by the three anthologies I have already discussed. Continuing the discussion of women's under-representation, France sees her anthology as a 'neccesary sister volume' or corrective to Bloodaxe's *The New Poetry*, published in the same year (with seventeen women and thirty-eight men). France's aesthetic criterion for inclusion is that the poem should 'successfully order thought, emotion and imagination into a form that communicates itself effectively and unequivocally to the reader'. She considers the poems to be characterised by a need to balance opposing forces, a new frankness about the erotic, an honesty that extends the boundaries of conventional English autobiography, amounting to a 'new openness' but not a 'post-feminist dawn'. France argues that the themes of her chosen poems are the perennial ones of poetry: 'love, death, work, family, childhood, art, time, memory, place, nourishment and dreams'. In terms of approach two factors need mentioning: first, the poetry contains more humour and satire than most previous work, in the selections included by, for example, Carol Ann Duffy, Jo Shapcott, Selima Hill, U.A. Fanthorpe, and Anne Rouse; second, there is a strong sense of affirmation in many poems such as Paula Meehan's 'The Man Who Lives in the Clouds' or Elaine Feinstein's 'Getting Older'. Many of the poems also 'answer back' to male perspectives (Carol Ann Duffy's 'Standing Female Nude') or writers (Elma Mitchell's 'Thoughts About Ruskin'). By focusing on a period, after 1971, rather than a 'generation', France manages to select a wide spectrum of poets from an older group including Ruth Pitter (mentioned earlier in the chapter on the 1930s) and Elizabeth Jennings (discussed in connection with the Movement), who are placed alongside the best new writers such as Jo Shapcott and Jackie Kay.

Sex, the family, and gender[2]

The postwar period saw significant changes in almost every area of sexual practice and representation: advice on contraception (family planning), tolerance of homosexuality, and public debate of sexual matters all increased. In the 1960s sex manuals, pornography, and even sex education were more widely available and more graphic. Divorce increased and the emphasis on virginity at marriage, especially for women, decreased (see Fiona Pitt-Kethley's 'Losing Your Virginity' in *Private Parts*: 'Most girls are technically deflowered / quite young, by tampons or a sudden sneeze'). Female sexuality became the subject of fierce debate after the release of Kinsey's second report, *Sexual Behaviour in the Human Female* (1953), and then again at the height of the liberation movement with the publication of Masters and Johnson's *Human Sexual Response* (1966). Women's experience of sex was no longer portrayed solely in terms of men's; female masturbation was seen as healthy; and the sexual importance of the clitoris was emphasised (cf. Carol Rumens's poem about a 1960s housewife, 'Houses by Day': 'Adjusted now, I have learned my role is to wait /.../ and light up at a flick of my clitoris'). Sex was seen less in terms of marriage, procreation, and morality, and more in terms of pleasure and diversity – at the same time, for Herbert Marcuse in his influential *Eros and Civilization* (1955), private desire was the key to counter-cultural revolt. While the political right saw the late 1950s and the 1960s as a descent into moral turpitude, to most campaigners reforms were minimal and sexual control was simply deflected from monolithic laws to more diverse forms of surveillance and containment. From the Wolfenden Committee's report on prostitution and homosexuality (1959) through the 1960s, reforms were aimed at refining the means of policing sex and health as well as bolstering the institution of the family.[3] However, in the dozen years before the Thatcher government came to power, there were still more key reforms, such as: the Abortion Act, legalising termination of pregnancy, and the Sexual Offences Act, decriminalising homosexuality, both in 1967; the Divorce Reform Act in 1969, making divorce available through mutual consent; and the Sex Discrimination Act banning employment and education discrimination against women in 1975. But, in the name of 'the family', the Conservative rule from 1979 to 1997 saw several retrograde steps, such as Clause 28, outlawing positive gay and lesbian images in schools in 1987, and the Child Support Agency in 1993, a government-authorised body pursuing child maintenance. The only outstanding progressive development was the Church of England Synod's vote for female ordination in 1994. From another perspective, however, women have seized higher political profiles since the 1960s. For example, while 1983 was the year that Margaret Thatcher was first re-elected, at the other end of the political process it was also the year in which the anti-nuclear women protesters at Greenham Common resisted eviction attempts and the year before the Women Against Pit Closures organisation emerged.

The period since the 1960s has in some ways been seen as a series of crises for the institution of the family. A higher number of couples do not have children (20 per cent), and those that do have them generally opt for smaller families. Childbearing is frequently postponed until the late twenties or early thirties and the often-quoted mean 'average' 2.4 children British family has now dwindled to 1.8, a trend which reflects the overall decline in the proportion of 'conventional' families. Only 24 per cent of contemporary British households now fall into the 'two adults plus dependent children' nuclear model, and this figure includes not only married couples but the increasing number of long-term cohabitees. At present, more than a third of marriages finish in divorce, making British rates the highest in Europe, and the number of lone parent families (90 per cent of which are headed by women) has risen dramatically to 20 per cent of all family units. However, the most important factor in the transformation of gender identities has been the irreversible trend towards female participation in the labour force: women's participation in paid employment rose dramatically in the late 1950s and has continued to increase in every decade since. Shifts in patterns of employment, particularly the expansion of secretarial, administrative, and clerical occupations in the 1960s and 1970s, and the rapid growth of the service sector in the 1980s, opened up new areas of female employment. Because this has been coupled with the demise of heavy industry, and a subsequent drop in the male dominated areas of unskilled manual work, the balance has tipped towards an almost evenly divided male and female labour force for the first time ever (however, despite hard-won legislation such as the Equal Pay Act, 1970, women still earn just under 80 per cent of men's pay). Moreover, there is a marked difference in the composition of the female labour force: in the first half of the century the majority of working women were either young and single or middle-aged with grown children, whereas the greatest increase in the 1970s and 1980s has been amongst those with partners and dependants.

The early years of the AIDS crisis, after Britain's first official AIDS-related death in 1982, that of Terrence Higgins, produced a wave of anti-gay hysteria, exacerbated by the popular press. Following the 1967

Sexual Offences Act's decriminalisation of homosexual acts in England (extended to Northern Ireland in 1979 and Scotland in 1980), a vibrant gay and lesbian subculture flourished in urban areas of England in the late 1970s and 1980s. A backlash came in the form of the Local Government Bill of 1987 inserting the notorious Clause 28, an amendment outlawing the presentation of 'positive' gay images by local authorities and demanding that traditional family values be promoted in British schools.

In the four anthologies I discussed above, many authors treat versions of identity in relation to gender differences, parturition and sexuality, while widening previous male limits for suitable subject matter in poetry. In France's collection, for example, Elizabeth Bartlett's poem 'Stretch Marks' compares poetry and birth, Sujata Bhatt's 'White Asparagus' explores the carnal desire of a pregnant woman, Jean Earle's 'Menopause' meditates on lost pregnancies, Rita Ann Higgins's 'The Did-You-Come-Yets of the Western World' dwells on male responses to female sexuality, Sylvia Kantaris's 'Toy Boy' satirises the idea of younger lovers as playthings, and Helen Dunmore's 'Safe Period' considers the occasions and non-occasions of sex. Another poet concerned with reappropriating women's experience from confining gender roles is Penelope Shuttle, more famous as a novelist. She writes poems of motherhood, pregnancy, and love, and has written a meditation on menstruation, 'Fosse', which takes as its starting point an epigraph from the poet Peter Porter: '...and from the menstrual ditch / The future runs...' (a fosse is a ditch or moat dug as a fortification). Shuttle has also written a study of menstruation, *The Wise Wound*, with her partner the poet Peter Redgrove. Mainstream poems about same-sex desire are now also common (e.g. Carol Rumens's 'Stealing the Genre' and Jackie Kay's 'Close Shave' are two excellent examples, the first about women, the second about men). The importance of such examples is to underscore the breadth and variety of recent poetry by women. As I will discuss below, in terms of poetry as well as sex – 'refusing late drinks / or a possessive caress' – there is in many senses a shared expedition to get, in the title of Marion Lomax's poem, 'Beyond Men', to a language and a desire that is not 'man-made'.

Two exemplary poets who explore gender in terms of difference and desire are Jo Shapcott and Selima Hill. Shapcott's 'Robert and Elizabeth' poems, in her first collection *Electroplating the Baby* (1988), offer alternative, gendered views of language and thought. Explorations of difference and possible creative union, the poems suggest two personalities, the one interested in terminology and denotation, the other in relations and patterns; they sit 'each listening to interpret the faint sounds / of the other's scouring on the paper' ('Fun with Robert and Elizabeth'). In 'Robert Watches Elizabeth Knitting', the composite man (Robert Browning, Robert Lowell, and Jonathan Swift are all suggested) wonders why he has a compulsion to label and name the woman (Elizabeth Barrett, Elizabeth Hardwick, or Esther Vanhomrigh), 'to call her a whole list of things / other than what she is?'. Watching Elizabeth rhythmically knit her wool, or weave her text, Robert realises an alternative reality in which 'meaning is all in the gaps': 'all sensuality and wholeness, with the independent life of every stitch'. The sequence ends with a hopeful poem suggesting that after the reciprocal observation in the preceding poems, there is the possibility of mutuality when 'Robert and Elizabeth Sit Down Again'. Published a year later, Selima Hill's *The Accumulation of Small Acts of Kindness* (1989) presents the diaries of a young schizophrenic woman before, during, and after her stay in hospital, 'menstruating on a stranger's blankets'. The surreal, disjointed writing seems to suggest the 'woman's language' of French feminist theory – bringing out the feminine speech that is the 'Other' of social language.[4] Creating its own non-linear, sensuous, semiotic narrative, the book begins with the question 'Whatever's the point of writing it all in code?' and then weaves four discourses seamlessly together: the woman's writing, imaginary voices, remembered words, and direct speech. Before the last part, each of the sections is titled with a plural masculine (though not always male) noun: 'Boys', 'Sons', 'Doctors', 'Masters', 'Strangers', and 'Monks'. The authoritarian language of these figures is contrasted with the woman's thoughts, which are structured in terms of desire, the flows of the body, and the unconscious: 'Feel between my legs two lips like lollies, / or like a blood-hound on the verge of tears.' The contrast of women's libidinal experience with the strictures of social authorities seems in many ways to exploit successfully the possibility of an alternative to phallocentric language through the linkage of the logic of desire with the formal experimentation of poetry.

Picking up from Plath

The strained, psychological subject matter of Hill's book recalls Sylvia Plath's semi-autobiographical 1963 novel, *The Bell Jar*, about the search for different types of female identity, leading to nervous breakdown. The possibility of an inheritance from Plath is by no means uncommon, and I'd like now to discuss briefly three particular writers who all feature in the anthologies discussed above as well as in the

Penguin Book of Contemporary British Poetry, and who can be seen, from one perspective, as indebted to Plath's poetry. Fleur Adcock, who said the 1980s was 'our decade' (Logan 1991: 235), writes at the start of her introduction to the *Faber Book of Twentieth-Century Women's Poetry* (1987) that 'What is different about poetry by women...is not its nature but the fact that until recently it had been undervalued and to some extent neglected.' All the same, her poetry is very much ambivalent towards men and her early work concerns her response to male predatory seduction. Adcock also plays with gender roles – often, she says, this simply creates poetry about her own experience and relationships. In 'The Ex-queen Among the Astronomers', one of her best-known poems, she seems to complicate the kind of sexual relations Plath discussed in poems such as 'The Applicant'. Alan Robinson writes that,

> the ex-queen represents all women, socialised into conformity with male erotic expectations and then abandoned when her novelty has been outgrown. The male astronomers are satirised as distractedly self-important rationalists, whose scientific pursuit of knowledge is, it is suggested, a quest for materialistic possession; their exploitative desire to reduce the universe to ordered control is the counterpart to their patriarchal oppression of women. Both are objectified sadistically by the males' scopophilic drive, manifest in their obsessional voyeurism: 'They serve revolving saucer eyes', 'they wait upon / huge lenses', 'they carry pocket telescopes / to spy through', 'Spectra possess their eyes'. To vie for attention the ex-queen (queen as well as ephemeral sexual icon) must degrade herself to a chattel rewarded by decorative bangles that are less a mark of affection than a brand of ownership, going through the excitational motions of foreplay in an automatism whose matter-of-fact enumeration records her revulsion: 'she sucks at earlobe, penis, tongue / mouthing the tubes of flesh'.
>
> (Robinson 1988: 189)

Seeing the sexual revolution as in many ways a gain made for men while women remain reified and powerless, Adcock's less surreal poems hint at a separatist politics. In a comic poem in couplets, 'Smokers for Celibacy', she concludes 'sex is a drag. / Just give us a fag.' In another short piece, 'Against Coupling', she suggests that the solution to male appropriation and oppression is self-sufficiency or, in sexual terms, masturbation. Though she feels that she must/will respond to her body's physical desire, in the sexual ritual the woman appears both objectified and stripped of identity: 'Just to avoid those eyes would help.' The poem works against a 1960s' view of promiscuity and sexual licence by suggesting that copulation is a biological urge overlaid by a loss of self-dignity, which is a preoccupation found in Plath's poetry on marriage, sexuality, and motherhood. Many of Adcock's poems deal with displacement (she herself has moved back and forth between Britain and New Zealand) and lack what Ian Gregson calls 'any reliable sense of ontological stability' (Gregson 1996: 89). The divisions of identity in her poems concern the self, sexual relations, nationality, and writing poetry – but she has come to see this primarily in terms of gender, asking on one occasion 'Are women natural outsiders?' (Couzyn 1985: 202).

Anne Stevenson has considered herself a poet in the same 'plight' as Sylvia Plath: married (then divorced) with small children. Stevenson, whose biography of Plath, *Bitter Fame*, was published in 1989, is also a poet caught between commitments to her writing and her family. Her ideas about poetry have a lot in common with those of Carol Rumens and she praises Rumens for her individual humanity, her seriousness, and for not adhering to any 'dogma' such as feminism or socialism (Montefiore 1993: 34). A sensitive poem of discontent such as 'The Marriage' (included in isolation in the Penguin anthology, but one of a sequence of poems in Stevenson's *Travelling Behind Glass*, 1974) seems directly indebted to Plath, and Stevenson compares herself with Plath before saying of her collection of epistolary poems, *Correspondences* (1974),

All the anger, the confusion, the misery, and the doubt I experienced during the fifties and sixties went into it, and because they were a woman's angers and miseries, they exposed part of the general consciousness of the age – a part that in the past had been suppressed.

(Stevenson 1979: 175)

Correspondences is

a fragmentary history of a bourgeois New England family called the Chandlers, told through imaginary letters, diaries and poems between 1828 and 1968. The story focuses mainly on women, particularly the constraints they endure and the limited options they can choose.

(Montefiore 1993: 34)

It is in part based loosely on Stevenson's family, and on her own experience in an early unhappy marriage. It chronicles the social and
economic restrictions placed on several generations of women in one
family steeped in a Puritan ideology of self-repression. The family are
shown as mutually supportive but subjugated by a patriarchal rule that
is internalised in both males and females. Stevenson herself writes:

> The central character in *Correspondences* is a woman like my
> mother – liberal, generous, self-sacrificing, devoted to good
> causes and prone to idealising her family. I called her Ruth after
> Ruth in the Bible.... Ruth sacrifices a lover to devote herself to
> her kindly but unexciting husband.... *Correspondences* is about
> more than women's predicament in American history. It was
> intended to be a study of puritan values in New England – of
> their strengths, their weaknesses, their corruption by ambition
> and greed, and their final overthrow in the world of Vietnam
> and Watergate.... Ruth...tries to follow in her mother's foot-
> steps, but falls in love with an English novelist – a plummy,
> selfish fellow whose pseudo-sophistication impresses her. She
> lives a secret, divided life with her husband until she dies of
> cancer, publicly virtuous but privately horrified and under-
> mined by a devouring sense of guilt. In a letter to her lover in
> 1945, she writes of this guilt...
>
> (Stevenson 1979: 169–72)

With referemce to the liberation movement of the 1960s, the sequence
of poems deals with a face-off between women's desire for economic
independence and their interdependence with men in families. It
documents 'the surely incurable pain of / living misunderstood among
many who love you' ('A Love Letter: Ruth Arbeiter to Major Paul
Maxwell'). Stevenson goes on to say in words that echo Woolf's theory
of androgyny:

> I am not convinced that women need a specifically female
> language to describe female experience. The question of
> language is in any case an extremely thorny one. For even if
> we agree that women have a less aggressive, more instinctive,
> more 'creative' nature than men (and I'm not sure that's true)
> language is difficult to divide into sexes. A good writer's
> imagination should be bisexual or trans-sexual.
>
> (Stevenson 1979: 174)

Stevenson seems to affirm a tradition of poetry over women's experience or female culture; a stance about which Jan Montefiore writes: 'there is an obvious irony apparent in a woman poet's affirmation of a tradition to which most women's poetry never officially belongs' (Montefiore 1993: 38). Also, despite her assertions to the contrary, much of Stevenson's work appears very aware of the restrictions placed upon women, female poets in particular, and also emphasises the differences in sexed experience if not the differences in poetry by men and women.

My third example is Medbh McGuckian, who was only born in 1950, shortly before Stevenson began her career as a poet. In some ways, McGuckian also seems a descendant of Plath because they share concerns with logocentrism, patriarchy, relationships, and parturition. Thomas Docherty observes how McGuckian's language, grammar and syntax have all been scoured for their interrogation of masculinism. He relates this to Luce Irigaray's work in a way that also illuminates Adcock's 'Against Coupling' and 'The Ex-queen Among the Astronomers':

> Irigaray, especially in *Speculum* and in *This sex which is not one*, has proposed that the entire history of Western thinking has been inescapably masculinist for the primary reason of its prioritisation of the specular gaze and of the sense of vision. If we replace this with tactility, she suggests, we might be able to counter the inevitability of masculinist thinking.
>
> (Docherty 1992: 196)

Docherty and also Patricia Boyle Haberstroh suggest that many of McGuckian's poems (e.g. 'Tulips' – also the name of one of Plath's most famous poems) express this preference for touch over sight (Haberstroh 1996: 125). Her exceptional syntax, which requires careful and repeated reading, commonly tackles unexceptional and familiar subjects such as horticulture, meteorology, and the female domestic sphere. She has a preference for the definite article and over half of the poems in her first collection *The Flower Master* (1982) have titles which begin 'The'. They are frequently poems 'About nature, greenery, insects, and of course, / The sun' ('The Sofa'). Changes in the seasons and the weather stand as parallels to alterations in human and particularly female identity. Solitary occupations, such as weaving, letter-writing or lace-making, encompass lives, and homes shape personalities. One of her best poems plays with the parallels between the flight of birds, house-movers, and personalities-in-transition: ' "You wouldn't believe all this house has cost me – / In body language terms, it has turned me upside down"' ('The Flitting'). Neil Corcoran writes:

> The method of a McGuckian poem is evolved to create a space in which some subjects (marriage, pregnancy, maternity) may be articulated with a new intimacy, and in which others (masturbation, menstruation, bisexuality) may, breaching taboos, be articulated exceptionally. The poem 'Slips' makes the method continuous with that slippage of language associated by Freud with subconscious revelation, slips of the tongue and slips of the pen. Including, like much of her work, an imagery of apples (which inevitably drags along in its wake Genesis-motifs of Eve, temptation, and fall), and references to a matrilineal line of grandmother and mother, the poem ends by offering an interlocutor the poem's own episodes or anecdotes as a series of duplicities.
>
> (Corcoran 1993: 223)

The poems are deeply personal, often forging a connection between an object, event, or occupation and the pervasive 'I' that seems to root nearly all McGuckian's work in a shared consciousness. Her poems are also steeped in an 'always / Sexed' discourse ('Prie-Dieu'), which sees gender as a kind of social clothing; in 'From the Dressing-Room' she considers the arbitrary allocation of a sexed experience and remarks that 'Left to itself, they say, every foetus / Would turn female.' Like many of the women discussed in this chapter, McGuckian's prime interest is in the shifts and slides of self as process: the fabrication, invention, arbitrary selection, and manipulation of identity. This emphasis on identity formation is very strong in one of her most-praised poems, 'The Seed-Picture', in which her narrator constructs a portrait of a woman in a sampler, 'Bonding all the seeds in one continuous skin'. The poem indirectly explores various resonances the seeds have in their arranger's life, to do with children, sex, new growth, changing home, and taking root. From the arbitrary patterns that the seeds make, the arranger selects different shapes and colours to build a picture which concludes with a single pearl barley which 'makes women / Feel their age, and sigh for liberation'.

Conclusion

Women's poetry since the 1980s has dealt more readily with everyday female experience. Marriage, the body, and childbirth take their place

alongside food, work, leisure, consumerism, fashion, the family, social-
ising, and sex. Identity features as a site of self-interrogation but also in
the frequent examinations of the roles of mother, daughter, wife, lover,
sister, grandmother, friend, and poet. The issue which often seems to
be underdiscussed is class, as the majority of the women represented in
the anthologies come from similar social backgrounds, and most
attended university. Otherwise, there is a richness of subject matter
which is reflected in a diversity of styles.

A significant trend, however, though it does not quite form the
dominant mode of the anthologies discussed in this chapter, has been
an increased use of humour. Wendy Cope and Carol Ann Duffy are
two poets who have established reputations since the Morrison and
Motion book (of the four women-only collections discussed above they
only feature together in the France anthology). Both excel at comic
writing and their barbs are usually aimed at modern living and at relationships with men. Cope is the more obviously satirical of the two,
and she foregrounds the male literary tradition in her work, only to
subvert both masculinism and the varieties of chauvinism that suffuse
and surround men's poetry. Both poets offer critiques of gender relationships while dwelling on the difficulty and deceptions of
contemporary relationships, but Duffy, in 'Valentine' and 'Adultery' for
example, writes complex, multi-layered poems of love and hate
without humour or pathos. Duffy is the more politically engaged poet,
and Alan Robinson concludes that she

> writes without affectation on the uncomfortable social issues
> in Britain in the 1980s: racial tension, child neglect, youth
> anomie and unemployment, moral callousness and drug addic-
> tion. Some of her finest poems adopt feminist perspectives on
> sexual relationships, often employing a speciously comic exag-
> geration that carries a barbed contempt.
>
> (Robinson 1988: 196)

From her *Selected Poems*, pieces such as 'Education for Leisure' and
'Psychopath' enter the minds of violent, self-aggrandising men who
consider the street a place in which they can assert their dominance.
Duffy attempts a ventriloquism in these poems that, in a critique of
1980s social values, mix a sense of purposeless lives with callous arro-
gance and extreme self-regard.

Duffy is also one of the few white poets who, in looking beyond
their own experience, consider the position of ethnic minorities (see
'Girl Talking', 'Comprehensive', 'Foreign', and 'Originally' in *Selected*

Poems). Many of her poems are also written from the standpoint of outsiders, and there is a double-voiced quality about much of her work. Repeatedly, she seeks to give two perspectives at once: explicitly that of the speaker and implicitly that of the poet. In this way the poems often seem in dialogue with themselves, and an awareness of identity and alterity runs through her poems, as in 'The Dolphins': 'The other has my shape. The other's movement / forms my thoughts'.[5] She also analyses the reinvented role of the poet in modern life – on the one hand she describes herself giving a reading to children before a teacher who wants her to 'Convince us there's something we don't know' in 'Head of English'; and on the other she imagines a tabloid headline writer considering himself a modern wordsmith in 'Poet for Our Times', where politics is not reduced to but indistinguishable from alliterative sound-bites.[6] The poet is seen as exotic and gifted in Duffy's poems (she is described as 'a real live poet' in 'Head of English'; the headline writer says he has 'a special talent'), but her overall point is that while language is devalued, poetry is only superficially valued for didactic and commercial reasons.

As often as they turn to literature for their intertexts, Duffy's poems turn to pop music ('$', 'Psychopath', 'The Captain of the 1964 *Top of the Form* Team') and art ('Oppenheim's Cup and Saucer', 'The Virgin Punishing the Infant'). The title poem of her first book, *Standing Female Nude*, uses the relationship between painter and model to examine male voyeurism and the continuing commodification of women's bodies. In a common gesture of contemporary women's poetry,

> Duffy reminds us that icons of female sexuality are not transparently natural, created disinterestedly as if by divine fiat, but instead are social constructs that arise from the complex intersection of economic forces whose formative influence is deceptively absent from the finished work.
>
> (Robinson 1988: 198)

In terms of her view of society more generally, Duffy is particularly astute when she is revealing the ways in which politically motivated ideals – of family life, marriage, sexuality, femininity, community – are naturalised. For example, the punningly titled 'Model Village' sets up a contradictory dialogue between an adult's description to a child of village life, from the farmer to the vicar, and the interjected, dark thoughts of each of the disturbed characters who appear in the one-dimensional story. Her division between an adult world of deception and violence, and a sanitised picture of communal life delivered to children, complements a more general tendency in her work to avoid sentimentality and to portray British society in contemporary rather than idealised, nostalgic versions.

Cope is also a poet who contrasts an adult reality with the version of it offered to children in elementary books. Her poem 'Reading Scheme', like Duffy's 'Model Village', uses the language of 'grown-up' explanations of life to children, in this case in a *Janet and John* book, to tell a clichéd adult story: the standard trio of girl, boy, and dog, are contrasted with the adult threesome: mummy, daddy, and the milkman. A story of petty infidelity is conveyed in double-coded children's language as 'fun': 'Go Peter! Go Jane! Come, milkman, come! / The milkman likes Mummy. Mummy likes them all.' Cope is a parodist who nearly always chooses male poets for her models. In this she writes back to a tradition which would have excluded her and mocks the high-principled aridity and studied gravity of that tradition. Cope is constantly undercutting the male literary canon and she has written poems on or to Wordsworth, A.E. Housman, Hilaire Belloc, and Kingsley Amis. 'So Much Depends' is a homage to William Carlos Williams' 'The Red Wheelbarrow', a poem which, by aesthetic arrangement, concentrates importance in the seemingly ordinary and trivial. Cope, here as elsewhere, invokes the weighty gravitas of a poetic intertext in order to subvert male pretension, solemnity, and competitiveness. Her frequent character, 'Mr. Strugnell', though no doubt a composite figure ('Strugnell in Liverpool' is dedicated to all the 'great men who have influenced my writing'), seems at first to owe a great deal to Philip Larkin and particularly to his poem 'Mr. Bleaney'. Strugnell is what Cope calls a 'Tump', a 'typically useless male poet' and her examples of his imitative poems have the form or style of, for example, Ted Hughes ('God and the Jolly Bored Bog-Mouse'), Edward Fitzgerald ('*From* Strugnell's *Rubáiyát*'), Ezra Pound ('Strugnell's Haiku'), and even Shakespeare (one of Strugnell's sonnets begins 'Let me not to the marriage of true swine / Admit impediments'). Using her own voice, Cope mocks the seriousness, literally the 'dryness', of Eliot's poem, in her 'Waste Land Limericks'. Yet, there is a serious side to her choice of poem: *The Waste Land* has been discussed by Maud Ellmann in terms of its patriarchal literary tradition, its invocation of a male reader, and its fascination with male lust. She argues that throughout the poem, the way that the female is included in the male suggests an Adam-and-Eve acceptance of female supplementarity, and Eliot's composite figure Tiresias is less a union of both sexes than an 'old man with wrinkled dugs'. Maud Ellmann sees the poem as largely misogynistic (in its portrayal of the women characters such as the society Lady and Lil in 'A Game of Chess') but also as fascinated by the femininity it constantly denigrates (Ellmann 1987: 91–113). For her part, Cope writes with both a love and a loathing for Eliot's poem, whose invocation and celebration of a male literary tradition and of abstruse spiritual and philosophical codes seems at once authoritative and remarkably self-satisfied.

While her 'Waste Land Limericks' flippantly distil the bleak message of Eliot's poem into the five-line form of Edward Lear's nursery rhymes, Cope's 'My Lover' is a homage cum parody of the famous lines from Christopher Smart's eighteenth-century poem *Jubilate Agno* which begin 'For I will consider my cat Jeoffry' (itself modelled on the psalms). Cope uses humour to defuse poems which stereotype male behaviour in terms of large but fragile self-opinions ('Men and Their Boring Arguments', 'Faint Praise'). She also uses her humour to deflate costly psychiatrists, voguish environmentalists, and opportunist publishers; on each occasion her target is the temporarily fashionable or the conceited and pompous. Her wry, sardonic poems about relationships and affairs ('Advice to a Young Woman' or 'Two Cures for Love') helped to make her perhaps the most popular poet of the 1980s and there are signs of her influence on the most recent work by younger poets (e.g. Simon Armitage's 'Very Simply Topping Up the Brake Fluid', which concludes *The New Poetry*).

Duffy and Cope are examples of mainstream writers who are expanding the range of contemporary poetry and reintroducing a level of popularity by combining serious subjects with humorous reflection. Like many of the other poets discussed in this chapter, their work approaches the social level through personal experience or observation, shifting and reversing sexual as well as poetical stereotypes. The 'anti- and post-colonial poets' examined in the next chapter are in some ways similar but their poetry often dwells on collective action and social legislation, showing less often that the personal is political than that the political is also personal.

9

ANTI- AND POST-
COLONIAL WRITING
Northern Irish and black British poets

Englishness, for a poet, is almost a taboo subject. Britishness is
altogether out. Whereas an American poet may speak to, or
on behalf of, his [sic] nation, this is hard for an English poet,
now that it is not clear what his nation is.

(Fenton 1990: 18)

Introduction

This chapter is concerned with identity, or, more specifically, with fractured, heterogeneous, and hybrid identities. As a final chapter, it aims
to highlight some of the most recent examples of the abiding concern
with national as well as personal identity that has run through this
book since discussion of the rallying-cries of Austin and Newbolt. I
intend to touch upon the separations and cross-overs between several
different ethnicities: British, Irish, Northern Irish, African, Indian,
Caribbean and black British.[1] As such, the importance and consequence of English imperialism is the chapter's premise, and the anti- or
post-colonial positions adopted by Northern Irish and black British
poets will be of cardinal interest. Considering the last chapter,
however, it is worth my first mentioning that although Northern Irish
poets have been well represented and repeatedly foregrounded in
anthologies since *The Penguin Book of Contemporary British Poetry*, only
one woman has come to prominence: Medbh McGuckian. The South
has produced many lauded women poets, especially Eavan Boland, but
mainstream poetry in the North remains a masculinised territory (see
Long 1997). By contrast, one of the very few anthologies to signal its
representation of black and white poets is a 1980s collection of
women's poetry: Illona Linthwaite's *Ain't I a Woman! Poems by Black
and White Women* (Virago, 1987). It would therefore be as wrong to

180

over- as to underestimate the shift in poetry away from a white, male English hegemony, despite the new voices and reorientations of the last twenty years.

Northern Ireland: colonialism and nationalism

when all of England to an Irish child
was nothing more than what you'd lost and how
(Eavan Boland, 'An Irish Childhood in England: 1951')

Seamus Deane has argued that if the Irish could throw off the notion of what it means to be 'essentially Irish', then a 'genuine independence' would follow: 'The idea of what is British continues to govern the idea of what is Irish. Both should be allowed to lapse back into the arms of the nineteenth century in which they were cradled' (Deane 1984: 90). Deane here does not argue against forging an identity through an anti-colonial stance, but against its continuance in a post-colonial country where such restrictive notions of self-constitution are no longer libera-tory but repressive, amounting to what Luke Gibbons calls the 'backward look of nationalism' (Gibbons 1991: 561).

The polarisation of Irish and British identities has taken many forms. Britain has often been characterised by its Protestantism and so the strength of Irish Catholicism has been read as reactive. Similarly, the opposite positions of rural, agricultural island, and urban, industrial country are also antithetically constructed. Consequently, Declan Kiberd believes that the Irish and British have created colonial reflections of each other which he describes as 'Anglo-Irish attitudes'. He also argues that because of colonialism the Irish cannot be said any more to live in a country of their own making and that 'the notion "Ireland" is largely a fiction created by the rulers of England in response to specific needs at a precise moment in British history' (Kiberd 1985: 83). He refers to the supe-rior position automatically adopted by the colonisers, which is so strong that the colonised are forced into fabricating and averring a rival and positive self-image to combat the range of subordinate positions thrust on them.

The relation of language, and therefore poetry, to identity in the colonial context is allied to the wider question of national culture, its existence, practices, and unificatory potential – both before and after independence. The members of the Field Day Theatre Company, whose directors have included Seamus Heaney, Tom Paulin, and the dramatist Brian Friel, have set themselves the project, through poetry, drama, essays, and anthologies, of contributing 'to the solution of the present crisis by producing analyses of the established opinions, myths and stereotypes which had become both a symptom and a cause of the current situation' (Field Day 1985: vii). Nationalism produces many of those established myths of identity and culture as it 'subverts *and* reproduces imperialism', in Deane's phrase (Deane 1995: 355). In his introduction to a Field Day collection of essays from 1990, Deane argues that: 'Irish nationalism is, in its foundational moments, a derivative of its British counterpart.... The collusion of Irish with British nationalism has produced contrasting stereotypes whose most destructive effect has been the laying of the cultural basis for religious sectarianism' (Deane 1990: 7–8). It is therefore not surprising that Northern Irish poetry, in particular, shows an awareness of such divisions; the pressures of a country which veers between British and Irish, Catholic and Protestant, loyalist and republican, are treated imaginatively and often allegorically, repeatedly raising questions of identity, cultural miscegenation, and history. As is pointed out in the introduction to *The Penguin Book of Contemporary Irish Poetry* (Fallon and Mahon 1990), while there was never really a Northern poetry 'School', the first generation of widely recognised Northern Irish poets, including Seamus Heaney, Derek Mahon, and Michael Longley did gather together at Queen's University in the early 1960s as the Belfast 'Group' and 'appeared more or less simultaneously and coincidentally with the present "Troubles"' (Fallon and Mahon 1990: xx). Neil Corcoran goes even further, to claim that the clash between the Civil Rights Movement and the Royal Ulster Constabulary in October 1968 may be 'the single most influential factor on the subsequent history not only of Britain and Ireland, but also of contemporary "English" poetry' (Corcoran 1993: 136).

Northern Irish poetry

The 'Troubles' have been treated in many experimental ways by Northern Irish writers. For example, Derek Mahon's poem 'The Snow Party' refracts the contemporary situation through the historical violence of seventeenth-century Japan, Brian Friel's play about the 1833 Ordnance Survey, *Translations*, considers the significance of language and map-making in bolstering colonialism, while Brian Moore's novel *Black Robe* approaches the contemporary conflict imaginatively and tangentially through a story of Jesuit settlers and indigenous natives in seventeenth-century Canada.

After Yeats and before Heaney, the giants of Irish poetry in the mid-century are Patrick Kavanagh (1904–67), who moved from the country to become a Dublin poet sceptical of the city's sentimental view of rural Ireland, and Louis MacNeice (1907–63), who was born in Northern Ireland but moved to England, and whom I discussed as a 1930s poet. Currently, Northern Irish poetry is, for many critics, having a long-lasting renaissance which some have seen partially as a result of the 1947 Education Act and others as the influence of the Arts Council of Northern Ireland (Fallon and Mahon 1990: xx and Kirkland 1996: 60). As the first sign of this, several poets arose from the capital around the mid- to late 1960s, as I mentioned above. A second wave included such poets as Paul Muldoon, Ciaran Carson, Medbh McGuckian, and, writing in England, Tom Paulin, who is one of the fiercest critics of Anglo-Irish politics, which he refers to as the 'English problem'. Apart from Carson, all of these poets are featured in *The Penguin Book of Contemporary British Poetry*, a collection which gives a greater number of pages to Heaney than to any other writer (even so, Heaney later objected in a Field Day pamphlet to appearing under the heading 'British Poetry'). Several of Heaney's entries are taken from his 1975 volume, *North*, which many critics see as representing a turning point in his engagement with the political situation in Ulster. It is on these poems that I shall concentrate.

After his early nature and autobiographical poetry, Heaney's increased political involvement dates from when he returned to Belfast in 1971, following a year teaching in America. He found that relations between the Catholic community and the British soldiers drafted into Northern Ireland during 1969 had deteriorated dramatically. Subsequently, Heaney felt an increased pressure on himself to take a political stance in his poetry. He resigned his post as lecturer at Queen's University Belfast in 1973 to become a full-time writer. He then moved to Wicklow, south of the border, and there wrote *North*, his fourth collection. *North* is a significant book for several reasons: it won a number of major literary prizes; it established Heaney as a considerable popular and critical success; it sold over 6,000 copies in its first month (more than even Larkin's *The Whitsun Weddings* or Hughes's *Crow*). It was the first widely recognised volume of poetry on the subject of the 'Troubles', and it seemed to some critics that Northern Ireland had found its equivalent to Wilfred Owen (Morrison 1980b: 103).

In *North*, Heaney addresses the idea of the Northern hemisphere from several standpoints. The title refers both to the north of Ireland and to other northern civilisations that have shaped and influenced Ireland, such as that of the Vikings. Heaney's chief aim is to trace connections, primarily through language, ritual, and archaeology, between the past (treated in poems in the first part) and the present (addressed in the second part). His purpose is to give a cultural and historical context to sectarian violence.[2]

North begins with two poems, 'Sunlight' and 'The Seed Cutters', which are paired under the heading 'Mossbawn: Two poems in Dedication'. They present scenes of domestic and communal harmony and act as a calming influence before the violent images that follow in the rest of *North*. They are simple, symbolic poems which are also ritualistic, like a prayer before battle or the saying of grace before a meal. The two poems refer back to Heaney's childhood, hence their overall title 'Mossbawn', which is the name of his family home. The eldest of nine children, Heaney grew up in a Catholic farming community in County Derry, Northern Ireland, and these opening poems are dedicated to the nurturing influence of his aunt, Mary. The poems fall outside the volume's general concern with conflict and public events, focusing instead on domestic calm and simple custom. I shall discuss the first poem, to show how Heaney is praising 'peace', the quality which is absent from the politics of Northern Ireland but which is also the desired outcome of the 'Troubles'. 'Sunlight' is written in Heaney's regular style: four-line stanzas without end-rhymes, by far the most common verse form throughout *North*. The poem describes two scenes of peace and harmony, one internal and one external. The two scenes are joined by the word, 'So,' in line 10, suggesting that they are alike. In the first section there is nobody present in the yard – but there is heat warming the pump and there is light making the water in a bucket look golden like honey. The sun presides over the atmosphere of calm and ease which lasts all afternoon. In the second section, there is a scene with the same aspects to it: not the sun giving out heat and light but the reddening stove; not an iron pump growing hot, but scones heating in the oven; water isn't turned golden like honey, but shins are 'measling', blotchy white and red, colours of light and heat. And presiding over this is Heaney's aunt. And again there is a lack of presence: a space. In the last stanza, the poem implies that in the absence of movement and action there is love. It likens love that is enduring and constant, to a familiar, comforting household object, a tin handshovel. Heaney has described the poem as an attempt to represent the comfort of the womb; thus he writes from the point of view of a body sensitive to heat and requiring tranquillity. At the end, the scone rises in the oven to the ticking of two clocks, imitating the growth of the baby to the rhythm of its heartbeat and that of its mother.

The opening two poems of *North* try to stress the positive, nurturing forces in Heaney's experience which might otherwise be forgotten in the later poems which deal with destruction. They also serve as a reminder that domestic life in Northern Ireland is mostly peaceful and unchanging. After these poems there are very few comforting or peaceful images in the book as Heaney tries to come to terms with the 'Troubles'.

'Funeral Rites', the next selection from Heaney in *The Penguin Book of Contemporary British Poetry*, is one of four poems in *North* which deal with the Scandinavian influence on Ireland. At the time Heaney was writing the book, archaeological sites were being discovered and excavated around Dublin, and all the Viking poems try to trace connections and continuities between past and present, in language or in the soil. In the poems, Heaney constructs 'parables' for his Irish present via contemplation of various objects and bones retrieved from the ground.

The next group of poems, 'The Tollund Man', 'Punishment', and 'Strange Fruit', Heaney himself has described (like 'Funeral Rites') as 'symbolic'. By this, he means they deal with histories of the northern lands through archaeological, linguistic, mythological, and other images. They have also been called 'Bog Poems' because they stem from Heaney's reading in 1972 of *The Bog People* (1969) by P.V. Glob, a book about Scandinavian discoveries of preserved iron-age men and women in peat bogs ('bog' is Gaelic for 'soft' and is a rare English borrowing from Irish). Through his reading of Glob, Heaney found a symbolic approach to what he calls Ireland's 'neighbourly murders' in the image of tribal sacrifices that occurred in Jutland during the few centuries before Christ. They were considered appropriate tribal sacrifices, which amounted to ritual hanging or beheading, of thieves, adulterers, or traitors, to the gods of harvest. After the killing, or as a way of drowning, the victims were disposed of in bogs, such that, in many cases, their bodies have been preserved for over 2,000 years by the chemical properties of the peat. A large number were discovered in Denmark in the four decades up to 1970. Heaney uses these figures as examples of victims of ritual murders resembling those in Northern Ireland. His aim overall is to try to convey his horror at Ulster violence without using the rhetoric of the tabloids. In one of his essays, he has said the following:

> The early iron age in Northern Europe is a period that offers very satisfactory imaginative parallels to the history of Ireland at the moment.... You have a society in the iron age where there was ritual blood-letting. You have a society where girls'

heads were shaved for adultery, you have a religion centring on the territory, on a goddess of the ground and of the land, and associated with sacrifice. In many ways the fury of Irish republicanism is associated with a religion like this, with a goddess who has appeared in various guises. She appears in Yeats' plays, and she appears as Mother Ireland.... It seems to me that there are satisfactory parallels between this religion and time and our own time.[3]

The first properly documented discovery of a human buried in peat was the unearthing of a woman's body near Belfast in 1781, so this is long before the discoveries which were made in Jutland comparatively recently. The body is presumed to be that of a Danish Viking, and this provides Heaney with a further historical connection between Ireland and Jutland. The horror he finds in the ritual murders is balanced by the beauty he finds in the amazing preservation of the bodies which seem to have become something more than human – closer to art or inanimate nature. This ambiguous response parallels his attitude to northern violence in the 1970s; he shares in the disgust but also feels his own ties of Catholicism and kinship. Eventually, the figures in the poems seem to shift in significance for Heaney, from being victims of an ancient ritual to deities of a natural religion with which he sympathises. Heaney's ambivalence is suggested by these two emotions – hatred of violence and love of nature, to which these iron-age people were supposedly sacrificed.

To take an example, in 'Strange Fruit', the metaphoric fruit is not hanging from a tree but has been cut down. The poem is about a young woman's head found in Denmark in 1942. It appears to have been a sacrificial offering because the head was discovered along with ancient clothing and artefacts, but no body has been found. The head was wrapped in sheepskin. In the poem, Heaney puns on the word 'prune' as both an image of the head cut from the woman's shoulders like a tree that has been pruned, and on the dried skin of the face wrinkled like a dried plum. Similarly, the word 'gourd' both describes the shape of the head, like an oval container, and the fruit, resembling large cucumbers, from which gourds are traditionally carved. As in several of the other bog poems, he describes the head in terms of nature, beauty, and buried treasure (and he uses the sonnet, a traditional form for love poetry). At the end, the twin pressures of violence and veneration – in the words 'axe and beatification' – are pushed away by the anonymity of the woman's face.

Finally, the horror felt at the images which are the subjects of these poems should remind the reader of the horror of violence in Northern Ireland which even in 1975 had numbed many people's emotions by appearing commonplace; Heaney's feelings appear ambivalent on this point, however, because he asks for a greater understanding of the causes of the violence.

'A Constable Calls' and 'Exposure' are two poems from an autobiographical six-poem sequence entitled 'Singing School', which ends the second half of *North*. Heaney calls the second part of the volume 'explicit' because it deals directly with contemporary issues of North(ern) Ireland. The volume's division into two halves is also for Heaney a way of representing the ambiguous nature of his response to the history and politics of his country. *North* reflects the need to think on the one hand and the need to act on the other – which is to say, the impulse to give a considered, deliberated response to events but also an instinctive immediate reaction. Heaney is also, as a poet, only indirectly involved with the 'Troubles', and so portrays himself in several poems as someone looking on – a voyeur simultaneously intrigued and repelled by what is happening. There is no attempt in *North* to offer a solution to the conflicts in Ireland, but there is an attempt to put them in a larger context, which is necessarily violent and mournful.

'Singing School' concerns some of the background which has influenced Heaney's cultural position. The title is taken from Yeats's poem 'Sailing to Byzantium', which I discussed in Chapter 4. For Yeats, the school for a poet's soul is other, inspiring works of art. Heaney's 'Singing School' concerns poetry but other key influences on him seem to have been ones of threat and guilt leading up to the 1970s. In one of his essays, he describes the culmination of this fear at Christmas in Belfast in 1971:

> Everywhere soldiers with cocked guns are watching you...on the streets, at the corners of streets, from doorways, over the puddles on demolished sites. At night jeeps and armoured cars groan past without lights...road-blocks are thrown up.... Fear has begun to tingle through the place. Who's to know the next target on the Provisional list? Who's to know the reprisals won't strike where you are?
>
> (Heaney 1980: 30–1)

These feelings of fear and suspicion are prominent in all the parts of 'Singing School', though they are often implicit rather than explicit, as in the second part, 'A Constable Calls'. The incident remembered is that of a policeman's visit to Heaney's farmhouse at Mossbawn when he was a boy. The constable has only stopped by as part of a routine survey to record the type and acreage of Heaney's crops. However, the poem is marked by a fear of the policeman's authority – particularly as Heaney knows his father is deceiving the constable over an undeclared line of turnips. The memory of this small misdemeanour suggests the influence on growing up that fear and guilt have had on Heaney and others in Northern Ireland. It evokes the constant presence of a police force to regulate the life of ordinary people in Belfast. None of this exists in the scene itself, but it is all there in the boy's mind; for Heaney, the scene is pervaded with suspicion and the fear of repri-mand. Throughout this poem are casual images of violence; for example, in the second verse the dynamo is cocked back like a revolver, followed by the implied threat of the words 'hanging' and 'boot'. The poem stands in stark contrast to the first poem in *North*, 'Sunlight', which it alludes to at the start of the second verse. 'Sunlight' conjured childhood images of love and tranquillity, of heat and light. At the close of this poem, the policeman's carrier-spring snaps closed like a trap and his bicycle chain ticks like a bomb. This is of course so different from the peaceful ticking of the two clocks at the end of 'Sunlight'.

The final poem of 'Singing School' considers three types of 'Exposure': media exposure, exposure to nature, and self-exposure (in poetry). On the occasion of a comet, it is a reflection on Heaney's retreat from Northern Ireland south of the border, 'Escaped from the massacre'. He sees himself as someone holed up, waiting for a sign that the battle is over. However, one dominant aspect of violence in *North*, in poems conspicuously absent from the Penguin anthology, such as 'Ocean's Love to Ireland' and 'Act of Union', is that of English incursions into Ireland. While 'Exposure' returns to a focus on a north/south divide, the contexts for the conflict in Northern Ireland in *North* have ranged over Greek mythology (Hercules and Antaeus), tribal sacrifice in iron-age Jutland, Viking settlement, and rapacious English Imperialism. Heaney said at the time of writing *North*: 'I always thought of the political problem...as being an internal Northern Ireland division. I thought along sectarian lines. Now I think that the genuine political confrontation is between Ireland and Britain' (Longley 1986: 168). It is therefore important to realise that the violence condemned and allegorised in *North* is as much colonial and English as it is sectarian and Irish. This shift is even apparent in *North*'s most well-known poem, 'Punishment', which likens the bog-sacrifice of an adulterous iron-age woman to the tarring and feathering of Northern Irish women accused of consorting with British soldiers. Heaney's distaste for the punishment is shadowed by his understanding of the sense of injury at tribal, or national, betrayal.

A poet who has been seen as countering Heaney's mythic approach in *North* because he embodies a self-conscious, anti-grand-narrative postmodernism is Paul Muldoon (Matthews 1997: 187). Muldoon was born in 1951 in County Armagh and is like Heaney a Northern Irish Catholic educated at Queen's University, Belfast. His poetry most often attracts the labels 'hybrid' and 'hermetic': its worlds seem both multiple and self-enclosed. He approaches the colonial status of Northern Ireland in oblique but imaginative ways: 'The More a Man Has the More a Man Wants', a fantastical story of the Protean terrorist adventurer Gallogly, is declared by Muldoon to be 'loosely based on the Trickster cycle of the Winnebago Indians'. Another piece, 'Meeting the British', is a short poem about the end of Pontiac's Rebellion in Canada. It ends by noting the introduction of smallpox to Ottawa Indians by the British in the mid-eighteenth century, about which Muldoon has said there are parallels with the decimation of Irish culture by the English. Again, in 'Crossing the Line', Muldoon approaches the 1985 Anglo-Irish agreement only indirectly, by making reference to the *Mabinogion* story of a deal between Gwydion and Pryderi which leads to betrayal and violence (Kendall 1996: 145). His poems therefore draw on history and literature to provide parallels and anecdotes for understanding the same situation Heaney approaches through grander frameworks of mythology and etymology. Yet Muldoon is also sceptical of the common attempt by critics to squeeze political meanings out of any poem by a Northern Irish writer (see his parodic 'The Frog').

Clair Wills writes that 'Muldoon's "Quoof" has become his trademark, signalling above all the desire to create in poetry a private, intransitive word' ('quoof' was the Muldoon family word for a hot-water bottle). She sees it as Muldoon's attempt

> to experience the world of poetry as a paradise, an Eden, untainted by the corruption of the 'real'. And in response to this perceived desire his poetry has been both championed for a certain reluctance to draw links between poetry and politics in Northern Ireland, and condemned for its irresponsible hermeticism.... [but] both readings ignore the ways in which Muldoon himself consciously problematises questions of the private and the political in poetic discourse.
>
> (Wills 1992: 123)

Some critics, for example, see reference to the situation in Ulster in Muldoon's fascination with hybridity and mixed identity, as in 'Mules' ('Why should we not have the best of both worlds?') or the multiple-identity figures in 'Paris' and the miscegenation of 'The Mixed Marriage' (ostensibly a poem about Muldoon's inheritance of his mother's love of reading and his father's skill at farming). 'Immram' – Gaelic for 'rowing around' – is the longest Muldoon selection in the Morrison and Motion volume. It is a quest-poem (son for a father) in the Irish classical tradition of voyage literature but written in the style of an American detective story. As a search for roots and belonging, the poem exemplifies Muldoon's general concerns and illustrates a way of reading his narrative poetry as an exploration of Northern Irish identity. On both a personal and a political level Muldoon's studied intertextual style is, as Blake Morrison has said, 'much concerned with plural genealogy...it has a fascination with mixed or shifting identities' (Morrison 1987: 197).

Most commonly, Muldoon's entwined narratives produce hybrids of an undecided significance, as in 'Whim', where two strangers become 'stuck' when copulating and are carried off 'like the last of an endangered species', a poem Morrison thinks may be an allegory of Ireland and England's union. In the playful and ironically titled 'History', Muldoon writes a seemingly ahistorical personal poem about the search for sexual origins as he lengthily but inconclusively asks his partner where they first made love; yet, Muldoon's questioning poetry is also sometimes overt in its references, as in 'Ireland', where the speaker wonders whether a 'ticking' parked car is a sign of lovers or terrorists nearby. However, considerable ambiguity remains: Muldoon dislikes 'opinionated' stances and no particular political position is suggested in his work despite its occasional references to hunger strikers, political prisoners, and the tarred and feathered. Edna Longley concludes that 'Muldoon's methods give the lie to the notion that language can operate politically in Irish poetry only by declaring allegiances' (Longley 1986: 207). The concern with half-states and cross-breeds, like the huskies of 'The Main-mast', 'Half-dog, Half-wolf', seems indicative of Muldoon's general emphasis on Northern Ireland's religious and national mixed loyalties. As Tom Paulin argues, Muldoon's poetry, like Leopold Bloom's objections to the Citizen in the Cyclops episode of *Ulysses*, seems to aim to 'deconstruct such a fictitious unity' as the single nation (Paulin 1992: 17). It opposes fixed unities or identities and in this seeks to offer an alternative to essentialist and separatist arguments.

Along these lines, the current post-colonial emphasis on hybridity, most noted in the work of Homi Bhabha, has been understood in the Irish context in terms of 'adulteration' (Bhabha 1993). David Lloyd contends that 'adulteration', sexual and 'racial', is the constitutive anxiety of an Irish nationalism which both fears contamination and accuses the nation of it. By contrast, Irish writing from street ballads through to Joyce has been heterogeneous, parodic, assimilating, and characterised by this 'adulteration' which Lloyd argues is a 'stylisation of the hybrid status of the colonised subject as of the colonised culture' (Lloyd 1993: 110). Such strategies are opposed to nationalist constructions but also to imperial identifications, and they constitute an anti-colonial resistance. Like the other texts Lloyd cites, it is the hybrid position between imperialism and post-colonial nationalism that makes Muldoon's poems the contested objects of persistent political struggles over meaning. For Lloyd, it is their ambiguity which makes such writings so contentious but which also makes them disruptive of fixed identities, whether promulgated by imperialist or nationalist voices.

The other poets from Northern Ireland featured in the Morrison and Motion anthology are Medbh McGuckian, Derek Mahon, Tom Paulin, and Michael Longley. McGuckian was discussed in the last chapter, and is more often considered in terms of feminist poetry than nationalist, but I will say a little about the other three here. Longley, a Protestant born in Belfast in 1939, was a contemporary and friend of Heaney at university in Belfast. He says he is obsessed with form, its extremities of control and points of disintegration. *Gorse Fires* (1991) is highly regarded and has brought him similar recognition to that accorded Heaney. Much of Longley's work is in the genres of pastoral and love poetry but he does engage with the political situation in several poems (often on themes of home, exile, and belonging), as in 'Wounds', where a man is casually shot in the head: 'By a shivering boy who wandered in / Before they could turn the television down'. Tom Paulin, born in 1949 in Leeds, was brought up in Belfast (his mother is Irish) from the age of 4 to 18, when he went to study English at Hull. Paulin's poetry has been described as obscure and puzzling, but also as over(t)ly political. As well as writing poetry and drama, he is editor of the controversial *Faber Book of Political Verse* (1986) and author of *Ireland and the English Crisis* (1984). He has argued that there needs to be a dictionary of Irish English to recognise the separateness of the language in Ireland. One of Paulin's most famous poems, 'Anastasia McLaughlin', allies Irish history with Russian, explaining the one in terms of the other. A more obviously socio-historical poem is 'Settlers', which deals with the Protestant migration from Scotland to Ireland that is one of the origins of the contemporary schism. In the light of the discussion of Heaney above, it is also worth noting that in Paulin's murder/retribution poem 'Under the Eyes' he alludes to the end of 'Punishment', through the phrase 'exact revenge'; the poems are directly comparable.

Derek Mahon was born into a Protestant family in Belfast in 1941, but has spent a considerable amount of his adult life in England. He is co-editor of *The Penguin Book of Contemporary Irish Poetry* and his writing is suffused with literary references to Yeats, MacNeice, Wilde, and others. Mahon often approaches his relation to Northern Ireland from a position of exile, as in 'Afterlives': 'the hills are still the same / Grey-blue above Belfast. / Perhaps if I'd stayed behind / And lived it bomb by bomb / I might have grown up at last, / And learnt what is meant by home.' Some critics suggest that Mahon has therefore rejected his past. He is better seen, however, as a syncretic poet, caught between two cultures: 'The rhyme of "bomb" and "home" registers a brutal kind of consonance while marking an ironic distance between what is usually meant by home and [Mahon's] actual home-town where he no longer feels at home' (Haughton 1992: 100). Mahon is another explorer of the present's history in language and soil; his 'Lives' is dedicated to Seamus Heaney and, with regard to Heaney's Bog Poems, charts a number of different archaeological and cultural antecedents to contemporary Ulster (including Celtic, Greek, Tibetan, and African). His most famous and anthologised poem is 'A Disused Shed in Co. Wexford', a meditation on Irish dereliction based on an anecdote about a forgotten shed in the grounds of a 'burnt-out' hotel. The poem is also a Yeatsian meditation on a time of civil war – the entrapped mushrooms are symbols of the victims of Anglo-Irish conflict, imprisonment and amnesia. Such poetry is sophisticated and oblique in its references. Like much of the Northern Irish poetry I have discussed, it aims to do at least two things at once and the subject of the poem appears distant from contemporary history, but its resonances and symbolism lead the reader to an understanding of how the 'Troubles' are ever-present in Northern Ireland and yet do not loom large in most people's day-to-day lives. Mahon's themes of exile and exclusion are as much a commentary on the continuing legacy of British colonialism as are Heaney's poems of violence and tribalism in *North*.

New black ethnicities

The first large numbers of arrivants from the Caribbean came to England on the *S.S. Empire Windrush* in June 1948. From the first, alongside physical hostilities in cities and ports, British politicians spoke against the West Indians who had been encouraged (by companies like British Rail) to come to work in Britain. In 1953, Beresford Craddock MP said in the Commons:

> Let us remember that 95 percent of them are primitive people. One of the reasons they are not generally accepted into hotels is because their sanitary habits are not all that could be desired….[Their] views and practices are due to the psychological make-up of those primitive people from time immemorial.
>
> (Dabydeen and Wilson-Tagoe 1988: 81)

In 1967, Duncan Sandys, who had been Secretary of State for the Commonwealth and Colonies from 1960 to 1964, decided about Britain that: 'The breeding of millions of half-caste children would merely produce a generation of misfits and create national tension' (Kureishi 1986: 11). The next year, Enoch Powell made his infamous 'rivers of blood' speech, which predicted mass rioting if immigration was not stopped. This was followed by a Gallup poll the next month that suggested 74 per cent of Britons supported Powell's views.[4] Three years later, in 1971, Powell's repeated calls for a massive repatriation scheme ended in the Immigration Bill which denied the right of Commonwealth workers to settle in Britain. Powell's rhetoric relied on a nostalgic appeal to an Imperial history and was premised on a narrow ethnic stereotype, insisting on an authentic British identity that is white Anglo-Saxon. The Powell years have been thought of as containing the worst examples of racism but white British fear of black immigration has persisted; in 1986 one tabloid headline read '3,000 Asians Flood Britain' just before new restrictions for visa applications were imposed. Margaret Thatcher appealed to this fear in 1978 when she promised in a television speech that she would not let Britain be 'swamped' by a different culture.[5] Such rhetoric is still in evidence in the 1990s, and many commentators likened a speech in May 1993 by the Conservative MP, Winston Churchill, in which Churchill claimed that the 'British way of life' was being overrun by 'immigrants', to Powell's 'rivers of blood' polemic.[6]

The response to such attacks has been on the one hand peaceful and on the other violent. In March 1981, the Black People's Day of Action was held, the largest black protest demonstration ever to take place in Britain. This was followed by urban 'race riots' in 1981 and 1985, especially in the old slave ports, London, Bristol, and Liverpool (see, for example, Benjamin Zephaniah's poem 'U-Turn'). While resistance against discrimination has taken the form of demonstrations, protests, and 'riots', blacks have more commonly turned to cultural forms to register their grievances, express solidarity, and contest the politics of representation. Another aim is to assert what Stuart Hall has called 'new ethnicities', which acknowledge, for example, that the term 'black' does not refer to a particular nation or race, but refers to 'shared experiences of discrimination and racism within the dominant, white, English culture' (Hall 1988; Fortier 1994: 218). Such 'new ethnicities' allow different kinds of allegiance and community from those validated by a concept such as 'the nation', which is associated with histories of jingoism and colonialism (see Fryer 1988 and 1984). In considering these 'new ethnicities', I want now to provide two contexts for discussing black British poetry: language and diaspora.

Tony Crowley has argued that early nineteenth-century politics prompted the founding of a Standard English: a campaign that continued over the next century (Crowley 1989). Amid political dissent, language was used as an emblem of underlying cultural connection, a bond that brought together otherwise disunited factions. Crowley notes that this striving for uniformity culminated in linguists such as Daniel Jones, in his *English Pronouncing Dictionary* (1917), advocating the educated pronunciation of the southern cities as the standard against which other forms were judged as not just deviant but uncouth, unintelligible and educationally subnormal. Such linguistic dictates not only functioned to exclude people from power and influence in terms of class, but also in terms of ethnic differences of dialect, vocabulary, and pronunciation. In the Irish context, this has long been recognised. In the year before Jones's dictionary was published, James Joyce had Stephen Dedalus in *A Portrait of the Artist As a Young Man* assert of his English lecturer 'The language in which we are speaking is his before it is mine.' More recently, Seamus Heaney, in his second collection of essays, *The Government of the Tongue*, has underlined the point that to use Standard English is to commit an act of linguistic perjury – a point made clear by the Scottish 'patois' poetry of Liz Lochhead and Tom Leonard. For Caribbean and subsequently black British writers this point has been equally significant, making language a site of cultural resistance and assertion. Black British poets in the 1970s have thus engaged with similar social and political issues to those which engaged the Liverpool poets and protest singers of the 1960s.

The authors of *The Empire Writes Back* argue that 'the crucial function of language as power demands that post-colonial writing define itself by seizing the language of the centre and replacing it in a discourse fully adapted to the colonized place' (Ashcroft *et al*. 1989: 38). Many post-colonial theorists follow this view that language is appropriable, but also needs to be localised. C.L.R. James has maintained that West Indian consciousness was fashioned by Europe's philosophical, linguistic, and literary models, which are as much a part of the West Indies as is creole. Similarly, the Barbadian poet and critic Edward Kamau Brathwaite writes of a Caribbean 'Nation Language' (instead of 'patois', 'dialect' or 'creole'): 'It may be in English: but often it is an English which is like a howl, or a shout or a machine-gun or the wind or a wave. It is also like the blues. And sometimes it is English and African at the same time' (Ashcroft *et al*. 1995: 311). Brathwaite calls this a 'submerged/emerging culture' which uses oral tradition, calypso, and different sound and rhyme patterns (e.g. that of the drumbeat) from those in the English literary canon (see Brathwaite 1984). For Brathwaite, Anglophone Caribbean writers create a language of their own nation by using music, as well as oral, popular, and colloquial forms, creating a poetry better suited to the hurricane of the Caribbean than the weather of Europe. When reinvented in Britain by black poets, this language is hybridised again into a new form of expression which draws on Brathwaite's ideas (his pioneering trilogy *The Arrivants* was published in 1973) on Jamaican reggae rhythms, and also on the experience of British racism, as in Linton Kwesi Johnson's 'Reggae Sounds': 'Rhythm of a tropical electrical storm / (cooled-down to the pace of the struggle)'. In terms of traditional British poetry, this new language mixes Standard English with regional terms and accents, Americanisms, urban estuary English, and, most importantly, an 'all-Islands' creole learned at school (D'Aguiar 1993: 59). The invention of British black English thus works socially to form a community of language users, and politically to express a resistance to the dominant culture through the manipulation of its language (see Sutcliffe 1982).

In his 'On Not Being Milton: Nigger Talk in England Today', David Dabydeen stresses that, inappropriately, 'Milton's ornate highly-structured, Latinate expressions...are still the exemplars of English civilisation against which the barbaric utterances of black people are judged' (Dabydeen 1990: 8). Creole, he argues, expresses black experience in a way that Standard English cannot and 'young British blacks have resisted white domination' through the creation of a patois evolved from the West Indian language of their parents. The language, Dabydeen says, is 'uncomfortably raw'. Some features are the incorporation of local words from one or more Caribbean islands, the disregard for past and future tenses, using only the present ('I bashing future with present tense', John Agard, 'Listen Mr Oxford Don'), and spelling words as they are spoken (so 'me' becomes 'mi' and 'for' becomes 'fi', while 'into' is 'inna', 'can't' is 'caan', and 'England' is 'Inglan'). The language, in contrast to Standard English, is terse, sometimes coarse, but also succinct, forceful, assertive, and politically sharp as in the Jamaican Mikey Smith's 'Nigger Talk'. (Dabydeen notes that creole's attack on English is reminiscent of Alvarez's attack on the 'gentility' of the Movement poets.)

However, language is both a product and producer of experience: all cultures develop and also develop from their own language or dialect. Paul Gilroy writes of a distinctive and shared black Atlantic culture which is particularly useful when considering the relation between Caribbean and black British poetry. Gilroy describes a culture made necessary by the slave-triangle of Europe, Africa, and the Americas; a culture shared by all who have an African heritage (the triangular movement of goods and people is explicitly and formally mapped in Grace Nichols's poem 'Out of Africa'). Gilroy argues that diaspora, a term taken up by historians of Africa and slavery in the 1950s, provides a way of understanding contemporary cultural identities.[7] He argues that the work of black writers should not

> be exclusively assimilated to the project of building an ethni-
> cally particular or nationalist cultural canon, because the logic
> of the great political movement in which these texts stand
> and to which they contribute operates at other levels than
> those marked by national boundaries.
>
> (Gilroy 1993: 218)

In the light of modern world history, Stuart Hall also recommends a new paradigm for viewing human identity as always moving, never arrived at, and therefore in some ways more related to a discourse of diaspora than of homelands and rootedness (such as Pan-Africanism or Anglo-Saxon Englishness). Hall contrasts this understanding of self as migration with a traditional view in the West of identity as self-evident, self-defining, and homogenous: a unity rather than a function of differences. Shifting to conceptions of diasporic experience, Hall rejects the idea of a communal identity which can be fixed by looking back to a sacred home and pure ethnicity. He concludes that, 'Diaspora identities are those which are constantly producing and reproducing themselves anew, through transformation and difference' (Hall 1993: 402). Given this redefinition of identity, which develops from Brathwaite's model of creolisation, Hall argues that diasporic culture is instrumental in post-colonial formations wherever there is a recognition of displacement, hybridity, colonial history, or creolised language. So Gilroy can argue that

> Black Britain defines itself crucially as part of a diaspora. Its unique cultures draw inspiration from those developed by black populations elsewhere. In particular, the culture and politics of black America and the Caribbean have become raw materials for creative processes which redefine what it means to be black, adapting it to distinctively British experiences and meanings.
>
> (Gilroy 1987: 154)

In its reclamation of black history to rework present cultural identities, the Guyanese-born David Dabydeen's own poetry provides a good example. Respectively, his three volumes *Slave Song* (1984), *Coolie Odyssey* (1988), and *Turner* (1994) chronicle the domination and sadomasochism inherent in plantation life; rework the journey to the Caribbean of indentured Indians, who were 'employed' to replace slaves after 1834, in a story of his mother's more recent journey to a cold, unwelcoming England looking for work; and examine the role of black experience in English art, particularly Turner's 1840 painting 'Slavers Throwing Overboard the Dead and Dying'. Of the first volume, written in a Caribbean creole but often accompanied by translations, Dabydeen says,

> The subject demanded a language capable of describing both a lyrical and a corrosive sexuality. The creole language is angry, crude, and energetic. The canecutter chopping away at the crop bursts out in a spate of obscene words, a natural gush from the gut.
>
> (Dabydeen 1990: 3)

In his reconstitution of a Guyanese patois, Dabydeen has used the European notion of creole as 'broken English', reflecting the brokenness and suffering of its original users, but he also emphasises that they are 'songs', reasserting the oral origins of Caribbean poetry. In this language, Dabydeen suggests there is not only an expression of slave experience but also one of 'linguistic, gestural and sexual' resistance, as in the slave's desire for the plantation mistress: 'Let yuh come wid milk in yuh breast' ('Love Song') (see Lawson Welsh 1996: 419). Dabydeen's three volumes are all concerned with migration: from

Africa, from India, and from the Caribbean. Each constructs an identity that is forged through displacements of culture and people, through
the relocations of diaspora and of language.

Black British poetry

'English' poetry has a strong if not always prominent history in the
British Empire. As a subject for study, English literature was first tried
in the nineteenth century in India, and only subsequently imported to
Britain. Its purpose was to instil correct 'English values' in colonised
subjects and to project a vision of all that was finest and most
admirable in English culture. As a cultural signifier of racial and class
hierarchies it has remained a site of contestation into the post-colonial
world. Ezra Pound wrote near the start of the century of the need for
modernist poetry to break free from the iambic pentameter and in
1984, in *The History of the Voice*, Edward Brathwaite put forward the
same argument for West Indian poets. Brathwaite's point was that
language has to be shaped to experience and that the forms of literature also have to be moulded: 'The hurricane does not howl in
pentameters' (Brathwaite 1990: 33). Brathwaite's ideas, along with
those of other Caribbean writers, have affected and inspired a generation of poets in England who have framed discussions of black British
experience since the 1970s, for example Linton Kwesi Johnson, James
Berry, Grace Nichols, and Fred D'Aguiar.

In terms of developments in the UK since the 1970s, a key voice
has been Linton Kwesi Johnson who came to Britain from Jamaica at
the age of 11 in 1963 and published his first poetry book *Dread Beat
and Blood* in 1975. Influenced intellectually by Frantz Fanon, Aimé
Césaire, and Edward Brathwaite, musically by Rastafarian band The
Last Poets and DJ Big Youth, Johnson became a part of the Race
Today Collective with Darcus Howe and always worked for the
London organisation when not on tour. Johnson has consistently
placed himself as a voice for his generation of British blacks rather
than for himself, and despite his influence has repeatedly argued that
'poetry is never a substitute for concrete political action' (Johnson
1996: 77). To emphasise the importance of Johnson's influence, Fred
D'Aguiar has said that he created 'the newest and most original
poetic form to have emerged in the English language in the last
quarter century'.[8] D'Aguiar is referring to what has become known as
'dub', a fusion of reggae and poetry (sometimes with Rastafarianism)
which Johnson championed in the 1970s (see Morris 1997). Johnson
says

I wanted to do with Jamaican speech what Americans were doing but I incorporated Rasta dread talk and street slang, infusing it with reggae rhythms. The music's there in the structure of the speech. I always have a bass line at the back of my mind when I write.[9]

Johnson's poetry has a similar rhythm to reggae music, working with a series of double beats separated by pauses. James Berry writes:

Linton Kwesi's work reveals a fresh sharpness of mind that expresses itself through the sounds of 'Nation Language': it has an infectious and readily imitated rhythmic structure that accommodates both the presence and the absence of a musical (dub) backing, and it has all the immediacy of the calypso.

(Berry 1986: 90)

Johnson's poems often have their roots in events that epitomise institutional and cultural discrimination: 'Sonny's Lettah' about the SUS laws which gave the police the power to arrest on suspicion; 'Di Great Insohreckshan' about the 1981 'race riots'; and 'New Craas Massakhah' about a firebombing that killed fourteen blacks in 1981 (and was followed by a protest march by 20,000 people). In the late 1970s and early 1980s, popular music was more politically engaged in Britain than ever before, and, against the rise of the British National Front, Johnson was also part of a large union of punk and reggae acts that were establishing a new youth agenda through movements such as 'Rock against Racism', 'Red Wedge', and others (cf. Benjamin Zephaniah's poem 'Call it what yu like'[10]). The union of oral poetry and the music scene is fundamental to dub: Johnson honed his drum and bass poems in performance in the 1970s, touring with a band and a sound system. Unsurprisingly, his work has always been available in recorded form (*Forces of Victory*, 1979, on Island records made him an international reputation) as well as in print.

Johnson greatly influenced performance poets such as Levi Tafari and Benjamin Zephaniah, who was the centre of a major academic controversy when he was shortlisted for the position of Professor of Poetry at Oxford University. Zephaniah writes political and satirical poetry about black experience in Britain (such as 'A modern slave song', 'Black Politics of Today', and 'How's dat'), but he also 'rants' about traditional British institutions and stereotypes (e.g. 'The SUN' or 'Royals do it too') in a dub poetry which defamiliarises the subject matter because 'Dis poetry is designed fe rantin / Dance hall style, Big

mouth chanting' ('Dis Poetry'). His work concerns the power of performance, the delivery of a specific piece by a poet in a particular time
and place, and Zephaniah has gone as far as to say of the written
variety: 'today's poetry is dead. I don't like poetry' (Habekost 1986:
37). However, by contrast, the Jamaican British performer Jean 'Binta'
Breeze, who has been seen as the first woman dub poet, has voiced a
concern that the form of dub poetry may become as constraining as the
iambic pentameter if there is not more experimentation. She also challenges gender assumptions in asking why dub poetry had previously
been associated with men – a sense of exclusion reiterated in her poem
'I Poet' (Breeze 1996: 498).

If Zephaniah is indebted to Johnson he also draws from James Berry,
a lighter, more playful writer perhaps best known for his epistolary
collection, *Lucy's Letters* (1975), and his volume on colonialism and
slavery, *Chain of Days* (1985). Berry was born in Jamaica in 1924 and
came to England with the first West Indians to arrive in 1948 (a year
in which there were the first anti-immigration race-riots in England).
As well as writing poetry he has published two important anthologies
of Caribbean verse: *Bluefoot Traveller* (1976) and *News for Babylon*
(1984). In his spelling, Berry commonly uses the phonetics of Jamaican
creole and introduces Jamaican proverbs into his poems' conclusions,
but his work, especially in *Lucy's Letters*, is frequently about the difference between British and Caribbean experience. Lucy, a young woman
from the Caribbean in London in the 1950s, writes to her friend in a
Jamaican village, and contrasts not just Standard English with creole
but also the city with the island, affluence with poverty, purposeful talk
with gossip ('Labrish'), impersonal lives with friendly communities.
Berry acknowledges two important moments in his appreciation of
creole as a viable language for poetry: Brathwaite's releasing of creole
from the dungeon of a 'dialect' to the heights of a 'Nation Language',
and independence in the Caribbean, which was for him as important
in terms of identity and language as it was in terms of politics (Berry
1989: 175–7). In contrast to the oppositions between Jamaica and
England drawn in *Lucy's Letters*, in *Chain of Days* Berry pessimistically
considers the continuity between colonial and post-colonial experience. Elsewhere, he explains how

> The Westindian finds himself in a situation that amounts to a
> continuation of the old ways of life. Around him white people
> are still dominant, still in control.... He has missed out on the
> real experience of Independence, of being his own master.
>
> (Berry 1996: 359)

Chain of Days ranges over West Indian history from slavery to 'The Testing of the Ideal Third World New Man'. The emphasis is very much on the present, however, and in a poem like 'I am Racism' he assembles over six stanzas the multitude of ways in which 'an ethnic difference is the sign / of nonspecial people', while in 'Confession' he describes how a young black girl in Britain comes to realise, against a lifetime of indoctrination, that 'Black people were not cursed' but instead were constantly 'in struggle'. The poems also celebrate the rise of black literature and the growing body of classic texts of the black Atlantic, from the Nigerian Amos Tutuola's *The Palmwine Drinkard* to Toni Morrison's *Song of Solomon*: 'We the new poems, we carry no roses, / no snow or rhymes of rhetoric play.'

Foremost among younger British poets is Fred D'Aguiar. His first collection, *Mama Dot* (1985), draws on his early Guyanese childhood and celebrates in mock-heroic terms his grandmother's influence over his family in their rural village. It describes a fullness of life and a sense of warmth and wisdom that allies Mama Dot with the Caribbean, even in her anger: 'She gesticulates and it's sheet lightning on our world. / Our ears cannot be stopped against her raised voice' ('Angry Mama Dot'). D'Aguiar, born in London, dislikes the term 'black British' literature because it separates him from his white poet peers. However, he says:

> Britain is a plural society. You can't surgically remove the black British contribution from what it means to be British – though I know there are many English people out there who still do that with passion and relish.... I want to opt into the intellectual combat defining where this culture is going. Being West Indian doesn't mean you're outside it. From the moment the Englishman Hawkins collected his first slave cargo, that was an act of engagement. After that, I belonged.[11]

His latest collection is *British Subjects* (1993), which, in keeping with Hall's diasporic aesthetic, takes as its premise the idea that 'Home' is 'always elsewhere' as D'Aguiar travels between Guyana, Britain, and the US. Several of the poems range over British landmarks which represent 'home' but are also soaked in colonial history – the slave port of Bristol, the Thames at Greenwich, the customs entry point at Heathrow – building up to a celebration of the Caribbean-in-Britain found at the 'Notting Hill' carnival. The book is also, D'Aguiar says, about describing

Caribbean experience as a part of a British cultural identity. Nowadays Caribbean culture in Britain is no longer exotic, marginal, remembered, or in the process of being introduced to a host nation. The British host identity itself actually consists of Caribbean elements.

(Birbalsingh 1993: 142)

Despie this, D'Aguiar's poems deal with police brutality ('A Gift of a Rose'), racial prejudice ('Colour'), and violence ('Inner City'). Overall, exploring a new Britishness that the metropolitan orthodoxies try to exclude ('Friday, Tonto or Punkawallah / Sponging off the state' as he puts it in 'Letter from Mama Dot'), D'Aguiar says he is considering Britishness in terms of Salman Rushdie's 'mongrelization', Hall's 'hybridization', and Homi Bhabha's theories of difference and plurality (Birbalsingh 1993: 143). Most importantly, D'Aguiar, as in his 1997 novel *The Slave Ship*, sets about recovering or unsilencing black Atlantic and black British voices, for reasons similar to those of Johnson and Dabydeen: 'Check your history and you will see / throughout it some other body speaking for we' ('Dread' in *British Subjects*).

In the UK at present, the most well-known woman poet from the Caribbean is Grace Nichols. Nichols celebrates the body and uses metaphors of sexuality and colonisation to undermine each other, as in 'Configurations': 'her wide legs close in slowly / Making a golden stool of the empire of his head.' She also invokes or refers to magic in several of her poems or their titles, as in 'Spell Against Too Much Male White Power', suggesting that obeah serves both as an emblem of resistance and as a source of African comfort. Another of the techniques in her poetry is to emphasise multiplicities, denying the fixities of colonial or stereotypical identities.[12] Nichols first came to wide notice in 1983 with *I is a Long Memoried Woman*, a series of poems modelled on Brathwaite's *The Arrivants* but re-imagining the middle passage from a female slave's perspective. As a corrective to the stereotype of the 'African Queen' fantasy, her most frequently used creation is the 'Fat Black Woman', an alter ego whose assertiveness works against most of the imagery associated with each of the three attributes by which she anonymously labels herself. The 'Fat Black Woman' also uses spells, and many of Nichols's most comical poems are aimed at the men who try not to succumb to her powers, which operate as a kind of sexual counter-colonisation of her white lovers. Nichols can be seen to be working in the tradition of Louise Bennett, whose 'Colonization in Reverse' is one of the most famous literary comments on 1950s emigration/immigration to England. Bennett, who spent ten years in Britain, is one of the first and most influential twentieth-century Caribbean poets. She weds the oral tradition of songs, stories, and proverbs to a written form, adding humour, pathos, and a self-consciously unliterary language (e.g. see 'Independance'). She describes her political stance on creole thus:

> Dem say Jamaica language a corruption of de English language. But dem never say English a corruption of di Norman, Greek, Latin, French an' Anglo-Saxon – no: English derived from. You hear de word?! 'Derived from': English derived from an' Jamaican corrupt. No sah! Jamaican also derived.
>
> (Habekost 1986: 21)

Her common form is Jamaican dialect, which she feels best expresses the joy, irony, and comedy of her subject matter and her self-presentation in performance. An influence on poets like James Berry, Bennett uses the persona of 'Miss Lou' in many of her poems to express a social serious-ness through laughter.[13] Such playfulness serves a political purpose, asserting a difference from, and challenging the authority and gravity of, English poetic orthodoxies; but it is also integral to her view of creole:

> The nature of the Jamaican dialect is the nature of comedy, I feel. As it is used by the people to express their feelings, the dialect is very adaptable. You can twist it, you can express your-self so much more strongly and vividly than in standard English.
>
> (Scott 1989: 45)

As with the poetry by women discussed in the previous chapter, it is through the use of a distinctive voice and language, combined with a suitable style, in this case humour, that new poetic forms arise. According to some critics, it is also the impetus of a social or emotional situation to respond to that is the best catalyst for innova-tive poetry – a view which adds weight to the general impression that it is largely work by women and by Northern Irish or black British writers that is breaking fresh poetic ground and still following Ezra Pound's prewar instruction to 'make it new'.

Conclusion

There is a wealth of poetry by black writers being published in Britain at the moment. Other well-known poets with a Caribbean heritage are

John Agard, John Lyons, Leroy Jones, Jackie Kay, Merle Collins, and Valerie Bloom, but there are also prominent poets from South Asia, such as Tariq Latif, Iftikhar Arif, Rukhsana Ahmad, Moniza Alvi, and Sujata Bhatt (these are supplemented by the poets who write in non-English languages such as Hindi and Urdu). However, the major anthologies that have been published over the last twenty years have often omitted black poets: *The Penguin Book of Contemporary British Poetry* has none and neither has Edward Lucie-Smith's revised *British Poetry Since 1945* (1985). This has changed with Paladin's *New British Poetry* (1988) and Bloodaxe's *The New Poetry* (1993), which have substantial selections from black poets.

The acknowledgement of black British writers in many ways focuses the relation of poetry to its historical moment. Their struggle to be recognised involves several questions: the definition of 'poetry'; the relation of oral to written literature; the (non-)separability of politics and poetry; the ownership and identity of 'British' poetry; the biases of anthologists and the publishing business; and the need to struggle over the 'English' language. All of these issues are present throughout the century's poetry and all highlight the importance of thinking about literature not as just 'the words on the page', but as texts weaved by and weaving the historical discourses that surround them.

NOTES

INTRODUCTION

1 New Criticism takes its name from an essay collection by John Crowe Ransom in 1941. It is used to encompass a large body of critics and approaches to literary study, united by a diligent and strict adherence to analysing the precise words of the text, dominant in English studies from the 1920s to the 1960s.

2 For a thorough discussion of these issues, see Easthope 1983.

3 The story is 'Pierre Menard, Author of the *Quixote*' in Borges 1970.

4 For a short but thorough overview of these issues, see Jenkins 1991.

5 This belief is best known from the work of Jacques Derrida and is a round-about way of expressing the view he summarises as 'there is nothing outside the text'.

6 The Apocalypse poets' anthologies were *The New Apocalypse* (1939), *The White Horseman* (1941), and *The Crown and the Sickle* (1943).

7 Another one of these key publications surveys the last decade before the war: Robin Skelton's 1964 *Poetry of the Thirties*. With no mention of empire and only one woman poet (one more than Allan Rodway's 1967 *Poets of the 1930s*), Skelton's was the definitive 1930s collection for thirty years (its success prompted Penguin to bring out Skelton's follow-up collection *Poetry of the Forties*).

8 This is worth considering in the light of Harold Bloom's theory that all poets in the canon write in the shadow of those who have gone before (as though wanting to overthrow the 'father') in *The Anxiety of Influence* (1973).

9 Auden's line comes from 'In Memory of W.B. Yeats'.

10 On *English* modernism see Hobsbaum 1970. That Hardy had shown the way for the modernists was the view of the influential contemporary novelist, poet, and critic Ford Madox Ford. See Schmidt 1979: 24.

11 For example, neither is mentioned in anything more than passing in Day and Docherty's collection on poetry from 1900–50 (1995) or in Bell's collection on the context of English literature from 1900–30 (1980).

12 For a review of Hardy's position, see Widdowson's (1997) edited collection, which includes a helpful introduction and a critical commentary on previous editions and opinions.

13 Silkin 1987 gives considerable space to each.

14 See Shklovsky 1972. For a discussion of Brecht see Chapter 3.
15 This book is highly selective in its choice of poets and poems, focusing for the greater part on the most commonly studied. A substantial overview of the century which covers both English and American poets is to be found in Perkins 1976 and 1987.

1 'UNION JACKS IN EVERY PART': PREWAR AND GEORGIAN POETRY

1 The view that what a text leaves out, its silences and omissions, is as important as what it puts in is promulgated in Macherey 1978.
2 The best-known case for this is George Dangerfield's *The Strange Death of Liberal England* (1936).
3 Thomas Carlyle, perhaps the greatest influence on British cultural thought in the nineteenth century, had referred to the Elizabethan era as 'that strange outbudding of our whole English existence' in *On Heroes, Hero-Worship and the Heroic in History* (1841).
4 For example, there is Conrad's *The Secret Agent* (1907) about anarchists in London, H.G. Wells's novel *Ann Veronica* (1909) about women's emancipation, and John Galsworthy's play *Strife* (1909) about industrial conflict between capital and labour.
5 This is taken from Marsh's preface to the first volume, *Georgian Poetry, 1911–12*. For a discussion of Marsh, see the chapter on him in Ross 1967.
6 For a collection of contemporary reviews for all five volumes, see Rogers 1972.
7 See Fitzgerald 1984.
8 Marsh 1942: 75. There is of course much irony attached to Brooke's intention to make half of his 'contributors' women.
9 James Reeves's 1962 Penguin anthology of *Georgian Poetry* includes Thomas because of a shared style. Reeves excludes Lawrence, who appeared in all but one of Marsh's collections, on the same grounds.
10 Review in the *Daily Chronicle*, 19 November 1902, quoted in Longley 1986: 118.
11 In the *Daily Chronicle* in January 1913, quoted in Smith 1983: 2.
12 Longley compares Thomas's view with that of E.M. Forster, who wrote in his early novel *The Longest Journey* (1907): 'People at that time were trying to think imperially. Rickie wondered how they did it, for he could not imagine a place larger than England' (Longley 1986: 54).

2 'NOT CONCERNED WITH POETRY': WORLD WAR I

1 *The Times* 6 August 1915: 7; cited in Khan 1988: 3.
2 For an example, see the extract from the Introduction to the 1914 volume *Songs and Sonnets for England in War Time*, in Hibberd 1981: 31.
3 Letter dated 28 April 1915, extracted in Hibberd 1981: 39.
4 See letter from Wilfred Owen to Leslie Gunston, 29 October 1918, in Bell 1985: 360 and Buitenhuis 1989: 136. Beaverbrook also sought advice from Kipling and said he 'adopted everything he recommended'. Other influential writers such as John Buchan and Arnold Bennett had prominent

official posts in the orchestration of war propaganda, but Kipling refused to join Beaverbrook's staff.

5 Letter to Edward Marsh, 30 July 1917, in Rosenberg 1979: 260.

6 Janet Montefiore, 1994: 65–70. Montefiore did not revise her argument for this second edition but has qualified her views in her 1993 essay.

7 On the propaganda of the war machine, Randall Stevenson writes:

> A lifelong suspicion of the press was one lasting result of the ordinary man's experience of the war. It might even be said that the current devaluation of the letterpress and even of language itself dates from the Great War.
>
> (Stevenson 1993: 185)

8 Paul Fussell estimates that the trenches totalled 25,000 miles – enough to encompass the earth (1975: 37). The argument about gender is advanced in 'Soldier's heart: Literary Men, Literary Women and the Great War', Gilbert and Gubar 1989: 301.

9 See extract of letter of 2 August 1924 in Hibberd 1981: 65.

10 It was the ruling class rather than the various associations of 'England' that drew such hostility. Wilfred Owen wrote in disgust to his mother on 19 January 1917:

> They want to call No Man's Land 'England' because we keep supremacy there. It is like the eternal place of gnashing of teeth; the Slough of Despond could be contained in one of its crater-holes; the fires of Sodom and Gomorrah could not light a candle to it.... To call it 'England'! I would as soon call my House(!) Krupp Villa or my child Chlorina-Phosgena.
>
> (Silkin 1987: 201–2)

While Owen despised the generals who led the war from behind, he also considered the country to be sacred.

11 In a letter to Richard Aldington dated 7 April 1921. Quoted by Donald Davie in *Poetry Nation Review*, May/June, 1991: p. 24.

3 'BIRTH, AND COPULATION, AND DEATH': THE 1920s AND T.S. ELIOT

1 The articles by Hulme and Eliot, as well as Pound's patchwork essay 'A Retrospect' are all reprinted in Lodge 1972.

2 It is a historical coincidence that the rules of chess were finally codified in 1922 by the creation of the Fédération internationales des Echecs (FIDE).

4 'DEMON AND BEAST': THE 1920s AND W.B. YEATS

1 Macrae 1995: 79. Pound also strongly approved of fascism and Eliot confessed to a preference 'for fascism in practice' (from an essay by Eliot in *The Criterion* in July 1929, quoted in Smith 1982: 12).

2 See 'The Phases of the Moon' in *The Wild Swans at Coole*, and Yeats's note to the poem.

3 See the extract from the essay 'Magic' in Yeats 1964: 80.
4 'Owen Aherne and His Dancers' was in fact written before 'Michael Robartes and the Dancer'. Dates for the composition of each of Yeats's poems can be found at the end of Ellmann 1954.
5 The poem's publishing history is complex and parallels key moments of Irish resistance from 1916 to 1921, when it appeared in *Michael Robartes and the Dancer*, Yeats having decided against including it in *The Wild Swans at Coole*. For a discussion of this, see 'Yeats's Hunger-Strike Poem' in Paulin 1992: 133–50.
6 This is from Yeats's note to the poem on its first publication.
7 As I mentioned above, Hugh Kenner (1956) explains this in some detail with respect to *The Tower* (e.g. 'Sailing to Byzantium', 'Among Schoolchildren', and 'All Souls' Night' are beginning, middle, and end for a reason – they are philosophical poems concerned with the quest for something permanent beyond life's transience).
8 Letter to Herbert Grierson, 1922, cited in Smith 1990: 43–4.

5 IN/BETWEEN THE WARS: POETRY IN THE 1930s

1 This phrase was a standard thirties label to denote those sharing a (metaphorical) journey, usually to 'the north', always to the 'other side'. There is, for example, Spender's poem 'New Year' which compares the turning of the calendar to the turning of the earth at the North Pole: 'I ask that Time should freeze my skin / And all my fellow travellers harden'.
2 The term 'documentary' was translated from French into English for the first time in only 1926 by John Grierson. In the 1930s it became a by-word. For further information, see the essays by Ralph Bond, 'Cinema in the Thirties: Documentary Film and the Labour Movement', and Bert Hogenkamp, 'Making Films with a Purpose: Film-making and the Working Class' in Jon Clark *et al.* 1979. On the Mass Observation Movement see the compilation of first-hand reports of life on coronation day, 12 May 1937, in Jennings and Madge 1987.
3 The composite word 'MacSpaunday' was coined by Roy Campbell. The four poets worked together in pairs but as a group never met in the same room until 1947.
4 See the discussion of this in the chapter on 'High Failure' in Cunningham 1988. Cunningham, whose book has an excellent bibliography of 1930s material, lists key emblems as 'airmen, mountaineers, mountains, eagles, leaders, aerialism' and heroism; and Auden, in his plays as much as his poetry, is of course the representative practitioner.
5 For an extended discussion see Longley 1988 and also 'Louis MacNeice: *Autumn Journal* in Longley 1986.
6 A useful essay on Auden's childhood and his connection with Scandinavia is Isherwood 1964. Auden, in his 'Letter to Lord Byron', contrasts the dead poet with himself in this way: 'The North, though, never was your cup of tea; / "Moral" you thought it so you kept away.'

6 'PHILOSOPHICAL SUNDIALS OF HISTORY': POETRY AFTER THE WAR

1 At first associated with the Movement, and also with Ted Hughes, Gunn has moved sharply away from both to write his own style of contemporary gay poetry.
2 Here and elsewhere facts and statistics are indebted to Marwick 1982.
3 This is, for example, the view of A.T. Tolley in his introductory note to Tolley 1991.
4 Larkin condemned the obscurity of modernism and looked back to the huge sales of the Georgian poets. See *The Guardian*, 18 November 1958: 4.
5 See Gervais 1988. The phrase on Larkin is from Waugh 1995: 10.
6 See David Lodge 1977. Crudely, Lodge argues that literary taste swings between the poles of metaphor (modernism) and metonymy (realism): this movement has been mapped onto the literature of the 1920s, 1930s, 1940s, and 1950s as each decade reacts against the vogue of the previous one. The view has been opposed by later critics; see, for example, the reading of the 1930s in Williams and Matthews 1997.
7 Plath committed suicide in 1963, having never filled, through marriage, childbirth, or other relationships, the 'vacuum of her own ego', as she puts it in her novel *The Bell Jar*. At the time, she had separated from her husband, Ted Hughes, who has been accused by many of Plath's admirers of deserting her. Hughes's thirty-five-year near-silence on their marriage was only broken in January 1998 with the publication of the extraordinary eighty-eight-poem volume *Birthday Letters*, a verse-narrative account of their relationship as intense as Hardy's 1912–13 love poems for his deceased wife.
8 See Waugh 1995: 10 and Alvarez 1962.
9 See Jacqueline Rose's discussion of 'The Rabbit Catcher' and 'emergent female selfhood' in Rose 1991: 135–47.
10 Views on the uses of Jewish experience in 'Daddy' are summarised in Malcolm 1995: 63–66.
11 For an extended discussion of The Group see Garfitt 1972.
12 These poets are considered in Corcoran 1993 and elsewhere.
13 See the chapter 'The Mastering Eye: Douglas Dunn's Social Perceptions' in Robinson 1988: 82–99.

7 'TED HUGHES IS ELVIS PRESLEY': RECENT ANTHOLOGIES BY MEN

1 For an extended discussion see the chapter ' "Just the Facts, Just the": A Rough Guide to British Postmodernism' in Kennedy 1996: 79–119.
2 'The School of Eloquence' runs to sixty-four poems in the 1984 *Selected Poems* and its three sections split into political, personal, and reflexive political-personal poems.
3 Arthur Marwick (1982: 128) writing on Hoggart. Harrison's two-part poem 'Them and [uz]' is dedicated to Hoggart and to Leon Cortez (a comic who rendered Shakespeare in cockney).

4 Rosemary Burton, 'Tony Harrison: an Introduction' in Astley 1991: 16–17. Harrison says Loiners are 'citizens of Leeds...who bear their loins through the terrors of life, "loners" '.
5 This of course connects, somewhat problematically, British experience with African colonial liberation. Harrison taught for four years in Nigeria.
6 Terry Eagleton, 'Antagonisms: Tony Harrison's v.' in Astley 1991: 349.
7 A journalist as well as poet, critic, and essayist, Morrison went on in 1994 to write a searching and controversial work called *As If*, a book and monologue for television on the James Bulger case, in which two children murdered a baby.
8 For example, see the end of the chapter on 'The Working-Day' in Karl Marx, *Capital*, David McClellan (ed.), Oxford: Oxford University Press, 1995: 181
9 Alan Robinson (1988: 11) notes numerous other allusions in the poem.
10 One of the editors, David Kennedy, has deprecated 'the exclusive, superannuated and largely discredited London–Oxbridge centre', in a letter he wrote to Poetry Review, 85:4, 1995, 95.
11 For a discussion, see Conran 1997.

8 'MY HISTORY IS NOT YOURS': RECENT ANTHOLOGIES BY WOMEN

1 See Montefiore 1994: 180–7. Kristeva's essay is in Toril Moi (ed.) (1990) *The Kristeva Reader*, Oxford: Blackwell.
2 For a useful analysis of popular culture, modernity and women, which looks at changing British attitudes towards motherhood, marriage, sexuality, politics, and work, see Holdsworth 1988. Much of the information in this section has been taken from the chapter by Roberta Garrett on gender in Storry and Childs 1997.
3 An informative examination of the British legal and political system in relation to its treatment of gays and lesbians is Jeffrey-Poulter 1991.
4 For a discussion of French feminist thought, see Humm 1994: 93–113.
5 For a fuller reading along these lines, see the essay on Duffy in Gregson 1996.
6 In terms of the differences of time, gender, and authority, it is worth comparing her visit to a school with Yeats's in 'Among School Children', although she appears as a poet, he as an inspector.

9 ANTI- AND POST-COLONIAL WRITING: NORTHERN IRISH AND BLACK BRITISH POETS

1 This list is potentially very long and if room allowed there would be an obvious need to supplement the discussion at least with Welsh and Scottish ethnicities. Readers are referred to Crawford 1992 for further discussion.
2 The following are informative books on Heaney which discuss *North* in some detail: McGuinn 1986; Tamplin 1989; Morrison 1982; Corcoran 1986. My discussion of *North* is indebted to each of them.
3 See The *Listener*, 7 December 1972.
4 *Chronicle of the 20th Century*, D. Merced (ed.), Essex: Longman, 1988: 979.

5 Thatcher's speech is excerpted in Dabydeen and Wilson-Tagoe 1988: 82. One response was Linton Kwesi Johnson's lines in 'It Dread inna Inglan': 'Maggi Tatcha on di go / wid a racist show'.
6 The front page of *The Times*, 29 May 1993.
7 For a discussion of these issues, see Childs and Williams 1997.
8 Quoted by Maya Jaggi in *The Guardian*, 24 September 1996.
9 *Ibid.*
10 Zephaniah says the poem, in *City Psalms*, is 'A tribute to the Punks and Anti-Nazi campaigners who battled hard on 29th June when a group of National Front members invaded a rave at Ackham Hall, Ladbroke Grove, West London.'
11 See Maya Jaggi, 'On Being Here', *The Guardian*, 4 August 1993.
12 See 'Reinventing tradition: multiple identities in Grace Nichols' poems' in Montefiore 1994.
13 For an overview of Caribbean poets, see Paula Burnett's introduction to *The Penguin Book of Caribbean Verse*.

BIBLIOGRAPHY

Adcock, Fleur (ed.) (1989) *The Faber Book of Twentieth-Century Women's Poetry*, London: Faber.

Adorno, T.W. (1989) 'Lyric Poetry and Society' in S.E. Bronner and D.M. Kellner (eds), *Critical Theory and Society: A Reader*, London: Routledge.

Allnutt, G., D'Aguiar, F., Mottram, E. and Edwards, K. (eds) (1988) *The New British Poetry*, London: Paladin.

Alvarez, A. (ed.) (1962) *The New Poetry*, Harmondsworth: Penguin.

—— (1963) 'Sylvia Plath', *Review*, 9, October: 20–6.

Ashcroft, Bill, Griffiths, Gareth and Tiffin, Helen (1989) *The Empire Writes Back*, London: Routledge.

—— (eds) (1995) *The Post-colonial Studies Reader*, London: Routledge.

Astley, Neil (ed.) (1991) *Bloodaxe Critical Anthologies: 1. Tony Harrison*, Newcastle: Bloodaxe.

Auden, W.H. (1939) 'The Public *v.* the late Mr William Butler Yeats', from *Partisan Review*, VI:3, Spring, reprinted in Cullingford 1984.

Bantock, G.H. (1983) 'The social and intellectual background' in Boris Ford (ed.), *The New Pelican Guide to English Literature*, volume 7, Harmondsworth: Pelican.

Barrell, John (1988) *Poetry, Language and Politics*, Manchester: Manchester University Press.

Barry, Peter and Hampson, Robert (eds) (1993) *New British Poetries: The Scope of the Possible*, Manchester: Manchester University Press.

Barthes, Roland (1972) *Mythologies*, trans. Annette Lavers, London: Collins.

Bell, Ian A. (1995) 'Hugh MacDiarmid: Lenin and the literary left in the 1930s' in Day and Docherty 1995.

Bell, John (ed.) (1985) *Wilfred Owen: Selected Letters*, Oxford: Oxford University Press.

Bell, Michael (ed.) (1980) *1900–1930*, London: Methuen.

Belsey, Catherine (1980) *Critical Practice*, London: Methuen.

Benjamin, Walter (1973) 'The work of art in the age of mechanical reproduction' in *Illuminations*, trans. Harry Zohn, London: Fontana: 219–54.

Bergonzi, Bernard (1973) *The Turn of a Century*, London: Macmillan.

Berry, James (1986) 'The Literature of the Black Experience' in David Sutcliffe and Ansel Wong (eds), *The Language of the Black Experience*, Oxford: Blackwell.

—— (1989) 'Signpost of the Bluefoot Man' in E.A. Markham (ed.), *Hinterland: Caribbean poetry from the West Indies and Britain*, Newcastle: Bloodaxe, 175–7.

—— (1996) Introduction to *Bluefoot Traveller*, reprinted in Alison Donnell and Sarah Lawton Welsh (eds), *The Routledge Reader in Caribbean Literature*, London: Routledge.

Bertram, Vicki (ed.) (1997) *Kicking Daffodils: Twentieth-Century Women's Poetry*, Edinburgh: Edinburgh University Press.

Bhabha, Homi (1993) *The Location of Culture*, London: Routledge.

Birbalsingh, Frank (1993) 'An interview with Fred D'Aguiar', *Ariel*, 24:1, January.

Booker, Christopher (1992) *The Neophiliacs: The Revolution in English Life in the Fifties and Sixties*, 2nd edn, London: Pimlico.

Borges, Jorge Luis. (1970) *Labyrinths*, Harmondsworth: Penguin.

Brathwaite, Edward (1984) *The History of the Voice*, London: New Beacon Books.

—— (1990) 'History, the Caribbean writer and *X/Self*' in G. Davis and H. Maes-Jelinek (eds), *Crisis and Creativity*, Amsterdam: Rodopi.

Breeze, Jean Binta (1996) 'Can a dub poet be a woman?' in Alison Donnell and Sarah Lawson Welsh (eds), *The Routledge Reader in Caribbean Literature*, London: Routledge.

Buitenhuis, Peter (1989) *The Great War of Words: Literature as Propaganda 1914–18 and After*, London: Batsford.

Burnett, Paula (ed.) (1986) *The Penguin Book of Caribbean Verse in English*, Harmondsworth: Penguin.

Butler, Judith (1990) *Gender Trouble*, London: Routledge.

Caesar, Adrian (1991) *Dividing Lines: Poetry, Class and Ideology in the 1930s*, Manchester: Manchester University Press.

Cairns, David and Richards, Shaun (1988) *Writing Ireland: Colonialism, Nationalism, and Culture*, Manchester: Manchester University Press.

Childs, Peter and Williams, Patrick (1997) *An Introduction to Post-Colonial Theory*, Hemel Hempstead: Harvester.

Clark, Jon, Heinemann, Margot, Snee, Caroline (eds) (1979) *Culture and Crisis in Britain in the 30s*, London: Lawrence and Wishart.

Cohen, Joseph (1975) *Journey to the Trenches: The Life of Isaac Rosenberg, 1890–1917*, London: Robson.

Connor, Steven (1995) 'British Surrealist poetry of the 1930s' in Day and Docherty 1995.

—— (1996) *The English Novel in History 1950–95*, London: Routledge.

Conran, Tony (1997) *Frontiers in Anglo-Welsh Poetry*, Cardiff: University of Wales Press.

Corcoran, Neil (1986) *A Student's Guide to Seamus Heaney*, London: Faber.

—— (1993) *English Poetry Since 1940*, Essex: Longman.

Couzyn, Jeni (ed.) (1985) *The Bloodaxe Book of Contemporary Women Poets*, Newcastle: Bloodaxe.

Coyle, Martin (1995) 'Language, class, death and landscape in the poetry of the First World War', *English*, 44:179, Summer.

Crawford, Robert (1992) *Devolving English Literature*, Edinburgh: Edinburgh University Press.

Crowley, Tony (1989) *The Politics of Discourse: the Standard Language Question in British Cultural Debates*, London: Macmillan.

Crozier, Andrew (1983) 'Thrills and frills: poetry as figures of empirical lyricism' in Alan Sinfield (ed.), *Society and Literature 1945–70*, London: Methuen.

Crozier, Andrew and Longville, Tim (eds) (1987), *A Various Art*, Manchester: Carcanet.

Cullingford, Elizabeth (ed.) (1984) *Yeats: Poems, 1919–1935*, London: Macmillan.

—— (1993) *Gender and History in Yeats's Love Poetry*, Cambridge: Cambridge University Press.

Cunningham, Valentine (1988) *British Writers of the Thirties*, Oxford: Oxford University Press.

Dabydeen, David and Nana Wilson-Tagoe (1988) *A Reader's Guide to West Indian and Black British Literature*, London: Hansib.

Dabydeen, David (1990) 'On not being Milton: nigger talk in England today' in Christopher Ricks and Leonard Michaels (eds), *The State of the Language*, 2nd edn, London: Faber.

D'Aguiar, Fred (1993) 'Have you been here long? Black poetry in Britain' in Robert Hampson and Peter Barry (eds), *New British Poetries: The scope of the possible*, Manchester: Manchester University Press.

Davie, Donald (1964) *New Statesman*, 28 August, extracted in Hibberd 1981: 110.

—— (1973) *Thomas Hardy and British Poetry*, London: Routledge and Kegan Paul.

Davies, Alistair (1995) 'Deconstructing the high modernist lyric' in Day and Docherty 1995.

Davies, W.H. (1942) *Collected Poems*, London: Jonathan Cape.

Day, Gary (1993) 'The poets: Georgians, Imagists and others' in Clive Bloom (ed.), *Literature and Culture in Modern Britain. Volume One: 1900–1929*, Essex: Longman, 33–41.

—— (1995) 'Introduction: poetry, society and tradition' in Day and Docherty 1995.

Day, Gary and Docherty, Brian (eds) (1995) *British Poetry 1900–1950: Aspects of Tradition*, London: St Martin's Press and Macmillan.

—— (eds) (1997) *British Poetry from the 1950s to the 1990s: Politics and Art*, London: St Martin's Press and Macmillan.

Deane, Seamus (1984) 'Remembering the Irish future', *The Crane Bag*, 8:1.

—— (1985) *Celtic Revivals*, London: Faber.

—— (1990) 'Introduction' in Terry Eagleton, Fredric Jameson and Edward Said, *Nationalism, Colonialism and Literature*, Minneapolis: University of Minnesota Press.

—— (1995) 'Imperialism/Nationalism' in Frank Lentricchia and Thomas McLaughlin (eds), *Critical Terms for Literary Study*, 2nd edn, Chicago: Chicago University Press.

De Beauvoir, Simone (1972) *The Second Sex*, trans. H.M. Parshley, Harmondsworth: Penguin.

Dentith, Simon (1997) 'Thirties poetry and the landscape of suburbia' in Williams and Matthews 1997.

De Selincourt, Basil (1921) *Times Literary Supplement*, 6 January, extracted in Hibberd 1981: 59.

Docherty, Thomas (1992) 'Initiations, tempers, seductions: postmodern McGuckian' in Neil Corcoran (ed.), *The Chosen Ground: Essays in the Contemporary Poetry of Northern Ireland*, Glamorgan: Seren.

Dowling, David (1991) *Mrs Dalloway: Mapping Streams of Consciousness*, Boston: Twayne.

Dowson, Jane (ed.) (1996) *Women's Poetry of the 1930s: A Critical Anthology*, London: Routledge.

—— (1997) 'Anthologies of women's poetry: canon-breakers, canon-makers' in Day and Docherty 1997.

Doyle, Brian (1982) 'The hidden history of English studies' in P. Widdowson (ed.), *Re-reading English*, London: Methuen.

Eagleton, Terry (1976a) *Criticism and Ideology*, London: New Left Books.

—— (1976b) *Marxism and Literary Criticism*, London: Methuen.

—— (1983) *Literary Theory*, Oxford: Blackwell.

Easthope, Antony (1983) *Poetry as Discourse*, London: Methuen.

Eliot, T.S. (1932) *Selected Essays*, London: Faber.

—— (1972) [1919] 'Tradition and the individual talent' in David Lodge (ed.), *20th Century Literary Criticism*, Essex: Longman.

—— (1975) *Selected Prose of T.S. Eliot*, ed. Frank Kermode, Faber: London.

Ellmann, Maud (1987) *The Poetics of Impersonality*, Brighton: Harvester.

Ellmann, Richard (1948) *Yeats: The Man and His Mask*, London: Macmillan.

—— (1954) *The Identity of Yeats*, London: Macmillan.

Emig, Rainer (1995) 'The symbolic approach and its limits: W.B. Yeats (1865–1939)' in *Modernism in Poetry*, Essex: Longman.

Fallon, Peter and Mahon, Derek (eds) (1990) *The Penguin Book of Contemporary Irish Poetry*, Harmondsworth: Penguin.

Featherstone, Simon (1996) *War Poetry*, London: Routledge.

Fenton, James (1990) 'Ars Poetica' in *The Independent on Sunday Review*, 10 June: 18.

Field Day (1985) *Ireland's Field Day*, Field Day Theatre Company, London: Hutchinson.

Fitzgerald, Penelope (1984) *Charlotte Mew and Her Friends*, London: Collins.

Fortier, Anne-Marie (1994) 'Ethnicity', Paragraph, 17:3, November.

France, Linda (ed.) (1993) Sixty Women Poets, Newcastle, Bloodaxe.

Freyer, Grattan (1981) Yeats and the Anti-Democratic Tradition, Dublin: Gill and Macmillan.

Friedman, Susan (1981) Psyche Reborn, Bloomington: Indiana.

Fryer, Peter (1984) Staying Power, London: Pluto.

—— (1988) Black People in the British Empire, London: Pluto.

Fussell, Paul (1975) The Great War and Modern Memory, London: Oxford University Press.

Garfitt, Roger (1972) 'The group' in Michael Schmidt and Grevel Lindop (eds), British Poetry Since 1960, Oxford: Carcanet, 13–69.

Gervais, David (1988) '"Something Gone": "England" in Modern English Writing', English, 37:158, Summer: 103–26.

Gibbons, Luke (1991) 'Challenging the canon: revisionism and cultural criticism' in The Field Day Anthology of Irish Writing, volume 3, Field Day Publications: Derry.

Giddings, Robert (1997) 'Radio in Peace and War' in Gary Day (ed.), Literature and Culture in Modern Britain, Volume Two: 1930–1955, Essex: Longman.

Gilbert, Sandra and Gubar, Susan (1989) 'Soldier's heart: literary men, literary women and the Great War' in Sexchanges, volume 2 of No Man's Land: The Place of the Woman Writer in the Twentieth Century, New Haven: Yale University Press.

Gilroy, Paul (1987) There Ain't No Black in the Union Jack, London: Unwin.

—— (1993) The Black Atlantic, London: Verso.

Greening, John (1994/5) 'The quest for the seven virtues', Poetry Review, 84:4, Winter.

Gregson, Ian (1996) Contemporary Poetry and Postmodernism: Dialogue and Estrangement, London: Macmillan.

Habekost, Christian (1986) Dub Poetry: 19 poets from England and Jamaica, Neustadt, Germany: Michael Schwinn.

Haberstroh, Patricia Boyle (1996) Women Creating Women: Contemporary Irish Women Poets, New York: Syracuse University Press.

Hall, Stuart (1988) 'New ethnicities' in L. Appignanesi (ed.), Black Film, British Cinema, ICA Documents, 7, London: ICA.

—— (1993) 'Cultural identity and diaspora' in Patrick Williams and Laura Chrisman (eds) Colonial Discourse and Post-colonial Theory, Hemel Hempstead: Harvester Wheatsheaf.

Hall, Stuart and Schwarz, Bill (1985) 'State and society, 1880–1930' in Mary Langan and Bill Schwarz (eds), Crises in the British State 1880–1930, London: Hutchinson.

Hampson, Robert and Barry, Peter (eds) (1993) New British Poetries: The Scope of the Possible, Manchester: Manchester University Press.

Hassall, Christopher (1972) Rupert Brooke: A Biography, London: Faber.

Haughton, Hugh (1992) '"Even Now There are Places Where a Thought might Grow": place and displacement in the poetry of Derek Mahon' in Neil Corcoran (ed.), *The Chosen Ground: Essays in Contemporary Poetry of Northern Ireland*, Glamorgan: Seren.

Heaney, Seamus (1980) *Preoccupations: Selected Prose 1968–78*, London: Faber.

Henn, T.R. (1984) *The Lonely Tower*, excerpted in Cullingford 1984.

Hibberd, Dominic (1973) 'Introduction' in *Wilfred Owen: War Poems and Others*, London: Chatto and Windus

—— (ed.) (1981) *Poetry of the First World War*, London: Macmillan.

Hobsbaum, Philip (1961) 'The road not taken', *The Listener*, 23 November, reprinted in Martin and Furbank, 1975.

—— (1970) [1965] 'The Growth of English Modernism', reprinted in Lucie-Smith 1970.

Hobsbawm, Eric (1987) *The Age of Empire*, London: Weidenfeld and Nicholson.

Hoggart, Richard (1991) 'In conversation with Tony Harrison' in Astley 1991.

Holdsworth, Alison (1988) *Out of the Dolls House: The Story of Women in the Twentieth Century*, London: Butler and Tanner.

Holloway, John (1956/7) 'New lines in English poetry', *Hudson Review*, 9: 592–7.

Hulse, Michael, Kennedy, David and Morley, David (eds) (1993) *The New Poetry*, Newcastle: Bloodaxe.

Humm, Maggie (1994) *A Reader's Guide to Contemporary Feminist Literary Criticism*, Hemel Hempstead: Harvester Wheatsheaf.

Hynes, Samuel (1972) *Edwardian Occasions*, London: Routledge and Kegan Paul.

—— (1976) *The Auden Generation: Literature and Politics in the 1930s*, London: Faber.

Isherwood, Christopher (1964) 'Some notes on Auden's early poetry' in Monroe K. Spears (ed.), *Auden: A Collection of Critical Essays*, Englewood Cliffs: Prentice Hall.

Jameson, Fredric (1971) *Marxism and Form*, New Jersey: Princeton.

Jeffrey-Poulter, S. (1991) *Peers, Queers and Commons: The Struggle for Gay Law Reform from 1950 to the Present*, London: Routledge.

Jenkins, Keith (1991) *Re-thinking History*, London: Routledge.

Jennings, Humphrey and Madge, Charles (eds) (1987) *Mass-Observation Day-Survey*, London: Faber.

Johnson, Linton Kwesi (1996) 'Interview: Linton Kwesi Johnson talks to Burt Caesar', *Critical Quarterly*, 38:4, Winter.

Kendall, Tim (1996) *Paul Muldoon*, Bridgend: Seren.

Kennedy, David (1996) *New Relations: The Refashioning of British Poetry 1980–94*, Glamorgan: Seren.

Kenner, Hugh (1956) 'The sacred book of the arts', *Sewanee Review*, LXIV, 4, reprinted in Cullingford 1984: 136–45.

Kermode, Frank (1988) *History and Value*, Oxford: Clarendon.

Kettle, Arnold (1979) 'W.H. Auden: poetry and politics in the Thirties' in Clark *et al.* 1979.

Khan, Nosheen (1988) *Women's Poetry of the First World War*, Hemel Hempstead: Harvester.

Kiberd, Declan (1985) 'Anglo-Irish attitudes' in Field Day 1985.

Kidd, Helen (1993) 'The paper city: women, writing, and experience' in Hampson and Barry 1993.

Kirkham, Michael (1983) 'Philip Larkin and Charles Tomlinson: realism and art' in Boris Ford (ed.), *The New Pelican Guide to English Literature*, volume 8, Harmondsworth: Pelican.

Kirkland, Richard (1996) *Literature and Culture in Northern Ireland Since 1965: Moments of Danger*, Essex: Longman.

Knight, G. Wilson (1971) *Neglected Powers: Essays on Nineteenth and Twentieth Century Literature*, London: Routledge.

Kureishi, Hanif (1986) 'The Rainbow Sign' in *My Beautiful Laundrette and The Rainbow Sign*, London: Faber.

Larkin, Philip (1983) *Required Writing: Miscellaneous Pieces, 1955–1982*, London: Faber.

—— (1992) *Selected Letters of Philip Larkin 1940–1985*, ed. Anthony Thwaite, London: Faber.

Larrissy, Edward (1994) *Yeats the Poet: The Measures of Difference*, Hemel Hempstead: Harvester.

Lawrence, D.H. (1971) [1923] *Fantasia of the Unconscious/Psychoanalysis and the Unconscious*, Harmondsworth: Penguin.

Lawson Welsh, Sarah (1996) 'Experiments in brokenness: the creative use of Creole in David Dabydeen's *Slave Song*' in Alison Donnell and Sarah Lawson Welsh (eds), *The Routledge Reader in Caribbean Literature*, London: Routledge.

Leavis, F.R. (1972) [1932] *New Bearings in English Poetry*, Harmondsworth: Penguin.

Lindop, Grevel (1980) 'Being different from yourself: Philip Larkin in the 1970s' in Peter Jones and Michael Schmidt (eds), *British Poetry Since 1970: A Critical Survey*, Manchester: Carcanet.

Lloyd, David (1993) *Anomalous States: Irish Writing and the Post-Colonial Moment*, Dublin: Lilliput.

Lloyd, T.O. (1986) *Empire to Welfare State: English History 1906–1985*, 3rd edn, Oxford: Oxford University Press.

Lodge, David (ed.) (1972) *20th Century Literary Criticism*, Essex: Longman.

—— (1977) *The Modes of Modern Writing*, London: Edward Arnold.

—— (1989) *After Bakhtin*, London: Routledge.

Logan, William (1991) 'A letter from Britain', *Poetry*, 1 and 2.

Long, Declan (1997) ' "From Room to Homesick Room": women and poetry in northern Ireland' in Bertram 1997.

Longley, Edna (1986) *Poetry in the Wars*, Newcastle: Bloodaxe.

—— (1988) *Louis MacNeice: A Study*, London: Faber.

—— (1996) 'Signposting the century', *Poetry Review*, 86:1, Spring, 8–12.

Lucas, John (1986) *Modern English Poetry from Hardy to Hughes*, London: Batsford.

—— (1996) 'Poetry and Politics in the 1920s' in Kate Flint (ed.), *Poetry and Politics*, Essays and Studies 1996, No. 49, Cambridge: The English Association.

Lucie-Smith, Edward (ed.) (1970) *British Poetry Since 1945*, Harmondsworth: Penguin.

Lukacs, Georg (1972) [1957] 'The ideology of Modernism' in David Lodge (ed.), *20th Century Literary Criticism*, Essex: Longman: 474–87.

McGuinn, Nicholas (1986) *Seamus Heaney: A Student's Guide to the Poems 1965–75*, Leeds: Edward Arnold.

Macherey, Pierre (1978) [1966] *A Theory of Literary Production*, trans. G. Wall, London: Routledge.

Macrae, Alasdair D.F. (1995) *W.B. Yeats: A Literary Life*, London: Macmillan.

Malcolm, Janet (1995) *The Silent Woman: Ted Hughes and Sylvia Plath*, London: Macmillan.

Markham, E.A. (ed.) (1989) *Hinterland*, Newcastle: Bloodaxe.

Marsh, Edward (1942) 'Memoir' in *Rupert Brooke: The Collected Poems*, 3rd edn, London: Sidgwick and Jackson.

Martin, Graham and Furbank, P.N. (eds) (1975) *Twentieth Century Poetry: Critical Essays and Documents*, Milton Keynes: Open University Press.

Marwick, Arthur (1982) *British Society Since 1945*, Harmondsworth: Pelican.

Massingham, H.W. (1917) *Nation*, 16 June, extracted in Hibberd 1981: 43–4.

Matthews, Steven (1997) *Irish Poetry: Politics, History, Negotiation*, London: Macmillan.

Mendelson, Edward (1981) *Early Auden*, New York: Viking.

Mew, Charlotte (1982) *Collected Poems and Prose*, ed. V. Warner, London: Virago.

Millard, Kenneth (1991) *Edwardian Poetry*, Oxford: Clarendon Press.

Moi, Toril (1985) *Sexual/Textual Politics*, London: Methuen.

Montefiore, Janet (1991) 'How to avoid being canonized: Laura Riding', *Textual Practice*, 5:2, Summer.

—— (1993) '"Shining Pins and Wailing Shells": Women Poets and the Great War' in Dorothy Goldman (ed.), *Women and World War One: The Written Response*, London: Macmillan.

—— (1994) *Feminism and Poetry*, 2nd edn, London: Pandora.

—— (1996) *Men and Women Writers of the 1930s*, London: Routledge.

Moretti, Franco (1988) *Signs Taken for Wonders*, revised edn, London: Verso.

Morris, Mervyn (1997) 'A note on "dub poetry"', *Wasafiri*, 26, Autumn, 66–9.

Morrison, Blake (1980a) *The Movement: English Poetry and Fiction of the 1950s*, Oxford: Oxford University Press.

—— (1980b) 'Speech and reticence: Seamus Heaney's *North*' in Peter Jones and Michael Schmidt (eds), *British Poetry Since 1970: A Critical Survey*, Manchester: Carcanet.

—— (1982) *Seamus Heaney*, London: Methuen: London.

—— (1987) 'The filial art: a reading of contemporary British poetry' in C.J. Rawson (ed.), *The Yearbook of English Studies*, volume 17, London: MHRA.

Morrison, Blake and Motion, Andrew (eds) (1982) *The Penguin Book of Contemporary British Poetry*, Harmondsworth: Penguin.

Morton, Brian (1993) 'The world of popular music' in Clive Bloom (ed.), *Literature and Culture in Modern Britain. Volume One: 1900–1929*, Essex: Longman.

Motion, Andrew (1980) *The Poetry of Edward Thomas*, London: Routledge.

—— (1993) *Philip Larkin: A Writer's Life*, London: Faber.

Mottram, Eric (1993) 'The British poetry revival, 1960–75' in Hampson and Barry 1993: 15–50.

Murry, John Middleton (1918) 'Mr Sassoon's war verses', *Nation*, 13 July, extracted in Hibberd 1981: 43–4.

Newbolt, Henry (1898) *The Island Race*, London: Elkin Mathews.

—— (1932) *My World as in My Time: Memoirs*, London: Faber and Faber.

—— (1995) [1922] *The Teaching of English in England*, extracted in Judy Giles and Tim Middleton (eds), *Writing Englishness 1900–1950*, London: Routledge, 153–60.

Newton, K.M. (1990) *Interpreting the Text*, Hemel Hempstead: Harvester.

Orwell, George (1943) Review of V.K. Menon's *The Development of William Butler Yeats*, *Horizon*, VV, 37, reprinted in Cullingford 1984.

—— (1962) *Inside the Whale and Other Essays*, Harmondsworth: Penguin.

—— (1965) 'Rudyard Kipling' in *Decline of the English Murder and Other Essays*, Harmondsworth: Penguin.

Parfitt, George (1990) *English Poetry of the First World War: Contexts and Themes*, Hemel Hempstead: Harvester.

Parkinson, Thomas (1970) 'W.B. Yeats' in Bernard Bergonzi (ed.), *The Twentieth Century*, Sphere History of Literature in the English Language, volume 7, London: Sphere.

Paulin, Tom (1976) '*Letters from Iceland*: Going North' in *Renaissance and Modern Studies*, Special Number: The 1930s, vol. 20.

—— (1992) *Minotaur: Poetry and the Nation State*, London: Faber.

Perkins, David (1976) *A History of Modern Poetry. Volume 1: From the 1890s to the High Modernist Mode*, Cambridge, MA: Harvard, Belknap Press.

—— (1987) *A History of Modern Poetry. Volume 2: Modernism and After*, Cambridge, MA: Harvard, Belknap Press.

Poster, Jem (1993) *The Thirties Poets*, Buckingham: Open University Press.

Press, John (ed.) (1969) *A Map of Modern English Verse*, Oxford: Oxford University Press.

Pykett, Lyn (1997) 'Women poets and "women's poetry"' in Day and Docherty 1997.

Reeves, James (ed.) (1962) *Georgian Poetry*, Harmondsworth: Penguin.

Reilly, Catherine (ed.) (1981) *Scars Upon My Heart: Women's Poetry and Verse of the First World War*, London: Virago.

Robinson, Alan (1988) *Instabilities in Contemporary British Poetry*, London: Macmillan.

Rogers, Timothy (ed.) (1972) *Georgian Poetry 1911–22: The Critical Heritage*, London: Routledge.

Rose, Jacqueline (1991) *The Haunting of Sylvia Plath*, London: Virago.

Rosenberg, Isaac (1937) *The Collected Works of Isaac Rosenberg*, ed. Gordon Bottomley and Denys Harding, London: Chatto and Windus.

—— (1979) *The Collected Works of Isaac Rosenberg*, ed. Ian Parsons, London: Chatto and Windus.

Ross, R.H. (1967) *The Georgian Revolt: Rise and Fall of a Poetic Ideal 1910–22*, London: Faber.

Rumens, Carol (ed.) (1985) *Making for the Open*, London: Chatto & Windus.

Said, Edward (1990) 'Yeats and decolonization' in Terry Eagleton, Fredric Jameson and Edward Said, *Nationalism, Colonialism, and Literature*, Minneapolis: University of Minnesota Press.

—— (1993) *Culture and Imperialism*, London: Chatto and Windus.

Schmidt, Michael (1979) *An Introduction to Fifty Modern British Poets*, London: Pan.

Scott, Bonnie Kime (ed.) (1990) *The Gender of Modernism*, Bloomington: Indiana University Press.

Scott, Dennis (1989) 'Interview with Louise Bennett' in E.A. Markham (ed.), *Hinterland: Caribbean Poetry from the West Indies and Britain*, Newcastle: Bloodaxe.

Seeley, J.R. (1883) *The Expansion of England*, London: Macmillan.

Shklovsky, Victor (1972) [1917] 'Art as technique', reprinted in David Lodge (ed.), *20th Century Literary Criticism*, Essex: Longman.

Silkin, Jon (1987) *Out of Battle: The Poetry of the Great War*, London: ARK, Routledge.

Sisson, C.H. (1981) *English Poetry 1900–1950: An Assessment*, Manchester: Carcanet.

Skelton, Robin (1964) *Poetry of the Thirties*, Harmondsworth: Penguin.

—— (1968) *Poetry of the Forties*, Harmondsworth: Penguin.

Smith, Stan (1982) *Inviolable Voice: History and Twentieth-Century Poetry*, Dublin: Gill and Macmillan.

—— (1983) *20th Century Poetry*, London: Macmillan.

—— (1986) *Edward Thomas*, London: Faber.

—— (1990) *W.B. Yeats: A Critical Introduction*, London: Macmillan.

Spencer, Luke (1994) *The Poetry of Tony Harrison*, Hemel Hempstead: Harvester.

Spender, Stephen (1977) [1951] *World Within World*, London: Faber.

Spiers, Logan (1996) 'The New Poetry', *English Studies*, 77:2, March.

Stevenson, Anne (1979) 'Writing as a woman' in Mary Jacobus (ed.), *Women Writing and Writing about Women*, London: Croom Helm.

Stevenson, Jon (1984) *British Society 1914–1945*, Harmondsworth: Penguin.

Stevenson, Randall (1993) *Modernist Fiction*, Hemel Hempstead: Harvester.

Storry, Michael and Childs, Peter (eds) (1997) *British Cultural Identities*, London: Routledge.

Sutcliffe, David (1982) *British Black English*, Oxford: Blackwell.

Symons, J.A. (1899) *The Symbolist Movement in Literature*, London: Heinemann.

Tamplin, Ronald (1989) *Seamus Heaney*, Milton Keynes: Open University Press.

Tarn, Nathaniel (1968) 'World wide open', *International Times*, 28 June–11 July, extracted in Lucie-Smith, 1970.

Tate, Alison (1988) 'The master-narrative of Modernism: discourses of gender and class in *The Waste Land*', *Literature and History*, 14:2, Autumn: 160–71.

Thomas, Edward (1914) 'War poetry', *Poetry and Drama*, II:8, December, extracted in Hibberd 1981.

—— (1928) 'This England', in *The Last Sheaf*, London: Jonathan Cape.

Thwaite, Anthony (1996) *Poetry Today: A Critical Guide to British Poetry 1960–1995*, Essex: Longman.

Tolley, A.T. (1975) *The Poetry of the Thirties*, London: Victor Gollancz.

—— (1985) *The Poetry of the Forties*, Manchester: Manchester University Press.

—— (1991) *My Proper Ground: A Study of the Work of Philip Larkin and its Development*, Edinburgh: Edinburgh University Press.

Trivedi, Harish (1995) ' "Ganga was sunken...": T.S. Eliot's use of India' in *Colonial Transactions: English Literature and India*, Manchester: Manchester University Press.

Trodd, Anthea (1991) *A Reader's Guide to Edwardian Literature*, Hemel Hempstead: Harvester Wheatsheaf.

Trotter, David (1988) 'Modernism and empire: reading *The Waste Land*' in Colin MacCabe (ed), *Futures for English*, Manchester: Manchester University Press.

Walter, George (1995) 'The rise and fall of Georgian poetry' in Day and Docherty 1995.

Waugh, Patricia (1995) *Harvest of the Sixties: English Literature and its Background 1960 to 1990*, Oxford: Opus.

Weeks, Jeffrey (1985) *Sexuality and its Discontents*, London: Routledge.

Widdowson, Peter (1997) *Thomas Hardy: Selected Poetry and Non-Fictional Prose*, London: Macmillan.

Williams, John (1987) *Twentieth-Century Poetry: A Critical Introduction*, London: Edward Arnold.

Williams, Keith and Matthews, Steven (eds) (1997) *Rewriting the Thirties: Modernism and After*, Essex: Longman.

Williams, Linda R. (1992) ' "Rule and Energy in View": the poetry of modernity' in Linda R. Williams (ed.), *The Twentieth Century*, London: Bloomsbury.

Williams, Raymond (1973) *The Country and the City*, London: Chatto and Windus.

—— (1979) *Politics and Letters*, London: New Left Books.

Wills, Clair (1992) 'The lie of the land: language, imperialism and trade in Paul Muldoon's *Meeting the British*' in Neil Corcoran (ed.), *The Chosen Ground: Essays in Contemporary Poetry of Northern Ireland*, Glamorgan: Seren.

Winterbottom, Derek (1986) *Henry Newbolt and the Spirit of Clifton*, Bristol: Redcliffe.

Winters, Yvor (1984) 'Yeats's silly ideas', reprinted in Cullingford 1984.

Woolf, Virginia (1952) *Three Guineas*, London: Hogarth Press.

Yeats, W.B. (1925) *A Vision*, excerpted in Yeats 1964.

—— (1936a) Letter to Dorothy Wellesley, 21 December, extracted in Hibberd 1981: 80.

—— (ed.) (1936b) *The Oxford Book of Modern Verse*, Oxford: Oxford University Press.

—— (1964) *Yeats: Selected Criticism*, ed. A. Norman Jeffares, London: Macmillan

—— (1972) [1900] 'The symbolism in poetry', reprinted in David Lodge (ed.), *20th Century Literary Criticism*, Essex: Longman.

INDEX

Cope, Wendy, 161, 162, 166, 176–9
Corbin, Alice, 54
Corcoran, Neil, 120, 162, 175, 182
Cornford, John, 105, 111
Costello, Elvis, 145
Counter-Attack (Sassoon), 47
Country Life, 22
Couzyn, Jeni, 164, 171
Craddock, Beresford, 193
Crawford, Robert, 158
Cripps, Stafford, 151
Crowley, Aleister, 57
Crowley, Tony, 194
Crozier, Andrew, 129, 130, 151
Cullingford, Elizabeth, 91, 97, 99
Cunard, Nancy, 112
Curtis, Tony, 159
Cut (Plath), 139

D'Aguiar, Fred, 151, 194, 198, 201–2
Dabydeen, David, 193, 195, 196, 197, 202
Daily Express, 22
Daily Mail, 22
Dante, 15, 81
Daryush, Elizabeth, 102, 118, 119
Daughters of War (Rosenberg), 52
Davie, Donald, 8, 46, 124, 127, 128, 130, 133
Davies, Alistair, 72
Davies, W.H., 13, 26–7, 29
Davitt, Michael, 87
Day Lewis, Cecil, 6, 105, 108, 109, 110, 114, 117
Day, Gary, 10, 30
De Beauvoir, Simone, 163
De la Mare, Walter, 26, 127
De Selincourt, Edward, 49
De Valera, Eamon, 88, 95
Dead Man's Dump (Rosenberg), 51–2
Dead Men's Love (Brooke), 32
Deane, Seamus, 93, 181, 182
Decadents, 16, 29, 57
Delaney, Shelagh, 144
Demon and Beast (Yeats), 90, 92, 93
Derby, Lord, 58
Derrida, Jacques, 72, 78
Des Imagistes, 5
Dickens, Charles, 3, 81

Dickinson, Emily, 164
Dilke, Charles, 16, 25
Disabled (Owen), 49
Docherty, Thomas, 174
Dockery and Son (Larkin), 136
Does It Matter? (Sassoon), 50
Dolphins (Duffy), 177
Don Quixote, 2
Donne, John, 81, 131
Dooley, Maura, 160
Douglas, Keith, 120
Dover Beach (Arnold), 4
Dowling, David, 50
Dowson, Ernest, 16
Dowson, Jane, 109, 119, 160
Doyle, Brian, 65
Drafts (Bomford), 53
Drake's Drum (Newbolt), 24
Drake, Francis, 24
Duchamp, Marcel, 17
Duffy, Carol Ann, 158, 160, 166, 176–9
Duffy, Maureen, 146
Duhig, Ian, 156
Dulce et Decorum Est (Owen), 49
Dunmore, Helen, 169
Dunn, Douglas, 123, 142–3, 148, 158
Durrell, Lawrence, 129, 141
Dymock Poets, 34

Eagleton, Terry, 1, 2, 12, 68, 73–4, 154
Earle, Jean, 169
Easter 1916 (Yeats), 91, 93
Easter Monday (Farjeon), 34
Easthope, Antony, 10
Education (Barrington), 54
Edwards, Ken, 151
Ellis, Havelock, 64
Egoist, 10, 39
Einstein, Albert, 18, 64
El Heroe (S. T. Warner), 112
Eliot, George, 20
Eliot, T.S., ix, 2, 9, 10, 16, 17, 33, 39, 45, 60, 83, 92, 99, 102, 104, 105, 106, 115, 116, 120, 124, 126, 133, 134, 136, 147, 178–9
Ellmann, Maud, 178–9
Ellmann, Richard, 84

Kendall, Tim, 189
Kennedy, Michael, 7, 144, 148
Kenner, Hugh, 93
Kermode, Frank, 113
Kettle, Arnold, 115
Khan, Nosheen, 53, 55
Kiberd, Declan, 181
Kidd, Helen, 162
Kinnock, Neil, 158
Kinsey, Alfred, 167
Kipling, Rudyard, 2, 8, 9, 14, 19, 27, 45, 46, 57, 102
Kirkham, Michael, 136
Kirkland, Richard, 183
Knight, G. Wilson, 31
Kristeva, Julia, 163
Kumin, Maxine, 166
Kuppner, Grank, 158
Kureishi, Hanif, 193

Lament of the Demobilised (Brittain), 54
Lamming, George, 144
Lane, Homer, 115
Larkin, Philip, 6, 8, 9, 40, 122, 123, 124, 125, 127, 128, 130, 133–40, 148, 151, 154, 178, 183
Larrissy, Edward, 96
Latif, Tariq, 204
Lawrence, D. H., 4, 16, 27, 73
Lawton Welsh, Sarah, 197
Lear, Edward, 179
Leavis, F. R., 16, 17, 66, 109
Leavis, Q. D., 66, 109
Leda and the Swan (Yeats), 97
Lehmann, John, 111, 128
Leonard, Tom, 157, 158, 194
Lessons of War (Reed), 120
Letters from Iceland (Auden and MacNeice), 117
Lewis, Alun, 120, 131, 141, 159
Lewis, Wyndham, 16, 39
Lindop, Grevel, 134
Linthwaite, Illona, 180
Lloyd, David, 191
Lloyd, T. O., 127
Lob (E. Thomas), 35
Lochhead, Liz, 158, 194
Lodge, David, 80, 124, 134

Logan, William, 171
Logue, Christopher, 142
Lomax, Marion, 169
Long, Declan, 180
Longley, Edna, 7, 35, 37, 96, 188, 189
Longley, Michael, 182, 191
Longville, Tim, 151
Louse Hunting (Rosenberg), 51
Lowell, Amy, 39
Lowell, Robert, 132, 170
Loy, Mina, 39
Lucas, John, 15, 25, 93–4, 160
Lucie-Smith, Edward, 6, 141, 161, 204
Lukacs, Georg, 69
Lust (Brooke), 32
Lyons, John, 204

MacBeth, George, 126, 141
MacCaig, Norman, 6, 121, 128, 131, 132, 158
MacDiarmid, Hugh, 103, 110, 131, 158
MacDonald, Nina, 53, 55
MacDonald, Ramsay, 106, 124
MacInnes, Colin, 144
Maclean, Sorley, 158
MacNeice, Louis, 6, 102, 105, 106, 107–8, 109, 113, 114, 116, 117, 118, 131, 158, 183, 192
Macrae, Alasdair, 83, 84, 86, 87
Madeleine in Church (Mew), 28
Madge, Charles, 104
Mahon, Derek, 182, 183, 191, 192
Making for the Open, 161, 163, 164–5
Mallarmé, Stephen, 17, 68
Man He Killed (Hardy), 45
Marcuse, Herbert, 167
Marsden, Dora, 39
Marsh, Edward, 5, 27, 28, 30, 31, 32, 34, 42, 45, 62, 88
Martian Poetry, 149–50
Marx, Karl, 113
Masefield, John, 27, 102
Mask of Anarchy (Shelley), 1
Mass Observation, 104
Massingham, Hugh, 46
Masterman, C. F. G., 14
Masters and Johnson, 167

INDEX

Winters, Yvor, 99
Winterson, Jeanette, 146
Wittgenstein, Ludwig, 64
Women He Liked (E. Thomas), 37
Woolf, Virginia, 20, 24–5, 160, 165, 173
Word (E. Thomas), 37
Words (E. Thomas), 37
Wordsworth, William, 8, 10, 36, 138, 178
Wright brothers, 18

Wright, David, 6, 121
Wright, Kit, 158

Yeats, Anne, 90
Yeats, W.B., ix, 7, 8, 10, 13, 14, 20, 40, 48, 59, 65, 68, 82, 83–101, 102, 105, 106, 121, 124, 127, 139, 182, 186, 187, 192

Zephaniah, Benjamin, 194, 199–200